Vanessa Plate

The Impact of Off-Label, Compassionate and Unlicensed Use on Health Care Laws in Preselected Countries

Vanessa Plate

THE IMPACT OF OFF-LABEL, COMPASSIONATE AND UNLICENSED USE ON HEALTH CARE LAWS IN PRESELECTED COUNTRIES

ibidem-Verlag
Stuttgart

Bibliographic information published by the Deutsche Nationalbibliothek
Die Deutsche Nationalbibliothek lists this publication in the Deutsche Nationalbibliografie; detailed bibliographic data are available in the Internet at http://dnb.d-nb.de.

Bibliografische Information der Deutschen Nationalbibliothek
Die Deutsche Nationalbibliothek verzeichnet diese Publikation in der Deutschen Nationalbibliografie; detaillierte bibliografische Daten sind im Internet über http://dnb.d-nb.de abrufbar.

ISBN-13: 3-8382-0135-1

Printed in the United States of America

Yesterday's outsider-method is today's academic medicine
and tomorrow's error in treatment!

(Die Außenseitermethode von gestern ist die Schulmedizin von
heute und der Behandlungsfehler von morgen!)

G. Schroeder-Printzen, ehem. Vors. Richter am BSG

Für Hans-Joachim

List of abbreviations

ABDA	Federal Union of German Associations of Pharmacists
ABDATA	Pharma Data Service
ABO	Ordinance on the Operation of pharmacies (Austria)
ABPI	Association of the British Pharmaceutical Industry
ABGB	Austrian Civil Code of 1811
ÄG	Austrian National Law on Physicians
ADR	Adverse Drug Reaction
ADE	Adverse Drug Event
AERS	Adverse Event Reporting System (FDA)
AFSSAPS	French Health Products Safety Agency
AGES	Austrian Agency for Health and Food Safety
AKW	Vienna Pharmaceutical Chamber
ÄKW	Vienna Medical Chamber
AMA	American Medical Association
AMD	Age Related Macular Degeneration
AMG	German Drug Act as amended on 12.12.2005
AMG-Au	Austrian Drug Act as amended on BGBl. I Nr. 112/2007
AMGKostV	AMG Cost Ordinance
AMK	(ABDA) Drug Commission of the German pharmaceutical Association
APhA	American Pharmacist Organisation
ApBetrO	Ordinance on the Operation of pharmacies (Germany)
ASP	Drug Safety in Psychiatry (Austria, Germany)
ATC	Anatomical Therapeutic Chemical
ATU	Temporary Use Authorization (France)
AWEG	Austrian Medicines' Importation Act as amended on 02.01.2006
BÄO	German National Law on Physicians
BAG	Federal Office of Health (Switzerland)
BAH	Federal Association of Drug Manufacturers (Germany)
BAS	Biological Active Substance
BCCA	British Columbia Cancer Agency (Canada)
BfArM	Federal Institute for Medicinal Products and Devices (Germany)
BGB	German Civil Code as amended on 02.01.2002
BMG	Federal Ministry of Health (Germany)
BNF-C	British National Formulary for Children
BPCA	Best Pharmaceuticals for Children Act (U.S.)
CADRAMP	Canadian Adverse Drug Reaction Monitoring Program Adverse Reaction Database
CADRMP	Canadian Adverse Drug Reaction Monitoring Program
CADTH	Canadian Agency for Drugs and Technologies in Health
CAP	Compassionate Access Program
CAQDA	Computer-Aided Qualitative Data Analysis
CDC	Centers for Disease Control and Prevention (U.S.)
CDER	Center for Drug Evaluation and Research (FDA)
CHF	Swiss Franc
CHLIA	Canadian Life and Health Insurance Association
CHMP	Committee for Medicinal Products for Human Use (E.U.)
CIRS	Critical Incident Reporting System

CMS	Centers for Medicare & Medicaid Services (U.S.)
CNOM	National Medical Professional Association (France)
CNOP	National Council of French Pharmacists
COMP	Committee for Orphan Medicinal Products (E.U.)
CP	Centralized Procedure (E.U.)
CPA	Canadian Pharmacists Association
CPSO	College of Physicians and Surgeons of Ontario (Canada)
CRO	Contract Research Organization
CSP	Public Health Act (France)
CTEP	Cancer Therapy Evaluation Program (U.S.)
DCP	Decentralized Procedure
DDL	Dear Doctor Letter
DIN	Drug Identity Number (Canada)
DLH	German Leukemia and Lymphoma Group
DSP	Drug Shortage Program (U.S.)
DSRU	Drug Safety Research Unit (U.K.)
EAP	Expanded Access Programs
EC	European Commission
EDRP	Emergency Drug Release Program (Canada)
EEA	European Economic Area
EFPIA	European Federation of Pharmaceutical Industries and Associations
EMA	European Medical Association
EMEA	European Medicines Agency
EML-C	(WHO) Essential Medicines' List for Children
ESIP	European Social Insurance Partners
EU	European Union
EUnetHTA	European network for Health Technology Assessment
FD&C	Food, Drug and Cosmetic Act as amended through December 31, 2004
FDA	Food and Drug Administration
FDAMA	Food and Drug Administration Modernization Act of 1997
FDR	Food and Drug Regulations as amended in October 2006 (Canada)
FMH	Swiss Medical Association
G-BA	Federal Joint Committee (Germany)*
GCP	Good Clinical Practice
HAS	French National Authority for Health
HCC	(UK) Health Care Commission
HCP	Health Care Professional
HEK	Committee for Drug Evaluation (Austria)
HMG	Swiss Federal Law on Medicinal Products and Medical Devices 2002
HTA	Health Technology Assessment
HV	Main Association of Austrian Social Security Institutions
ICH	International Conference on Harmonization
IIT	Investigator Initiated Trial
IMPD	Investigational Medicinal Products Dossier

* self-governing bodies of service providers and health insurance funds

IND	Investigational New Drug
Interpharma	Association of Drug Manufacturers (Austria)
IQWIG	Institute for Quality and Efficiency in Health Care (Germany)
IRB	Institutional Review Board
JMA	Japan Medical Association
JPA	Japan Pharmaceutical Association
JPMA	Japanese Pharmaceutical Manufacturers Association
KAKJ	Committee for Children's and Adolescent's Medicines (Germany)
KVB	Association of Statutory Health Insurance Physicians (Bavaria)
LEEM	Union of the drug industry companies (France)
m	Million
MA	Marketing Authorization
MAH	Marketing Authorization Holder
MDK	Medical Service for Health Insurance Companies (Germany)
MHRA	Medicines and Healthcare Products Regulatory Agency (U.K.)
MICE	Medicines Investigation for the Children of Europe
MP	Medicinal Product
MRP	Mutual Recognition Procedure (EU)
MS	Member State (EU)
NCE	New Chemical Entity
NCI	National Cancer Institute (U.S.)
NDA	New Drug Application
NDU	Nonlicensed Drug Use (i.e., off-label, compassionate, unlicensed use)
NHI	National Health Insurance (Japan)
NHS	National Health Service (UK)
NICE	National Institute for Clinical Excellence (UK)
NIPH	National Institute of Public Health (Japan)
NME	New Molecular Entity
NOC	Notice of Compliance (Canada)
OMP	Orphan Medicinal Products
PAL	Pharmaceutical Affairs Law as of July 2002 (Japan)
PASS	Post-Authorization Safety Studies
PatG	German Patent Law
PCMA	Pharmaceutical Care Management Association
PCT	Primary Care Trust
PDCO	(EMEA -) Pediatric Committee
PDMA	Pharmaceuticals and Medical Devices Agency (Japan)
PEM	Prescription Event Monitoring
PGEU	Pharmaceutical Group of the European Union
Ph.Helv.	Swiss Pharmacopeia
Pharma Forum	Swiss Pharmacists Association
Pharmig	Association of the Austrian Pharmaceutical Industry
PhRMA	Pharmaceutical Research and Manufacturers of America
PIP	Pediatric Investigation Plan (E.U.)
PMDA	Pharmaceuticals and Medical Devices Agency (Japan)
PREA	Pediatric Research Equity Act (U.S.)
PSUR	Periodic Safety Update Report (E.U.)
PUMA	Pediatric Use Marketing Authorization (E.U.)

RCPLondon	Royal College of Physicians (U.K.)
(R)CT	(randomized) controlled trial
RPSGB	Royal Pharmaceutical Society of Great Britain
Rx&D	Canada's Research-Based Pharmaceutical Companies
SABRE	Serious Adverse Blood Reactions and Events (UK)
SAMS	Special Access Management System (Canada)
Santesuisse	Umbrella Association of the Swiss Social Health Insurance Sector
SAP	Special Access Program (Canada)
SAR	Special Access Request (Canada)
SmPC	Summary of Product Characteristics
SMUD	Safety Management System for Unapproved Drugs (Japan)
SPC	Supplementary Protection Certificate
SPSU	Swiss Paediatric Surveillance Unit
StGB	penal code
Swissmedic	Swiss Agency for Therapeutic Products
TEDDY	Task-force for Drug Development for the Young (E.U.)
U.S.	United States (of America)
UNCAM	Health Insurance Fund National Union (France)
VAM	Swiss Ordinance on Drugs
VAZV	Swiss Ordinance on the simplified approval of drugs
VDAK	Association of the Employees Health Insurance Companies (Germany)
VfA	German Association of research-based Pharmaceutical Companies
WHO	World Health Organization
ZAK	Licensed Medicines for Children (Germany)

Reference note

For reasons of readability, notations are simplified. Interviews are cited as N."digit" by their numbers corresponding to Table 4 in lower index.

Acknowledgements

I would like to especially thank Professor Dr. Harald Schweim for his support and for allowing me latitude.

I am also thankful to PD Dr. Harald Enzmann for his valuable contribution.

I am grateful to the Deutsche Gesellschaft für Regulatorische Angelegenheiten for their scholarship, to the Drug Information Association for their poster prize as well as student fellowship and to MeTra – Mentoring- und Trainingsprogramm für Wissenschaftlerinnen i.e. Prof. Dr. Daniela Gündisch, Mrs. U. Mättig as well as Dr. Martina Pottek, for their conceptual support.

My sincere and genuine thanks to Dr. Christian Behles, Dr. Helga Blasius, approved drug information pharmacist Petra Nies, Dipl. jur. Janna Schweim, pre-registration trainee Carina Kapoor and Dipl. Dok. Katharina Schirawski for their collaboration. Many thanks go to my colleague Daniel Lewinski.

This thesis would have not been possible without the contribution of all the interviewees and experts. I gratefully acknowledge your participation in the study.

I would like to thank all the employees of the department of pharmacy and the department of cellular biology.

I appreciate the time that Jenny, Tobi and Sophie took to share their ideas and experience. My biggest thanks to Monika, Patrick and Maja. Thanks Katja.

I wish to thank my significant other Hans-Joachim.

Finally I would like to acknowledge the BMG for encouraging the research group's activities.

There are many more who must be thanked. Thanks to all.

Table of contents

Table of contents

Abstract

In times of situational therapeutic impasse, pressure to conduct off-label, unlicensed and compassionate use, which are hereafter summarized under the term nonlicensed drug use (NDU) is exerted onto health care professionals (HCPs). Liability, contractual and penal risks are present when treating a patient in a nonlicensed way. There is a gap of knowledge about institutional and governmental methods of resolution concerning off-label, unlicensed and compassionate use. Hypothesize is however, that strategies to manage off-label, unlicensed and compassionate use have evolved in different countries. The research problem of this thesis is thus to compare the effects of NDU on pharmaceutical legislation in selected industrial countries and to determine strategies brought forth by NDU. Furthermore, the development of a general regulatory approach to the management of NDU is sought. A regulatory approach shall consider existing conventions and available means in the present regulatory world.

Semi-structured qualitative interviews, comparison of laws, and literature research i.e. triangulation, was the scientific methodology chosen to address the research problem. The study was undertaken in Canada, the U.S., U.K., Japan, France, Germany, Switzerland, Austria and the transnational E.U. 45 semi-structured qualitative interviews were conducted with 47 selected representatives of different roles from a) five areas of interests and b) each country. The emphasis of this comparison of the impact of NDU laid on terminology for NDU, supply and necessity of NDU, pharmaceutical promotion of NDU, legal responsibility for NDU and public policies related to NDU. Social legislation was not considered.

Key findings from the survey included miscellaneous synonyms for NDU, multiple definitions for NDU and different classes of off-label, unlicensed and compassionate use. Two important results from the current literature on supply and necessity derived: There is a circumstantial need for off-label, unlicensed and compassionate use, but isolated evidence suggested nonrational NDU intermittently. Furthermore, the comparison of laws showed legal obligations of physicians to perform off-label, unlicensed and compassionate use. Another outcome was proof of inappropriate off-label marketing on the part of MA holders (MAH). On the other hand, a demand for information on NDU on behalf of HCPs was present. Obtained results illustrated cross-liability for HCPs and MAH. Special use authorizations, which were recommended by interviewed representatives, were found. Pharmacovigilance in NDU was seen to be either intensified in the scope of special use authorizations or else relied on routine adverse drug reaction (ADR) reporting. Finally, results demonstrated regulatory strategies of different efficiencies: In the E.U. for instance, incentives for new indications were (a) limited to one year or (b) restricted to (i) pediatrics or (ii) rare disorders. This was found to probably be insufficient, because a drug may be appropriate for multiple indications or much-needed in fields of medicine other than pediatrics or rare disorders.

The absence of statutory terminology causes incoherent interpretation of NDU across the researched nations; harmonization is crucial for an effective concept development. There is a situational need for early access to unapproved treatments. Denial of (nonlicensed) treatment is considered unethical. Databases to combat data shortage about NDU are operated intermittently in different settings. On the other hand, isolated evidence also highlights inappropriate marketing of NDU, which perhaps causes irrational NDU. Different effective regulatory strategies are at hand for patient access to off-label, unlicensed and compassionate use of medications in the short term. If present, these so-called special use authorizations are accompanied by drug safety measures exceeding customary ADR reporting and providing for pharmacovigilance, which otherwise would be absent. Special use authorizations define the liability and provide legal certainty. In the long term however, demand-driven approach to marketing authorization (MA), not neglecting the fact that a single drug may be appropriate in many indications, is crucial. Proposed solutions for an enduring management of NDU are firstly, the amendments of templates by competent authorities to include appropriate off-label use, secondly full MA of innovative MPs used compassionately and thirdly an amended German standard MA for essential unlicensed drugs.

1. Introduction

The term 'off label use' is first mentioned by Higgins et al. in 1988.[1] The concept of using a drug in a way different from the stated method on the label is however, long-established: On June 1st 1961 the first oral contraceptive, Anovlar®, is marketed in Germany.[2] An approved indication for application is menstrual dysfunction. It was if used for contraception, only to be prescribed to married women according to the marketing authorization holder's (MAH's) information. To prescribe oral contraceptives only to married women is medically implausible. The drug's marketing authorization (MA) did not correspond to science.

Equal mechanisms of action can be effective in managing different conditions, i.e. menstrual dysfunction and contraception in the example given above. This leads to use of one drug in different therapeutic areas. MA need not have been granted. In our time the vascular endothelial growth factor inhibitor bevacizumab[i] for treatment of colon cancer is widely used "off label" in the treatment of wet age-related macular degeneration (AMD). Often, drugs are approved for a limited indication, while a wide range of possible indications is apparent. This is particularly the case for newly approved drugs with a very limited approved indication. Use beyond a label becomes common practice and is subject to criticism. Common keywords of disapproval are: corporate responsibility of the MAH to apply for an MA, circumvention of the licensing process by the MAH through marketing methods, liability of health care professionals (HCPs) and patient safety. Supporters of drug use beyond the product label presently bring forward ethical arguments of situational drug supply gaps and medical assistance for patients without adequate treatment options.

Lack of treatment options has led to emergency drug release long before off label use is first mentioned: The FDA is believed to have a compassionate use policy in place since the 1970s or before.[3] The areas of controversy at that time were and still are patient exploitation and live-saving therapy in cases involving investigational AIDS drugs. There is, even nowadays, a circumstantial need for nonlicensed drug uses, such as in patients with diseases for which therapeutic options are exhausted or unavailable. On the other hand, compassionate use is dismissed as experiments in humans.

MA is meant to ensure evidenced-based pharmacotherapy; absence of MA did however, not hinder use of drugs in the past: Records mentioning unlicensed use are found as early as 1975.[4] Therapeutic approaches or medicinal products unavailable in a patient's country of residency are nowadays widely acknowledged through international media, targeting both HCPs and patients. Demand for a specific medicinal product (MP), which has not received MA in a certain country, is therefore stimulated more easily today than it was in the pre-internet era.[N.16]

All three drug uses have been subject to thorough quantitative investigation: The research field of off-label, unlicensed and compassionate use, after this summarized under the term nonlicensed drug use (NDU), is yet relatively new. It is also growing, as evidenced by the increasing number of papers on the subject. NDU has attracted much attention in pediatrics, oncology and neurology with regard to prospective and retrospective cohort studies. Research on NDU is focused on the incidences of NDUs and does not examine the impact on legislation. It is unexplored as far as institutional and governmental strategies of resolution are concerned. Legislation affecting decisions related to NDU has not been reviewed in a cross-national survey. Transnational laws regulating NDU of MPs and assuring drug safety and supply have not been compared and contrasted. Regarding NDU, regulation for product liability for the MAH has also not been compared internationally. Means of preventing circumventions of the licensing process have not been subject to scientific investigation. Neither legal definition for NDU has been searched for worldwide. Nor have experiences by authorities, societies and organizations with making rules regulating NDU been evaluated across national boundaries. A stocktaking of laws applying to physicians, hospitals, pharmacists, authorities and MAHs has not yet been performed. An assessment of the shortfalls in legislation and solutions for such has not been presented. Surveys into (a) deficiencies concerning drug supply in different therapeutic areas, the (b) necessity and (c) conduct of NDU are absent. Criteria by which is it possible to extend indications in a simplified process have not been analyzed in the past. However, evidence from France and the U.S. suggests processes to be present.

Hypothesize is set that strategies to manage off-label, unlicensed and compassionate use have evolved and contribute to a safe and effective management of NDU. The research problem is therefore to compare different, national regulatory solutions brought forth by off-label, unlicensed and compassionate use. The main research aim is to develop a general regulatory approach to the management of NDU. The study focuses on nonlicensed use of human MPs. Veterinary MPs, medical devices, food supplements and cosmetics and their unauthorized use are not the subject of this study. The term "off label use" is assigned to a medication practice not indicated in the SmPC and prescribed as such by a physician.

Abusive misuse and unintentional, incorrect use were not regarded as off label use and therefore not assessed. It was necessary to not only pay attention to the terms and their synonyms, but also for similar concepts. Sources were only examined closely when associated with unlabeled drug use, which is anticipated to treat, identify or prevent disease or when conceptualizing off label use else wise. The term "unlicensed use" was assigned to the use of any product as a medicine that does not have a legitimate MA in the country considered, irrespective of the registration requirements in the country of origin. "Compassionate use" was also related to the use of active treatment investigational new drugs (INDs) in individuals or groups of patients not participating in a clinical trial. Compassionate und unlicensed use are also not restricted to the proposed area of application of a product. The primary focus of this study is health legislation affecting NDU. Health care law is defined as any pharmaceutical legislation and statutory provisions on MPs and the following of regulations such as directives or guidelines. Selected aspects of medical law and professional codes of conduct were taken into consideration. Social legislation is not covered and the researched countries are U.S., Canada, U.K., France, Germany, Austria, Switzerland, Japan and the E.U.

CURRENT STATE OF SCIENCE: RATES OF NONLICENSED DRUG USE The following review of the state-of-the-art of science aims at giving an updated overview of the multinational situation of nonlicensed drug use in different settings. There are conflicts in the literature concerning the percentage of NDU. Another major problem to overcome, when developing a general regulatory approach to the management of NDU, is its commonness in certain medical fields. The summary looks at off label, unlicensed and compassionate use, pediatric and oncological NDU in out- and inpatient care.

Bücheler et al. finds off label use in Germany to account for 13.2% of 1.74 m prescriptions by pediatricians from Baden-Württemberg, general practitioners and internal specialists in the first quarter of 1999.[5] In some medical sectors, however, he finds off label use rates of up to 64%. Results by Schütz indicate that misoprostol[i] is used for induction of labor by 42% of researched physicians, and 82.1% used misoprostol[i] for a practice period of more than two years. Nearly half (44.8%) prefer misoprostol[i] for induction of labor[6] (N.B. oxytocin is licensed for induction of labor in Germany). A survey by Conroy et al. suggests that off label use is common in specialized pediatric care. Her results show that 41% of the patients in Germany did not receive prescriptions in accordance with the MA.[7]

Questioning an E.U. expert revealed that three compassionate use programs took place in Germany in 2007.[8] Unlicensed use is partially measurable by the rate of MPs imported to Germany: Results from 1064 community pharmacies in 19 out of 54 districts and cities in North Rhine-Westphalia for the second half of 2003 reveal 10,729 import transactions (19,193 packages).[9] In oncology care, the federal government suggests that 70%–80% of cases involve off label use.[10] Estimations (without empiric survey) imply rates of 56% and 90% for off label prescriptions in pediatric inpatient and neonatal care, respectively.[11] Results in psychiatric hospitals confirm 20% off label prescriptions (additional 19% off label use probable) for 2001–2002 and 2% (additional 26% off label use probable) in 2003–2004.[12] SmPCs of some drugs require extra qualifications of the physician prescribing the MP, and so prescriptions issued by physicians without advanced training can be considered off-label: Lauktien reports that in an analysis of prescriptions for controlled drugs, 17% of methylphenidate[i] scripts are prescribed by physicians who did not qualify.[13]

Off label prescriptions occur at a rate of 20% to 50% in the E.U.[14] An up-to-date list of compassionate use products[15] is not yet available according to information provided by the EMEA, because surprisingly no decisions have been taken.[16] Data on unlicensed use in general in the E.U. is not available. In oncology units 33% off label and 19% unlicensed use takes place according to European studies.[17] In line with an announcement in 2005 by the European Commission, more than 50% of all drugs are prescribed to children on an off label basis.[18]

There are no data in Japan on the incidence of off label use, compassionate use or pediatric NDU. A study by the Division of Clinical Trial Design & Management in the Translational Research Center of the Kyoto University Hospital in 2003 reveal that 30% of anti-cancer treatments and 40% of the products of complementary oncology, standard products for American physicians according to 'Current Medical Diagnosis and Treatment – an easy-to-read Manual', are not licensed in Japan.[19]

The British Drug Safety Research Unit, a registered independent charity, finds a rate of 22% off label use in children.[20] Their study on Foradil® (formoterol[i]) suggests that 258 children, or 4.5% of the cohort, received the drug on an off label basis.[21] Data on compassionate use in the U.K. is unavailable (as of 2007). An inquiry of the regulatory agency on January 25th 2008 revealed 704,812 notifications on record since January 2002.[22] Data by Conroy et al. demonstrate that in pediatric oncology, every child was treated at least once in a way not in accordance with the drug's license.[23] A further study by Conroy et al. in children's wards suggests that 109 out of 192 patients (84.5%) were assigned drugs not meeting licensing specifications.[24] Of 205 prescriptions dispensed, 66 cases (32%) involve patients receiving a diverging dose or doses at diverging intervals, 79 prescriptions (39%) are not suited for the patient with regard to his or her age, 36 (17%) are used in another indication, and 24 (12%) are given via another route of application.

In France, off label use is as frequent as 25% to 40% of the prescriptions in specific medical areas (not representative).[25] The French expert N.34 (see) stated that each year, 200 products are granted an ATU (temporary use authorization) by the AFSSAPS (agence française de sécurité sanitaire des produits de santé), and 20,000 nominative ATUs are issued every year. Temporary use authorizations are ascertained statistically since 1994. From 1994 until 2006, 781 drugs were used on ATU basis in oncology, infectious diseases, endocrinology and neurology. By February 1st 2008, eleven valid ‚ATU de cohorte' were present.[26] Data on unlicensed use is absent in France as of 2008. In 2001, a scientific analysis of the Vidal formulary (French National Formulary) 2000 explored pediatric information with regard to cytotoxic chemotherapy. At completion, 416 products qualified for cancer therapy; however, only 76 MPs remained after a) "drugs not to be used in children" and b) "drugs available on an ATU basis" had been excluded. As few as 20 out of 76 drugs were seen to provide pediatric information classified as "satisfying", 37 MPs were found to provide moderate information, and 19 unsatisfactory information. Out of 48 drugs prescribed only to pediatric patients, only 14 are seen to have distinct pediatric indications. Pediatric information is found to be available for dosing in 27 cases and contraindications are available in 8 cases. Pediatric information for drugs commonly used in children is seen to be satisfactory in 23% of the cases, poor for 38% and unsatisfactory for 30% of all cases.[27] In outpatient care, off label use in French children is estimated at 20%-30%; for inpatient care the rate is 67% and in neonatal and intensive care it is 90%.[28 29 30]

As early as 1980, Erickson et al. published an analysis of the proportion of drugs that are "used in an unlabelled way" in the U.S. i.e. 46 out of 500 drugs in an outpatient clinic.[31] Thompson et al. report an incidence of 7% (62 out of 951) off label use in a survey of drug orders from 1987 in university teaching hospitals.[32] Results of a Delphi-analysis judge 24 (39%) drug orders as reasonable and 10 (16%) unsuitable. Consensus was not possible for 45% of the orders. Raybourn et al. report a survey of women who were examined before the 14th week of pregnancy and who then gave birth to their child at a university hospital in Oklahoma: 22.6% (165 out of 731) women are found to have been treated off label in terms of the drug's indication.[33] In 2001, an estimated 150 m (95% confidence interval, 127-173 m) off-label mentions (21% of overall use) are present in the U.S.[34] The Association of Community Cancer Centers report very frequent off label uses in the eighties.[35] Another study at the same point in time reveals that one third of all patients in oncology receive a drug off-label. Another scientific investigation reports that 44 out of 46 drugs licensed for cancer treatment are prescribed off label at least once and more than half of all cancer patients (56%) receive an off label prescription at least once.[36] Albuterol (a selective beta-2-adrenergic agonist) is an example of a commonly used off label drug for children that has pediatric disclaimers stating that "safety and efficacy has not been studied in children".[37] Three out of four prescription drugs marketed in the U.S. lack full pediatric approval in 1996.[38] During the period 1997 through 2005, the FDA receives an average of 4.6 treatment INDs per year and approximately 659 emergency INDs (INDs) per year.[39]

In Canada, statistics on off label use, unlicensed use or NDUs in pediatrics or oncology are absent as well. A Canadian expert estimates that on average 300 off label prescriptions are issued per year.[40] 30,000 special access requests per year are processed by Health Canada; thousands of requests are authorized per year.[41]

A telephone survey in Austria finds that 115 (66.5%) patients receive a psychotropic agent for an off label indication between 1996 and 1997.[42] Quantitative studies on the incidence of compassionate use and NDU in oncology care are found neither for the inpatient nor the outpatient sector. According to the Austrian Society for Child and Adolescent Care, 50% of all drugs used in children's wards (general medicine) and 90% of drugs in neonatal care are not licensed.[43] Although these figures may, by careful judgment, originally derive from the U.K. As to the import fraction of unlicensed use: 925 import declarations were registered at AGES PharmMed for 2006.[44]

In a prospective study about unlicensed and off label prescriptions Di Paolo et al. provide evidence over a period of six months in Swiss university hospitals and the Children's Hospital of Lausanne. Sixty patients aged 3 days to 14 years were included in the study, and 483 prescriptions were analyzed. More than half of the prescriptions (247; 51%) met licensing criteria, while 114 (24%) are classified as unlicensed use, and 122 (25%) as off label use.[45] Approximately 4500 requests and 3000 inquiries for special dispensation ("Sonderbewilligung") led to an approval of 3197 requests in 2002 by Swissmedic with a view to compassionate use.[46] Lambert's study assessing the prescription behavior in a pediatric hospital in Basel in 251 pediatric patients, analyzed 1,339 prescriptions and finds rates of 46% off label and 10% unlicensed use. In summary, 79% of the children are treated in an off label or unlicensed way. There is no information available on NDU in Swiss oncology. Another study analyzes 1,033 drugs used in 2002-2003 at the University Children's Hospital of Basel, the Island Hospital of Bern, and the Children's Hospital of Zurich; 296 active ingredients with pediatric information are found in the SmPCs.[47][48] For 187 active substances (63.2%) a need for action is postulated by the authors, and 95 active pharmaceutical ingredients (APIs) (32.1%) require updates or further specifications of the SmPC in the Swiss Formulary. Eight active ingredients (2.7%) had claims for dosages in children, but a pediatric pharmaceutical form is still crucial and 114 active substances (38.5%) require clinical trials on the safety and efficacy of age appropriate formulations by opinion of the researchers.

Data are also available for countries that are not focus of this thesis: In the Netherlands Schirm et al. finds a rate of 22.7% off label drug use in pediatric outpatient care.[49] The extent of off label and unlicensed use depends on the patients and the supply area.[50] O'Donell et al. find 58% of all Australian pediatric prescriptions are NDU.[51]

This summary with a focus on the afore mentioned medical areas, underlines the presumption that selected medical sectors are affected by NDU. However, research activities have merely focused heavily on the incidence of NDUs especially in pediatrics and oncology. In fact, NDUs are assumed to also be common in other areas of expertise.[52] More research is needed.

OBJECTIVE AND RESEARCH QUESTIONS Due to the commonness of NDU, its impact on legislation is expected to be considerable. The key objective of this study is therefore to contrast different regulatory strategies brought forth by off-label, unlicensed and compassionate use. Another key aim is to design an approach to the management of NDU.

The following key research questions are pursued in order to contrast legislative management in different countries: What are the legal definitions for NDU? Which surveys of deficiencies concerning first the drug supply in different therapeutic areas, second the necessity and finally conduct of NDU exist? Which laws regulate NDU in terms of drug safety and supply of MPs? Which laws apply to HCPs, hospitals, authorities and MAHs? What experiences with rules for NDU were made by authorities, societies and other organizations? How is liability for NDU regulated to the MAH? What legislation affects therapeutic decisions related to NDU? How can circumventions of the MA be prevented? Which criteria allow indications to be extended in a simplified application process, while assuring drug safety? Which shortfalls in legislation are in place and how can they be overcome?

The purpose of this project extends beyond recording the current state of affairs, to suggesting a procedure as a proposal for solution. Information on off-label, unlicensed and compassionate use is reported to often be insufficient; risk for patients due to a lack of data are described. Rules for rational, well-founded pharmacotherapy outside or without product licenses are said to be crucial. The review, analysis and documentation of firstly the legal state in bordering countries, secondly literature research and finally qualitative research shall contribute to identification of solutions.

2. Methodology and Materials

Triangulation i.e. use of two or more research methods in one study was achieved by using a combination of literate research, comparison of laws and qualitative research. While literature research and comparison of laws provides unrestricted information, new theories as well as confidential information and data that are either unpublished or inaccessible to the public, could not be captured by a simple subject matter search. Reliance on qualitative research to identify strategies alone, was judged to be error prone. Data collection, research into legislative provisions as well as qualitative interviewing and its analysis thus were combined to answer the research questions effectively. Triangulation ensures comprehensiveness and encourages a reflexive analysis of the data.[53]

2.1. Literature Research

Literature on NDU was available from an in-house database (Reference Manager®) managed since November 2005. The data provided for, derived from Medline®, HealthStar® and PsycInfo® by OVID, Embase® and SciSearch® (ISI Web of Knowledge).

Medline® was found to be a National Library of Medicine (NLM, U.S.) database. It was seen to contain bibliographic details and abstracts of papers from more than 4600 medical journals in 70 countries. Subject areas were said to include medicine, dentistry, veterinary medicine, psychology, public health, biology, chemistry, biomedicine and biophysics. Medline® was estimated to be one of the largest literature databases in the world. HealthStar® by Ovid was seen to be loaded with literature from Medline®, but was shown to contain own citations. HealthStar® was noted to specialize in public health, technology, administration/politics and scientific research in inpatient and outpatient care. For the in-house database, papers from 1966 onward were selected from both Ovid-Medline® and HealthStar®. PsycInfo® was designed to locate 2000 journals and covers psychology, neuroscience, law, medicine and service to the community. Its searches were observed to cover the period from 1967 until today. Embase® by Elsevier (Amsterdam/The Netherlands) was found to retrieve 9.5 m publications (mostly European journals) and provide coverage of human medicine and biological sciences, focusing on drugs, active substances (pharmacology, efficacy and adverse reactions), health economics and hospital affairs, environmental medicine, ecology, forensic science and drug addiction. SciSearch® (ISI

Thomson Scientific, U.S.) was estimated to be the source for 23 m documents from 5900 international journals covering applied sciences, technology and medicine.

The MeSH®-Thesaurus (MeSH® = Medical Subject Heading) was the descriptor for Medline® and HealthStar®. The search strategy used to build the in-house database consisted of a search method by NLM (National Library of Medicine) in 1992 termed 'off label use of prescription drugs'. This method was outdated and was therefore changed. Keywords (a) "off-label", "unlicensed use" and "compassionate use" were consequently used. These keywords produced results specific to documents using the terms. In order to also identify documents not using the term "off label use", yet referring to the same concept, (b) unlabel$[i], unapprov$, nonapprov$, non-approv$ and in Medline from 2006 onward "not approv$" and (c) selected expressions from the MeSH®-Thesaurus were used. Results (b) and (c) were merged to (d). (a) and (d) were pooled and duplicates removed.

The search strategy was adapted for use with other databases. Psycinfo offered a thesaurus from which further terms were included in the search. The search of Embase® allowed entry of only one keyword, therefore „off-label", „unlicensed" and „compassionate use" were employed to locate relevant studies. SciSearch® was also subjected to this search strategy and further terms.

The descriptors "off label use", "unlicensed use" and "compassionate use", "inpatient", "outpatient", "language", "country", "full text" and "source of origin" were assigned to the record as a presentation of contents.

2.2. Research into legislative provisions

Regulation on NDU was identified from in-house country reports. A systematic study of internet sources was carried out to determine relevant literature and other sources of information (surveys and studies on NDU regulation) for the country reports. Scientific, legal and administrative information was obtained in order to compare legislative frameworks and to provide an overview of concepts in each country. The possibilities and limitations of incentives as well as enforcing measures were acknowledged.

Evaluation grids, a procedure in place for drafting laws, were used to classify approaches to unlicensed use of medications (see 3.6 Liability for nonlicensed

[i] $ stands for masking of terms to increase hits by including all grammatical forms and endings

drug use) [prohibition with an obligation to obtain a permit, obligation of notification (general authorization, where necessary, subject to prohibition) (relatively autonomous legal framework) and prohibition (restrictive rules), subject to the possibility of authorization].

2.3. Qualitative research in Regulatory Affairs

Qualitative research was historically a research instrument in social and geographical sciences. In health research, qualitative questioning of patients was seen to be common. In recent times, it was introduced to pharmaceutical sciences.[54] [55] [56] [57] Qualitative approaches have until now, not taken into account regulatory requirements. In this thesis, methods in qualitative health research were adapted to the exigencies of the regulatory field (see 2.3.1 Experimental design).

Qualitative research provided the interviewer with internal and otherwise inaccessible information. Nonlicensed drug use was seen to be a delicate topic e.g. for MAH due to liability issues and physicians because of the risk of recourse. Qualitative interviews were a valuable source of information for confidential data or intelligence not available in literature or else not accessible to the public. Unpublished information thus became accessible, reported or even provided directly to the researcher by the expert. Internal data and the level of knowledge and awareness in circles of experts was presented to the interviewer.

The absence of legal definitions has caused available studies to be incomparable. Former research nevertheless highlighted the extent of NDU in disciplines such as pediatrics, but failed to compare cross-national conventions, pharmaceutical legislation and handling of risks. Qualitative methods served as a technique for comparing law in comparison to effective practice. Experience from regulatory bodies, societies and associations, and hence shortfalls in practice, were surveyed with qualitative methods so as to overcome information difficulties and find lowest common denominators for definitions.

Qualitative research was seen to be able to a) contribute to measurement through the construction of simple scales and b) aggregate measures (typologies and taxonomies, see figure 7)[58] as well as c) the understanding of the reasons behind NDU. Qualitative interviews were described to be a precise source for description and explanation of patterns. Interviews supplied information on national options and needs. Primary, practical perspectives were captured.

Qualitative research was found to provide a more rich and deep understanding of a situation.[59] Descriptive statistics were judged to illustrate procedures accurately and to capture attributes. Everyday situations, daily practices and real life conditions can be revealed.[60] In particular, HCPs' experience with present procedures provided an insight into the success or failure of solutions. Findings in literature and law were confirmed or disproved. Qualitative interviewing allowed for continued reviewing of the in-house country reports during the data collection period. This detail was particularly important for the determination of conventions for informal proceedings.

A response to shifts and new questions is feasible in qualitative research.[61] Previous knowledge gained during literature research allowed the interviewer to take up national subjects and discuss them in greater detail. Recent incidents were addressed, and it was possible to re-sequence interview topics and omit questions to avoid termination of an interview.

A qualitative study design is generally explorative and based on multiple case reports. Research participants were seen to not be obligated to check boxes and select answers that may not represent their response adequately.[62] Qualitative research met the requirement of a timesaving technique that persuaded chief executives to participate in the survey. Interviewees were found to be allowed to talk at length and think about items in their own terms.[63] This explorative approach was essential to discover new theories and unpublished approaches to a problem. As a result of the qualitative survey, theories were developed from the observations.

2.3.1. Experimental design

Semi-structured interviews were selected due to their circumstantial flexibility whilst enabling comparison of covered topics. Yet, three major forms of interviewing were seen to be known to qualitative research: structured, unstructured and semi-structured[64] (see figure 1). Structured interviews were found to require the researcher to repeatedly ask the interviewee the same set of questions. With this form of interviewing, issues identified after the interview topic guide was passed, were likely to not be picked up and in-depth discussion of a topic is not stimulated. Furthermore, response categories were proved to be limited. Structured interviews were best to be used when literature in a subject area is highly developed.[65]

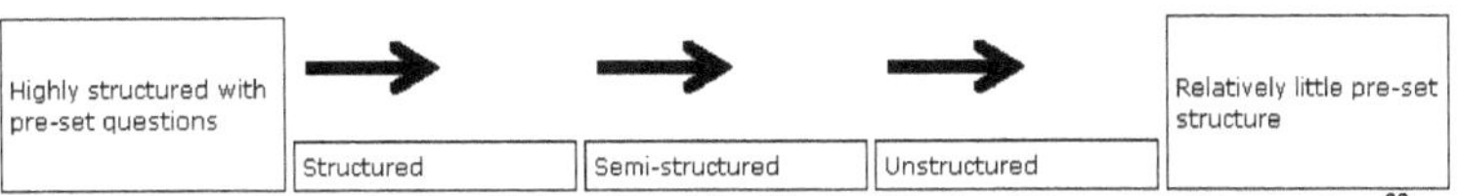

Figure 1 Types of interviewing (University of the West of England Research Observatory[66])

Unstructured interviews did not require preset questions. They were predicted to be difficult to replicate (see section 'Reliability') and they have a greater potential for bias. Unstructured interviews were rejected because of the risk of poor comparability of findings.

Semi-structured interviews were conducted using an interview topic guide that suggests questions to be covered by the researcher. Excursions were acceptable according to the researcher's discretion. 16 in-depth, semi-structured interviews involved face-to-face interviews, and 28 were conducted by telephone (see table 30). Sturges et al. found that face-to-face and telephone interviews yielded similar information and depth, provided that immersion in the environment is not necessary.[67] Up to two interviewers questioned one expert. In other cases interviews were scheduled with two participants or an expert decided to consult a colleague, who then joined the interview. This multi-method approach was found to be admissible.[68]

A semi-structured interview was seen to be best used when repeated interviewing is difficult and when there is more than one interviewer. Semi-structured interviewing was also chosen because a completely pre-designed questionnaire as in structured interviewing, would have limited the in-depth discussion of topics. Semi-structured interviews were also used because they allowed probing and clarification, thus preserving standardization and comparison in contrast to unstructured interviews. Interviewing was preceded by country reports to develop an understanding of local NDU. An interview topic guide was developed following U.S. and GB reports and based on research questions stated in the synopsis of the dissertation. Semi-structured interviews allowed participants to raise issues and concerns.

Selecting participants Six candidate roles were subject to recruitment in the eight countries and E.U.

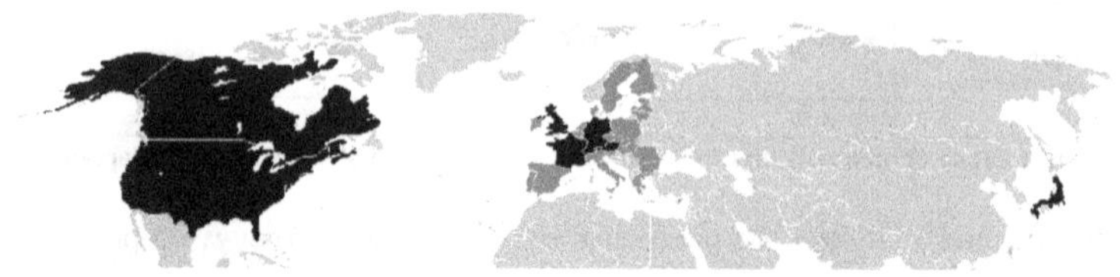

Figure 2 Researched countries (black) and E.U. member states (dark grey)

Representative roles from medical and pharmaceutical "societies", industry, regulatory agencies, academia, and funding agencies involved with NDU were invited to participate. Data collection was performed by in-depth interviews (t = 9 to 180 minutes) either face-to-face or by telephone survey at study sites in Germany, the U.K. and Austria. Qualitative sampling was meant to be purposive. Inclusion criteria for participation in this survey were (a) affiliation to a stakeholder, (b) point of contact to NDUs, and (c) willingness to provide insightful information.

A wide range of interests and stakeholders was selected in order to represent possibly all current opinions. Six categories were chosen: (a) medical or pharmaceutical societies, self help groups, HCP associations, federations and confederations, (b) "regulatory" bodies, either a supreme or higher federal authority and federal state authorities, (c) "MAH"s denoting pharmaceutical companies or enterprises or their federal associations, (d) funding agencies including institutes for cost benefit analysis, and (e) "academia" including research professors, lawyers and authors of scientific papers. Table 1 was set up to illustrate the organizations wherefrom research participants were recruited. In "academia", participants were authors of publications, which were identified in the interoffice database; those were contacted directly. All other organizations were first contacted not addressing a specific person. If two such approaches failed, publications on NDU by the institutions were checked for correspondence data and then addressed personally.

Category / Country	Society		Regulatory	Funding agencies		Coverage	Academia
	Medical	*Pharmaceutical*		**MAH**	**HTA**		
GERMANY	DLH	AMK	BfArM	VfA, BAH	IQWIG	MDK	University of Berlin
AUSTRIA	ÄKW	AKW	AGES PharmMed	Pharmig	HEK	HV	University of Innsbruck
SWITZERLAND	FMH	Pharma Forum	Swissmedic	Interpharma	BAG	Santé Suisse	University of Basel
GB	RCPLondon, BMA	RPSGB	MHRA	ABPI	NICE	HCC	University of London
JAPAN	JMA	JPA	PDMA	JPMA	NIPH	NHI	Keio University
U.S.	AMA	APhA	FDA	PhRMA	PCMA	CMS	Columbia University
CANADA	CPSO	CPA	Health Canada	Rx&D	CADTH	CLHIA	Dalhousie University
FRANCE	CNOM	CNOP	ASSFAPS	LEEM	HAS	UNCAM	Institut Gustave-Roussy
E.U.	EMA	PGEU	EC	EFPIA	EUnetHTA	ESIP	Not applicable

Table 1 Recruitment by candidate roles and country of employment (see list of abbreviations for written out words)

Call / COUNTRY	Initial [N]	Response [N]	Appointments [N]
JAPAN	7	1	2
CANADA	10	8	2
U.S.	68	13	7
E.U.	9	6	5
SWITZERLAND	7	7	4
U.K.	13	13	10
GERMANY	31	15	9
AUSTRIA	7	5	4
FRANCE	9	4	2
TOTAL [N] (%)	161 (100)	98 (61)	45 (28)

Table 2 Participation

Table 2 was created to illustrate the call report. In Japan, two acceptances but only one response was the result of a primary request for information on compassionate use in Germany to the department of Drug Regulatory Affairs at the School of Pharmacy of the University of Bonn by a Japanese delegation. This delegation was in return asked to participate in the qualitative interview in return. In North America, eleven written inquiries were forwarded to their destination via the U.S. Embassy in Frankfurt; only one letter was acknowledged in the telephone follow-up. Two appointments for interviews were arranged in the follow up period. After this unsatisfying follow-up in North America, publications of the interoffice database were searched for experts, who were contacted by email if an academical directory provided contact information. A total of 119 publications were identified from the interoffice database for Canada and the U.S. For 57 experts, contact information was available in an academical directory. Eleven addresses were invalid. Three experts referred to other specialists. Five denied participation. Five additional appointments were made. In the E.U., six experts responded to the initial inquiry, five participated. All experts responded in the U.K. und Switzerland; participation was good or sufficient respectively. Germany produced mediocre reaction and satisfying contribution. In Austria, six experts were interviewed on four occasions. A low rate of participation was obtained in France. A total of 47 experts was interviewed at 45 appointments (see table 30).

Countries cited in 3 "Results" and onward not being subject to the survey (i.e., Belgium, Ireland and the Netherlands) originated from interviews with representatives from the E.U. or research scientists working abroad e.g. in the U.S. who were referring to specific measures in their home countries.

INTERVIEW TOPIC GUIDE The interview guide consisted of two sections (pharmaceutical and social law) and 15 domains of inquiry on the basis of research questions: Determination of terms; reasons for off-label, compassionate and unlicensed use; functional implementation; relevance; necessity; adequacy; regulation; liability policies; scientific analysis; pharmacovigilance; scientific information/continuous training; ruling/legislature; transparency/nescience; reality of health care and references/recommended further reading.

The sequence of questions depended on the course of conversation. Interviews were conducted in German or English.

Recruiting participants Participants were contacted by mail, email or telephone (see table 3).

Call / Country	Initial consultation	Follow up 1	Follow up 2
Austria	Email	Telephone	–
U.K.	Email	Telephone	Telephone
U.S.	Mail	Telephone	Email
Canada	Mail	Telephone	Email
France	Mail	Email	–
E.U.	Mail	Email	Telephone
Japan	Email	–	–
Switzerland	Telephone	–	–
Germany	Mail	Telephone	Email

Table 3 In chronological order : Contact to organizations and experts

To increase participation, an allowance for special expenditures was offered; only one participant demanded remuneration for his efforts.

2.3.2. Composition of focus groups

Sixth parts of experts spoke per category, but a forth on behalf of academia (see figure 3). However, experts fitting two categories were assigned to the category matching the organization by which they had been contacted and whose views they were asked to take.

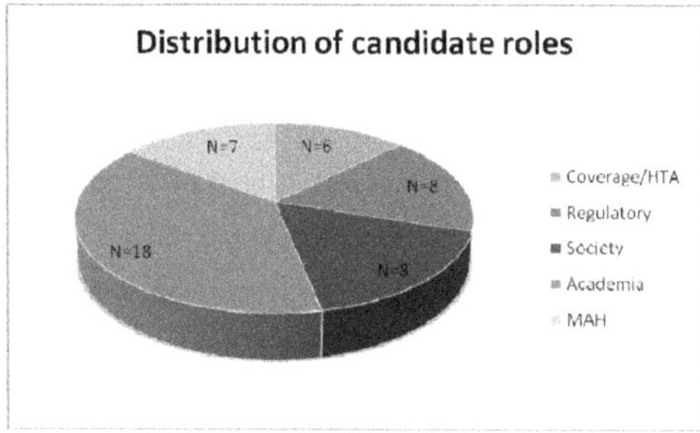

Figure 3 Absolute values of candidates per category

The category "coverage" includes "HTA" to merge pharmaco-economic interests.

SAMPLE SIZE AND NUMBER OF GROUPS The researched countries were selected on basis of official language in addition to the country's membership in the E.U. or its status as an observer in the International Conference of Harmonization of principles as a minimum. Japan was exempted from the language criteria and included for attainment of scientific knowledge. Greater differences were expected trans-continentally. For similarity reason, Belgium and Ireland were excluded despite meeting language criteria from the survey for few differences were expected, but Belgian and Irish people interviewed on behalf of the E.U. and U.S., addressed Belgian and Irish issues. Table 29 (appendix) was set up to illustrate the distribution of experts per country. It is also the key to the lower index citations.

Guidelines for sample sizes in applied research were found to be absent.[69] Sample size in qualitative research was seen to depend on the homogeneity of the group, data quality and the accuracy of the area of inquiry. An assessment of a variation for instance was observed to require larger groups. On the other hand, if a population is homogeneous, objectives are narrow and a similar set of interview questions is asked, as few as 12 interviews may provide data saturation.[70] In this study, the participants were homogenous: All had a university degree, filled similar positions and were acquainted with the subject of NDU; diversity in terms of genders and professions (physicians, pharmacists, chemists and attorneys amongst others) nevertheless led to desire for a larger sample. Sampling of one interview per category i.e. five per country was aimed at (Σ=45). Data saturation was calculated to prove the chosen sample size to be sufficient (figure 2).

The number of individuals expressing the same idea, content driven codes[ii] and novel insights were exhaustive. This lead to data saturation. Guest et al. measured data saturation at the point from where no or little change to the codes was produced. Most of the hither codes were developed in the initial coding (British interviews); few new codes derived later on. Codes typically evolved at the beginning of a new country set due to national features. Guest et al. confirms that important codes in the early stage of analysis remain essential. Figure 4 was created to illustrate the code changes during analysis of the interviews within this study (for interview numbers see table 29, appendix). No changes to data-de-

[ii] Keywords are applied to the textual data to dissect text into segments. Coding is naming segments of data with a label that categorizes, summarizes or accounts for a piece of data.

rived codes occurred after five out of nine i.e. British, Canadian, Japanese, Swiss and Austrian sets had been coded i.e. 19 interviews.

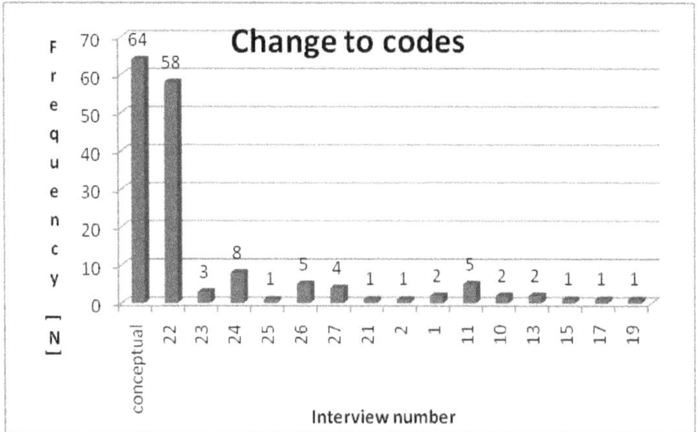

Figure 4 Fifteen out of 47 interviews (order of analysis) were accompanied by code changes

Data quality was also related to the depth of information, the duration of the interview and the purpose of participation. Depth of information was directly proportional to the duration of an interview. Although two interviews continued for less than 20 minutes, but the content was included into the study, because, upon consideration, both interviewees made invaluable statements, which contributed to the understanding of NDU. Interviews lasted 50 minutes on average.

The professional identity of the researcher was observed to play an important part and may provide for richer and more personal accounts.[71] In the present study, interviews in company of a physician took the longest, followed by interviews in company of an approved drug information pharmacist, and sole questioning by the research pharmacist. Thus presence of higher professional identity lengthened interviews. Chew-Graham et al. confirms that interviewing GPs (general practitioners) is easier when a GP researcher is known to the respondent.

The purpose of participation was an expectation on the behalf of the interviewees to contribute to future legislation, especially in Germany. Despite single interviews possibly aimed at exerting influence, the sample is nonetheless broad enough to counterbalance interests. The data quality additionally was assured by careful standardization (see 2.3.1 Experimental design).

ENSURING RIGOR A scientifically accepted research protocol allowed multiple case studies, assuring (a) currency of information; (b) data reliability (see next section) and (c) validity (see section thereafter). Data collection for descriptive purposes and theory construction was reported to have to be possible.[72]

Currency of information: All interviews were completed within a time frame of 19 months. During the survey period, the important issue of bevacizumab[i] and ranibizumab[i 73] moved into the center of attention of media. Interviews in Austria were completed before the topic became subject to daily press; the remaining interviews were completed after the controversy.

After data retrieval with MAXQDA 2007 R270608-ENG (for Windows 2000, Windows XP, Windows Vista). Belous, I., n.p., data description and theory building were accomplished by interpretation. Reoccurring themes were identified and analyzed. A topic was elaborated if it was not a direct subject of the question or project description but emphasized or represented a novel consideration. Certain patterns, such as approval procedures, notification requirements, etc., were searched for. Differences in country-specific attitudes were explored and contrasted (see table 22). Descriptive processes contributed to the constructing of theories.

RELIABILITY The semi-structured interview topic guide (see appendix) assured standardized data collection; it was newly developed, piloted in Austria and validated by peers. Data collection was achieved by intensive questioning; audio records were transcribed verbatim using Transcriber 1.5.1 (for Unix systems (Linux, Sun Solaris, Silicon Graphics) and Windows NT). Geoffrois, E; Libermann, M; Wu, Z., n.p. (see section 'Validity').

However, reliability was seen to be the extent to which the investigation is free from unsystematic error. Reproducibility of results and freedom from bias was found to be crucial in qualitative research and best achieved by retesting and reassessing. The limited availability of representative roles in this research field, however, caused repeated questioning by a second observer to be unfeasible. Also, the rapid development of the NDU field (e.g., new sentences or amendments to regulations in the area of interest or the NDU of bevacizumab[i]) did not allow assumption of consistency of opinion. The survey was therefore determined to be a current summary and can only provide an insight into strategies and opinions of 2009.

Because reliability was found to be defined as the likelihood of achieving consistency of measurement, it is dependent on data collection methods and settings, techniques of the data collectors, and interpretation of the data collection instruments by respondents.[74] Three data collectors performed the interviews, which were scheduled face-to-face or conducted via teleconference. The interviewer refocused the interview on the intention of a question if the participants' interpretation of the questions diverged from the preset purpose. Reliability was obtained, established and maintained by increased training, multiparty modification of the interview topic guide, and a system of consultation for all scientists.

VALIDITY, the extent to which qualities are captured, was tested by (a) face validation, (b) piloting of the interview topic guide, and (c) content validation. It should be pointed out here that structured interviews have been found to have higher validity than unstructured interviews.[75] A semi-structured interview guide was described to provide a clear set of topics to be covered for interviewers while presenting reliable and comparable qualitative data.[76] Nonetheless:

(a) Face validity was shown to be measurable through research participants recycling the analysis and then refining it according to their reactions.[77] This process was piloted in Austria but then discarded due to confidentiality, intellectual property and secrecy concerns.

(b) During piloting of the interview topic guide in Austria, qualities already identified in the country report were verified. For this reason the interviews were hereafter used to confirm or disprove literature findings.

(c) Content validity was seen to be assessed by presenting the interview topic guide to peers for rating its validity. Nine lecturers were contacted and provided with a rating form (see appendix). It was predetermined that a low rating would require amendments to the interview topic guide. These lecturers represented a cross-section of disciplines, and included a judge, a psychiatrist, a stakeholder (MAH), an oncologist, an executive (G-BA), a senior manager (CRO), a lawyer, a patient representative and a director (VDAK). Seven out of nine experts responded. Three assigned a high validity to the topic guide, three a satisfactory validity, and one a partial satisfactory and partial low validity to the interview topic guide.

RECORDING Written notes, minutes from memory and audio recordings were found to be the options for recording qualitative observations. In this study, all interviews were audio recorded with a Philips Digital Voice Tracer 7680 in order to reduce interview interference and to avoid loss of details. Written notes were kept to obviate data loss. The file format *.zvr was convertible to *.wav and managed with Voice Tracer 2.2. Philips, n.p. Interviewees gave their oral consent prior to recording.

TRANSCRIPTION All interviews were transcribed verbatim with Transcriber 1.5.1 (for Unix systems (Linux, Sun Solaris, Silicon Graphics) and Windows NT). Geoffrois, E; Libermann, M; Wu, Z., n.p. as well as proofheared with f4 3.0.3. dr. dresing & pehl GmbH, n.p. and USB-Footswitch f-pro. Interjections, repetitions and verbal errors were replaced by three full stops in squared brackets. All interviews were proofheared at least once by a second listener and forwarded to the interviewee to ensure correctness. Red highlighting marked words, which were not understood and, which required special attention. In three cases the record broke off and the interview was completed by minutes from memory. As a seen to be a standard procedure in qualitative research participants were sent a transcript of their interview, to amend within a given time frame. One participant answered questions in written form beforehand. Both the interview and written reply became subject to analysis.

PRIVACY AND CONFIDENTIALITY Ethics of qualitative research deserved special attention. As the representative roles in this survey at the time occupied major positions, their identities should not be revealed. Numbers were assigned to all interviews. The experts' organization was replaced by a corresponding 'category'. The country of residence, rather than his home country is assigned to each expert. Passages in which experts declared statements to be off-record were unaccounted for.

QUALITATIVE CONTENT ANALYSIS Content analysis was performed for evaluation. Mention of legislation, preambles and publications was assessed in order to identify effects and to learn about the as-is state in a country. There, interviews produced invaluable information, genuine insight into strategies and views from key decision makers and industry experts.

Content analysis was seen to be a qualified methodology for drawing valid meaning from qualitative data and involved interpreting texts through coding (indexing), classification and categories. It was found to allow comparative enumeration of reoccurring themes and evaluation as well as correlation of elements. Qualitative data analysis was performed in three steps:

1. Data reduction,
2. Data display and
3. Conclusion drawing and verification.

Conventional, directed and summative content analysis were shown to be three research techniques used to interpret qualitative texts.[78] Inductive analysis was observed to be used when no previous studies have dealt with the event. The researcher allows the data to define results without the use of predefined parameters or a pre-existing coding frame (ad-hoc codes). Deduction was to be used when the structure of analysis is parameterized on the basis of previous knowledge (conceptual codes). Summative analysis was designed to identify and quantify words and content of texts. All three techniques were combined to analyse the interview protocols.

CAQDA (COMPUTER-AIDED QUALITATIVE DATA ANALYSIS) Graphical analysis was found to be time consuming when handling large quantities of data. With graphical procedures, a clear cut display of data was seen to be a challenge; retrieval is error-prone. Therefore, use of software to accomplish analysis was preferred. With computer-aided qualitative data analysis software (CAQDAS), text material was coded electronically allowing for fast coding, undemanding display and sound scientific retrieval of all statements on a subject and thus an overview. MAXQDA 2007 R270608-ENG (for Windows 2000, Windows XP, Windows Vista). Belous, I., n.p. was used to perform computer analysis. MAXQDA is a means for making the analysis process easier in terms of data management, and is indicated when dealing with large amounts of material.

FEATURE / ENTITY	Quantity [N]
TEXTS	46
N° OF EXPERTS	47
CODES (CREATIONS)	191
CODING (ASSIGNMENTS)	11364
CODE SETS	31
COUNTRIES	9
CONTINENT SETS	3

Table 4 Key parameters of the MAXQDA project

In this study, 191 codes were developed. 11,364 assignments were made to 45 texts from 44 interviews with 47 experts. Three sets of countries were built (North America, Europe and Japan), and 31 code sets were analyzed (see table 4). The interviews were coded by one assessor between 16th and 31st of July 2008. Data retrieval was completed by August 22nd 2008.

To assess the effects of identified laws in 3.5 "Operating experience with provisions for nonlicensed drug use", segments coded "law" NEAR "feasibility" and "positive" as well as "negative" were retrieved for all countries (N=310). The statements were narrated and verified or disproved with literature data and wording of law.

The offer of information was put through a sub-investigation in 3.7 “Circumvention of drug approval: Law on advertising”. The code set “information” („second opinion“, „initiatives“, „evidence“, “data”, “documentation”, “compendia” und “circulation”) was analyzed. Commercial (e.g., „off-label.com“) and non-commercial as well as public and offers of information with restricted access were identified see 3.7 Circumvention of drug approval: Law on advertising.

2.3.3. Limitations to qualitative regulatory research

The limitations of qualitative research were found to be well recognized. Amongst other potential nonconformities investigators' internal persuasion was seen to possibly falsify conclusions. Integrity and criticality were therefore described to be represented through recursive and repetitive checks of interpretations and a reserved presentation of findings.[79] Good practice was seen to dictate that subjective processes be shared with the reader.[80] Conflicts of interests, expected findings, the process of forming outcomes, material provided to the interviewees and influence of the media on the investigator were therefore illustrated below:

Conflicts of interests were not present with the investigator. She had no financial affiliations to pressure groups.

EXPECTED FINDINGS Preceding knowledge on NDU was gained during a symposium in the spring of 2006 at the Bonn School of Pharmacy by the chair for Drug Regulatory Affairs. The researcher hence did not expect to find incoherent terminology.

PROCESS OF FORMING OUTCOMES British institutional guidelines, problem solving strategy for quality assurance beared problems of decentralized assessment and unequal management of patients, which led to early dismissal of this strategy. Second opinion procedures were not pursued due to time-intensity, problems of unequal treatment and high expenses. Research was soon focused on a) CPs, ensuring equal access for all patients and b) on the national management of risks, because problems for decentralized management of NDU were identified (DHCP-letters, batch recalls and important notification). Limitations of suggested improvements will also be discussed in 4 Discussion.

MATERIAL PROVIDED TO THE INTERVIEWEES The interview topic guide was given to the interviewees with a letter of inquiry and the project description (see appendix) enclosed in order to improve participation and demonstrate integrity. Only one interviewee in Germany strongly referred to the project description. Citations of the project description were excluded from the analysis.

INFLUENCE OF THE MEDIA ON THE INVESTIGATOR Recent topics e.g., bevacizumab[i] and ranibizumab[i] or the U.S. "Draft Guidance for the Distribution of Medical Journal Articles and Medical or Scientific Reference Publications on Unapproved New Uses of Approved Drugs and Approved or Cleared Medical Devices" were discussed in accordance with the methodology.

Further common errors of qualitative research apart from subjectivity were found to include (a) the failure to legitimize research findings, (b) the generalization of findings beyond the sample and (c) failure to estimate and interpret effect sizes.[81] Techniques to avoid these errors were seen to include review, reclassification and reassessment by other members of the research group. Subjectivity was thus leveled in an interdisciplinary team. The presentation of two independent analyses anchors the discussion in an evaluation of the objectivity and reliability of actual qualitative findings.[82] All interviews were presented to Dr. med. Christian Behles and Drug information pharmacist Petra Nies for independent evaluation. This final analysis of the impact of NDU on pharmaceutical law was presented to Dr. Christian Behles and Petra Nies for review and comparison. Discrepancies were discussed within the team.

Furthermore, the validity of the results is limited to the researched countries. Total response in the qualitative survey remained poor in Canada, France and Japan, with overrepresentation of the remaining countries. Grounds for underrepresentation of countries were possible linguistic barriers or administrative hurdles. Misrepresentation as discussed in 2.3.2 "Composition of focus groups" may have caused academic issues such as patient supply, therapeutic freedom, research and access to treatment to have headed findings. Reason for overrepresentation of interest groups were probably a greater time-based flexibility along with an interest in research. However, interests and problems of all groups were discussed well-balanced. Two U.S. and one British expert assigned to the "academic" group had previously worked for the regulatory agency and discussed regulatory concerns in detail. Many experts from academia, especially in the U.K., also acted for societies, representing its interests and cooperating with the industry. All arguments were also assumed to be identifiable in counter-arguments. Multi-professionalism and the interdisciplinary nature outweighed potential overrepresentation.

The methodology was standardized by the interview topic guide; however, presence of professional experience correlated, as shown in 2 Methodology and Materials, with prolonged interviews. Interview lengths were proportional to the interviewer's previous knowledge. Legislation in all German speaking countries had unexpected similarities to one another and across the E.U. had unexpected differences; basic principles in all German speaking countries were particularly well known to the investigators. These analogies simplified, but also lengthened discussion. In other countries, information content was counterbalanced by triangulation. Taken together, potential limitations are minor.

3. Results

3.1. Terminology

Medication that is not licensed for use in humans (unlicensed use), drugs used outside the terms of their product license (off label use)[83] or active INDs used outside of clinical trials (compassionate use)[84] are expressions, which are together referred to as 'nonlicensed drug uses' (NDU) in this thesis. Double meaning, ambiguous nomenclature and their spreading through international journals were assumed to cause complications in the (a) understanding across the world and (b) correct adherence of guidance. To give an example: Patients with brain metastases not participating in a trial give their informed consent for "off label use" of an IND to be designated for the "off-label" indication. Such drug use was more often referred to as compassionate use in this study, while off label use regularly was assumed to be the unlicensed use of a *licensed* medicine. Compassionate use is subject to more far-reaching measures than off label use in Germany. BfArM's proposed requirements for compassionate use may have not be met by the clinicians, who informed the patients about off label use. Patient's informed consent may be invalid. Explicit and – in the internet era – internationally harmonized definition of technical terms is important for the effective development of guidance. Definitions must also be designed carefully, because they determine the extent of NDU that is regulated. For this reason this chapter is devoted to terminology, to attribution, and to itemization. Recurring patterns were identified and the suitability of the definitions was tested by applying the definitions to national conventions. A variance of understanding and a desire for an umbrella term were found.

Use of an MP outside the terms of its license[85] was only one of many possible definitions for off label use. Compassionate use was said to be the use of an IND in patients not participating in a clinical trial,[86] while other authors said compassionate use was "*widely understood to be the accepted use of a medicine either outside its license or before it is licensed by authorities for compassionate reasons*".[87] Several authors regarded unlicensed use as the use of biological active substances as MPs, the modifications of proprietary MPs[88] or the use of proprietary MPs without an MA valid in the country of consideration. Not only understanding but also designation of NDU varies. Table 5 displays designations, collected throughout the three year period of the project, which conceptualize NDU (sorted by languages). There was no consistent terminology.

	Types of Nonlicensed drug use		
	Off label use	*Unlicensed use/medicines*	*Compassionate use/access*
FREQUENTLY APPLIED SYNONYMS	Nicht lizensierter Gebrauch		Named patient use
	Nicht zertifizierter Gebrauch		Single patient use[iii]
	Unapproved use		Special access program (SAP)
	Usage out of labeling	Extra-label (drug) use (ELDU)	Parallel track/trial
			Extended Access Program (EAP)
	Off license use		Individual patient use
	Not registered indications		Named patient supplies
	Beyond label use		Expanded/Early/Emergency access
	Non approved use		Named patient pro-gram/project
	Out of label use	No label use	
	Unlabelled use	Unauthorized products	Emergency drug release program (EDRP)
	Not in accordance with designation	Use of MPs not (yet) licensed	compassionate use pathway
	l'utilisation hors AMM	médicaments sans AMM	Usage compassionnel

Table 5 German, English and French terms with similar concepts (not comprehensive)

For off label use, three major definitions were present: post-licensing drug use outside the terms of the a) license[89], b) label[iv 90 91 92], and c) indication[93 94 95 96 97 98]. The "beyond label" definition was seen to be competitive with unlicensed use, as extemporaneous products and imported MPs also carry labels. The "not registered indication" perspective did not explain prominent off label uses e.g. (a) of iloprost[i] inhalation used in registered indication or (b) off label use in pediatrics but adult indication. Moreover, authors long have categorized off label use into indication, dose, age, route and contraindication levels.[99] For these reasons the label and indication definition failed verification tests.

Seven categories of off label use were identified in this study:

1. Indication[100]
2. Population[101]

[iii] ≠ single-use instruments

[iv] The term "labeling'" means all labels and other written, printed, or graphic matter (1) upon any article or any of its containers or wrappers, or (2) accompanying such article

3. Dose[102]
4. Application[103]
5. Contraindication[104]
6. Qualification[105]
7. Generic[106]

Subtypes of off label use were distinguished (table 7). Indication-based off label use was the use of a licensed drug to treat a different disease[107 108 109 110 111 112 113 114 115 116], entity [117 118 119] or stage (early, advanced/extensive, end/late). Population-based off label use was in different gender-[120] or age-groups[121 122 123 124]. Dosage-based off label use occurred in terms of different intervals,[125] overdose/sub therapeutic doses and defiant duration (short- or long-term treatment). Off label use in contraindications[126] included going against warnings and interactions.[127] Qualification-based off label use was where a drug should be prescribed by a specialist but was not.[128] Generic off label use[129] was again a result of cost saving attempts or mandatory generic substitution. Application-based off label use was the irregular administration of a licensed drug. Specifically, the "method of application" was seen changed, for example, suppositories applied reversely.[130] Moreover, the "way of application" was observed to be altered, i.e. iloprost[i] inhaled as opposed to injected.[131 132] Finally, the "type of application" was detected to have been changed, i.e., while iloprost[i] was systemically effective by both ways of application, intravitreal bevacizumab[i] suddenly had local action. Routes of application were therefore additionally subdivided by (a) the site of pharmacological action e.g. systemic or local and (b) site of administration for instance pulmonary, intravenously or rectal (table 6). The mode of application is mentioned for completeness, but was not of importance for NDU.

Site TERM	of effect*	of application	example
METHOD OF APPLICATION	Identical	Identical	Reversed suppositories (systemic effect)
MODE OF ADMINISTRATION	Dissimilar	Identical	Hormone (systemic effect) vs. copper releasing IUD (local effect)
WAY OF APPLICATION	Dissimilar	Dissimilar	Intravitreal (local effect) vs. intravenous (systemic effect)
TYPE OF ADMINISTRATION	Identical	Dissimilar	Inhalation vs. injection (systemically effective)

Table 6 Application techniques (*systemic or local, IUD= intrauterine device)

It was detected that there are blurred boundaries between off label administration by a different route and unlicensed use. Galenic manipulation to an MP for it to be administered by a different route is legally judged to be "manufacture" e.g. in Germany according to § 4 para. 14 German Drug Act (AMG) and classified as unlicensed use in the U.K. Unlicensed use was often used synonymously with off label use. Iloprost[i] solution for example though not reformulated, was used pulmonary as an inhalation; bevacizumab[i] injection solution was used intra-vitreally after dilution and refilling,[133] thus affecting the product's quality. Quality is determined by physical properties of a drug e.g. (§ 4 (15) AMG). Osmolarity and osmolality of a medicine for instance was most probably not adequate for application of the medicine into a different compartment. Also, bioavailability is untested in extemporaneous preparations.[N.24] These observations led different ways and types of application to be assigned to unlicensed use, because off label use falsely leads to the assumption that a licensed pharmaceutical form will be used, of which quality is secured.

CLASS	Variance	MP/ active ingredient/ formulation	MA	Off label use
INDICATION (ALSO DIFFERENT CLINICAL STAGE, ENTITY, TREATMENT REGIMEN)	Disease	Sandoglobulin®	Guillain-Barré-Syndrome, Kawasaki Syndrome or idiopathic thrombopenic purpura with a high risk of bleeding	Primary chronic-progressive multiple sclerosis
	Form	Genotropin®, Humatrope®	Microsomia due to insufficient endogenic growth hormone production and children with microsomia due to Ullrich-Turner-Syndrome or chronic kidney failure	Microsomia due to Silver-Russell-Syndrome or idiopathic microsomia
POPULATION	Age	Sotalol[i]	Adults	Children
	Gender	Duloxetin[i]	Women	Men
DOSE	Interval	Valette®	21 days + 7 day pause	Continuous
	Excess/under usage	Gentamycin[i]	Every 8 to 12 hours	Once-daily
	Duration of treatment	Dona®	Six weeks	Long term
ROUTE	*Way**	*Avastin®*	*Systemic application*	*Local application*
	Method	Suppository	Headlong	Contrary wise
	*Type**	*Proleukin®*	*i.v.*	*Inhalative*
CONTRAINDICATED	Also warnings, interactions	Dobutamine[i]	Heart failure	Stress echocardiography
QUALIFICATION	No variance	Methylphenidate[i]	Specialist	General practitioner
GENERIC	Cost saving/ mandatory generic substitution	Omeprazol[i] 20mg Ratiopharm	Antacid	Eradication of helicobacter pylori

Table 7 Examples of off label use (not comprehensive) *application in a different compartment represented a new dosage form and for this reason unlicensed use

It was not only off label use that was understood miscellaneously or for which several circumscriptions were found. Compassionate use was found to be a term historically used by physicians to refer to the use of investigational drugs outside formal trial.[134] N.40 On the other hand, two German authors argued that compassionate use was an individual treatment attempt, that expanded access was to be distinguished from compassionate use and that named patient use was related to the importation of MPs.[135] Attorney N.46 stated that *"in Germany, compassionate use is featured as (a) off label use, (b) unlicensed use and (c) state of emergency."* Originally, it was the supply of an IND by a sponsor for compassionate reasons to responding, former participants after completion of RCTs says expert N.39. Expert N.41 verified that compassionate use bridges the supply gap for patients eligible for the new drug after positive outcomes in RCT and before MA. So far compassionate zse was seen to be unrestricted or performed post-licensing, pre-licensing or else post-RCT. To further clarify this issue, programs meeting the compassionate principle were investigated more closely: In figure 5 the special access program in Canada (SAP, sections C.08.010 and C.08.011 Food and Drug Regulations) formerly known as emergency drug release program (EDRP), the ATU in France, U.S. treatment-, emergency- and single patient IND (regulated by 21 CFR 312.34 and 312.35), the E.U. compassionate use procedure and the Swiss special dispensation are arranged on a regulatory timescale to depict at what point of time of drug development compassionate access has been granted in the past.

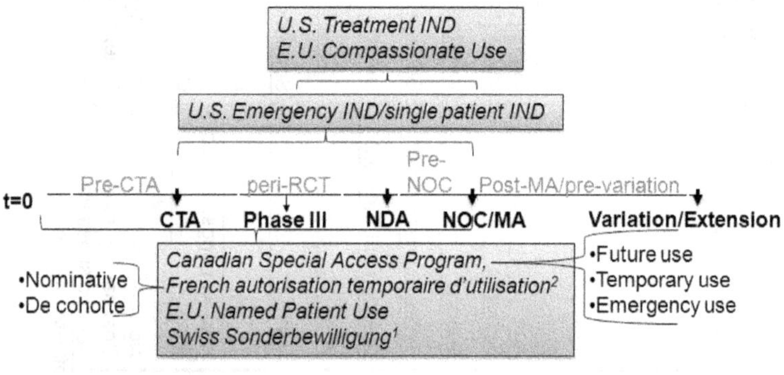

Figure 5 Drug Release Programs on a regulatory timescale

Simultaneously, the product's identity and the number of patients were frequent criteria for compassionate use. In the US and France for instance, compassionate treatment INDs and ATUs can be filed for a single patient, not eligible to the RCT or group of patients e.g. former participants in an RCT. Some compassionate use programs provide access to INDs, while others also regulate access prior to clinical investigation. Briefly, compassionate use was seen to be medication of active investigational treatment or unlicensed products and was broken down into: (a) the number of concerned patients, i.e., individuals (henceforth named patient use) and groups (hereafter referred to as expanded access), (b) the point of regulatory progress, i.e., as early as pre-CTA, post-CTA or post-Phase-III etc. and (c) off-protocol (patients do not meet RCT inclusion criteria)[136] or in-protocol (patients meet RCT inclusion criteria). This parameterization was tested and verified with off label and unlicensed use.

"Unlicensed use" means *'all uses of a drug, which has never received a European Marketing Authorisation as medicinal for human use in either adults or children'.*[137] Expert N.7 reports that *"the entire class of herbal remedies is unregulated and therefore unlicensed by the FDA".* Unlicensed use was also said to be a synonym for off label use.[138] [139] The Guideline on conduct of Pharmacovigilance for Medicines used by the Paediatric Population was found to conceptualize unlicensed use, excluding extemporaneous products and including imported MPs.[140] Choonara, Conroy and other authors gave (a) modifications to licensed MPs, (b) reformulated MPs, (c) biological active substances used as MPs, (d) novel MPs available as specials (see 3.2 Investigations into supply shortages of drugs and the necessity as well as procedure of nonlicensed drug use) and (e) imported MPs as examples of unlicensed drug use in the U.K.[141] [142] [143] Taken together, unlicensed use was predominantly separated from off label use and subdivided into the use of MPs, which were

(a) formerly licensed (expiry, suspension or waiver),

(b) seemingly licensed (extemporaneous products, shortage/supply shortfall) or

(c) not yet licensed (imported MPs, biological active substances [BAS]).

The definitions included MPs requiring registration, such as imported MPs and BAS, and even extended to extemporaneous products needing no approval.

NDU statements from literature, legislation and expert questioning of different countries are summarized in table 31 depicting criteria assigned to the expressions. Where no definition was evident, "undefined" was assigned to a segment.

One concept of law was identified for compassionate use in the E.U. Though one interviewee$_{N.40}$ claimed that in the E.U. a legal concept was also passed for off label use. The guideline[144] in question however, has no force of law and solely addressed pediatric pharmacy. Though compassionate use was undoubtedly regulated in European legislation, it was yet unknown to a number of interviewees in the MSs (member states). To improve awareness of NDU, expert N.43 suggested definition in professional codes of conducts; whereof HCPs are more conscious than of state law.

In total, uniform international concepts were absent for all NDU. Mutual agreement was present that off label use concerns licensed MPs and occurs post-licensing. No predominance was observed across the countries as to whether compassionate use is more associated with groups or individuals. For this reason both were assumed to apply. Compassionate use served as a superordinate concept for use of an active investigational treatment or unlicensed product between pre-CTA and pre-MA as well as off-protocol (patient[s] do not meet inclusion criteria) and in-protocol (patient[s] admitted after recruitment closed). No consensus was seen in unlicensed use with regard to its validity only for MPs requiring registration or also for seemingly licensed products. Therefore it was implied that both was effective practice.

The overall trends hence were: Off label use was described post-NOC and is limited to the point of variation of MA. In most cases, compassionate use was detected in parallel to clinical trials in a research setting. Unlicensed use was majorly associated with pre-RCT medication. All types of NDU have a predominant regulatory time segment in common. The legal impact of misunderstanding NDU and its legal consequences for medical practice suggested an accurate separation of compassionate and unlicensed use. Unlicensed use was therefore assigned to any use of an MP prior to clinical investigation or any use for which MA was withdrawn, renounced or suspended. Compassionate use most likely displayed the use of 'active treatment' INDs while clinical trials take place or when a new drug application (NDA) was filed. These outcomes were plotted on a product life cycle (figure 6).

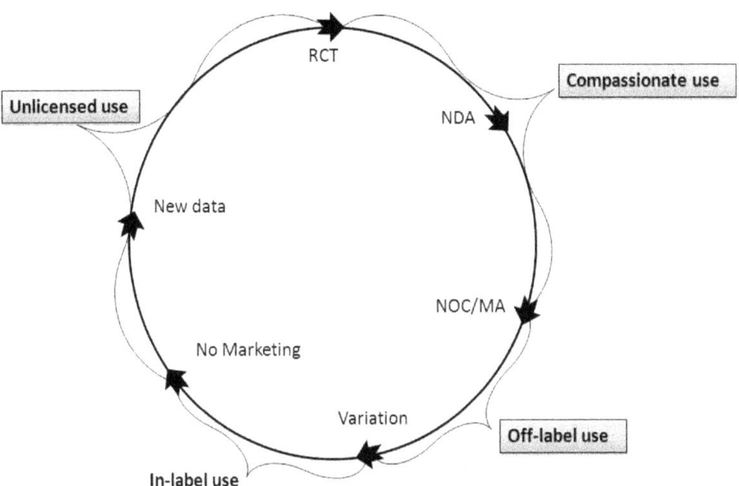

Figure 6 A regulatory lifecycle

As mentioned before, there was also a general tendency for all expressions to be assigned to certain patients, products and reasons. These designations are hereafter referred to as dimensions of NDU. The four dimensions of NDU were the

(a) regulatory point of time (pre-RCT, post-RCT/pre-NDA, pre-NOC/post-NDA),

(b) addressees (e.g. groups, individuals or severely ill patients),

(c) product classification (investigational, extemporaneous or proprietary) and

(d) cause (e.g. lack of licensed options, intolerance of alternative products).

To a certain extent, all NDUs were argued to apply to (c) severely ill patients and (d) by reason of inadequate alternatives. Off label use primarily had time (post-NOC) and product (liable to labeling, licensing or indication) dimensions. For closer examination, it has to be repeated that off label use was interpreted narrowly as 'every prescription outside the label' or read more broadly as off-license use (requiring authorization from the regulatory authority for the amendment by the MAH). Other authors merely interpreted any breaches of preset indication as off label use.[145] The label, license and indication interpretations presupposed that labels, MAs and a field of indication are present with the product used off label. In Germany, if limited to indications off label use only referred to proprietary medical products. Avastin® however, was reformulated to an extemporaneous product when used to treat age-related macular degeneration. The "indication interpretation" did not classify intravitreal bevacizumab[i] as an off label use, because extemporaneous preparations have no range of application. Assuming "out of label use" as a legal concept in future, rules would be valid for large scale products, "chemists' nostrums", proprietary products, German standard admissions, INDs, extemporaneous formulations and small industrial scale products. Here, bevacizumab[i] in wet AMD was an off label use. In contrast, "off-license" use does not relate to extemporaneous or small industrial scale products, but affects large scale products, "chemists' nostrums", proprietary products and German standard admissions. Thereby nomenclature became fail-safe.

Compassionate use had time, addressee, product, and cause[146] dimensions. It was frequently related to a period during or before drug development. Terminally or seriously ill groups of patients or individuals resistant to licensed treatment were commonly named as subjects for compassionate use. In association with cohorts, either (a) former volunteers who are supplied with the IND after the end of the clinical trial or (b) even new patients before licensure were compassionate cases. Individual patients are treated with INDs on a compassionate use basis, either because they are eligible for a RCT but recruitment is closed, or patients are treated outside the protocol because they do not meet inclusion criteria. The MPs used were active treatment forms of INDs or imported MPs. An overlap with regard to unlicensed and off label use was observed. Imported MPs were also used or severely ill patients were treated for lack of adequate treatment before a medicine was approved for a purpose in unlicensed use. The greatest bandwidth of understanding was detected for compassionate use across all countries. On the other hand, written down definition was obtained most often within temporary use procedures.

Unlicensed use primarily had time and product dimensions. It was the use of medication in the absence or presence of clinical investigation and product license. The MP did not have an MA and was (as in the case of imported MPs) or was not (with extemporaneous products) liable to registration. Jassal et al. reported that *"[...] palliative care uses a number of drugs for indications or by routes that are not licensed by the manufacturer. In the U.K. such unlicensed use is allowed [...]".*[147] The term unlicensed use was also assigned to the use of extemporaneous products,[148] imported MPs[149] and INDs.[150] Twice in Germany and Switzerland, imported MPs were subdivided by origin, e.g., E.U. and third party country or countries with similar versus incomparable pharmaceutical law (EEA, New Zealand, Australia, U.S. and Canada). Extemporaneous formulations sometimes included reformulated proprietary MPs and BAS. The superordinate concept unlicensed use was used to address issues common to all NDU.[151 152 153] Figure 7 gives a forecast for a potential consensus understanding of NDU, which was used as common denominator in the following chapters.

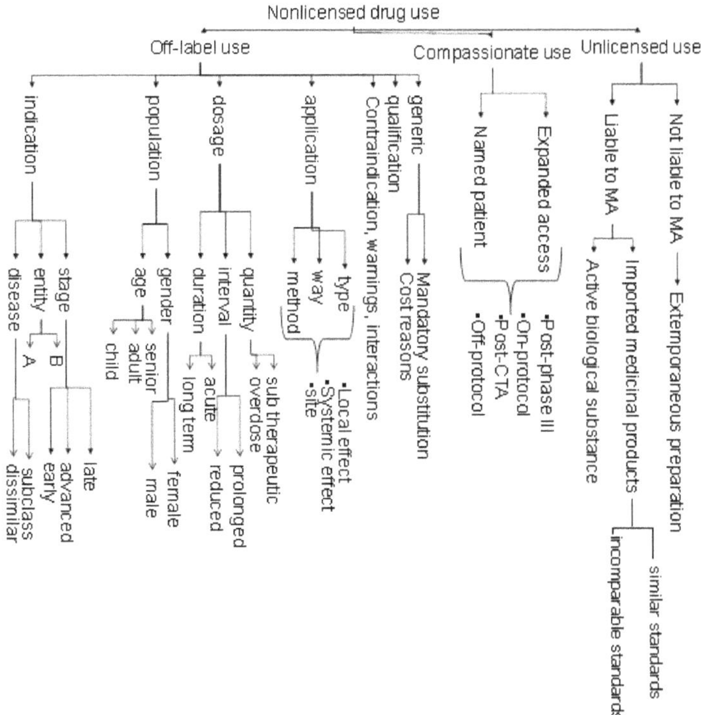

Figure 7 Fragmentation of NDU into macro-, meso-, micro- and submicrostructure

3.2. Investigations into supply shortages of drugs and the necessity as well as procedure of nonlicensed drug use

Methodical investigations into the supply shortages of MPs for the treatment of specific clinical pictures were not present in scientific literature. Nevertheless, there were reports on orphan MPs (OMPs), extemporaneous products and single APIs showing under-supply that has been present.

Findings suggested a circumstantial need for off-label, unlicensed or compassionate use under certain conditions.[154 155] The aim of two studies, identified in the course of this project, was to determine whether NDU prescriptions were necessary. According to a case presentation by Blumer, off label use of drugs in children was appropriate and was suggested to may be necessary.[156] Hanna et al. found that based on guideline definitions, appropriate off label use of IVIG was 89% in Canada.[157] In the opinion of the experts polled within this thesis, off label and unlicensed use were found to be necessary in children,[N.6 N.9 N.21 N.23 N.24 N.28] sometimes in cancer patients[N.26] and on occasion in adults with chronic diseases.[N.27] Off label use was said to be beneficial and in the patient's best interest in child psychiatry.[N.8] NDU were said to be required in obstetrics; the necessity of NDU was stated to be population-[N.5] and case-dependent.[N.32] In general practice, off-license use was judged to usually not be regarded as necessary.[N.25] Countries with a small population like Canada or Ireland were shown to not see all licensed products marketed and HCPs hence regarded NDU as necessary.[N.2 N.32]

Real patient access to OMPs was reported to be unsatisfactory in Europe in 2007.[158] A survey covered 22 OMPs authorized before the first of January 2006. Most OMPs (20 or 21 OMPs) had been available to patients in Finland, France, Germany, and Sweden. Between 15 and 19 OMPs had been obtainable in Austria, the Czech Republic, Denmark, Italy, the Netherlands, Norway, Spain, Switzerland, and the United Kingdom. Iceland, Latvia, and Lithuania only had up to four OMPs accessible. According to the authors, the 180 day legal delay for placing orphan MPs (OMPs) on the market was not followed frequently. Incidences of rare disorders per country did not correlate with the availability of OMPs. Unfortunately, the authors did not publish or explore whether and how OMP deficiency was overcome.

EFPIA also showed that MPs accessible to patients did not correlate with the number of MPs with MA in all countries, with the exception of Germany. EFPIA also reported several cases of reimbursement denied for new MPs licensed between January 1st and December 31st 2006 in its survey, though again none were reported for Germany.

A number of non-OMPs have been reported to be unobtainable: Shortages of injectable furosemide and injectable prochlorperazine have been identified in the U.S. when marketing was discontinued.[159] Intravenous immunoglobulin has been out of stock in the past.[160] A shortage of urokinase developed in the U.S. in early 1999.[161] A shortage of raw materials in 2002 had a considerable impact on the availability of isoproterenol hydrochloride in the U.K.[162] Recently (January 2009), a shortage of acetonitrile affected U.K. drug manufacture.[163] There were, however, no accompanying surveys into how many patients required each MP or into how shortages were managed by HCPs. One therapeutic area was seen to be permanently affected by a lack of suitable medication: drugs of proven quality as well as adequate license were detected to be infrequent for pediatric patients.[164] Various drugs used in children were reported not to be offered in suitable liquid dosage forms.[165] Liquid dosage forms were confirmed to have to be prepared extemporaneously using child-appropriate excipients.

Undersupply of age appropriate MPs and necessity of age related NDU is therefore explored further. Using drugs developed for adults in children was observed to be challenging because formulations and dosages often were not suitable for young patients, though the development of age-based MPs for children was perceived to be encouraged. Similar to children, seniors were classified heterogeneously. Age restrictions (for taxonomy see table 8) and a lack of fluid preparations were reported to be major difficulties in pediatrics and gerontology. Elderly people were also said to require liquid formulations because of swallowing difficulties and gavages. Until now, however, their need has only been discussed in terms of divisibility of tablets and handling of primary, secondary and tertiary packaging. Attempts to raise the awareness in wards that solid preparations may not be mortared together and prepared for liquid administration, illustrated further geriatric needs. Pientka et al. suggested that physicians should determine the pharmacokinetic status of seniors individually and classify resilient (go-go), comorbid (slow go) and elderly who must receive customized treatment according to a physician's professional judgment (no go).[166 167] Lack of age-specific studies has caused MPs to have age restrictions both for young and elderly patients. The elderly were also shown to make up the majority of carcinoma patients, but were proven to be a minority in clinical trials for cytostatic drugs.[168]

Body / MINORS	ZAK medicines for children database	ICH E11	FDA	EMEA	Age / MAJORS	[y]
PRETERM	n/a	Preterm	n/a	<36w	SENIORS	65- 74
NEW BORN	≤ 27d	0-27d	birth-1m	0-27d	ELDERLY	75- 79
BABY	28d-11m				AGED	80- 89
INFANT	12-23m				HIGHLY AGED	90- 99
PRESCHOOLER	2-5y	28d-23m	1m-2y	28d-23m	LONG LIVED	≥100
CHILD	6-11y	2-11y	2-12y	2-11y		
ADOLESCENT	<12y	12-16/18y	12-16y	12-17y		

Table 8 Classification of infancy & seniority (d=days, m=months, y=years, n/a=not available)

Among other causes, drug information and high insurance premiums were said to account for NDU: In the qualitative survey, expert N.37 claimed that 30%-40% of physicians used drugs off label because they did not know that a licensed alternative was available. This presumption was also the reason behind creating an approved children's medicines database (ZAK) in Germany. The reverse case of licensed MPs being extrapolated to untested populations was seen to be met by the Beer's list[v] in gerontology. However, only 51 out of 975[169] MAH contributed to ZAK as of June 28th, 2008. Due to insufficient contributions, the database was confirmed to be no reliable source of information for the availability or absence of drugs licensed for use in children.[170] Child protection and high insurance premiums for pediatric studies were evidenced to be causal for the supply shortage despite maximum fixed sums, e.g., setting an upper limit to indemnifiability in Germany (§§ 86-89 AMG). Another cause or reason for the small number of children's MPs in Europe was indicated to be the posterior registration process. Posterior registration caused licenses for treatments for the management of colds, herbal MPs, antibiotics, antihelminthic therapies and beta-sympatholytic suppositories to be cancelled. A sample survey, however, showed no intersection with an essential medicines list for children (EML-C) as listed by the WHO.

[v] list of agents to be avoided or used with extreme caution in elderly patients

On the other hand, MPs that are currently licensed for use in children were suggested not to necessarily be suitable for the target group. For example, U.S. experts stated that certain drugs (e.g., ketorolac[i]) are licensed for use in newborns, although studies had never been conducted in the age group. Earlier period extrapolations did not mirror current levels of knowledge of these drugs and require reassessment. MA renewal was explained to be excellent: MA is valid for five years in the E.U. (article 24 Directive 2001/83/EC) and becomes invalid if the product is not marketed within the three years after approval or if the produce is not marketed for three consecutive years. However, there is only one renewal in the E.U. that is followed by, given periodic safety update reports (PSURs) and far-reaching no risk event, unlimited validity.

Aside from these age groups another population, women of child-bearing age were said to have access to hardly any treatments, which are demonstrably harmless in pregnancy. Even when licensed MPs are available, physicians and midwives were sometimes confirmed to use nonlicensed drugs (see 1 Introduction). Although oxytocin[i] is licensed for induction of labor, misoprostol[i] or a mixture of ricinus oil, apricot juice and sparkling wine were also being used to induce labor in addition to a number of methods assigned to drug misuse. While data to license misoprostol[i] for this indication was suggested to be promising, pharmaceutical companies were said to resent licensure because misoprostol[i] is known to be misused for abortion. A reluctance to license MP to use during pregnancy was reported even for essential drugs. Until May 2009, Tamiflu® and Relenza® had not been licensed for use in pregnant women and nursing mothers.

The literature hence gave evidence for the circumstantial absence of specific MPs. Several publications additionally gave evidence for strategies to circumvent a lack of suitable MPs. Guidance supported importation (e.g., of Ritalin SR®)[171] and extemporaneous preparations as possible solutions for supply shortages. In Germany, extemporaneous formulations were associated with compassionate use and OMPs.[172] Continued use of biological active substances or extemporaneous products was reported because of the costs of licensed, OMPs in the U.K. by Nunn.[173] However, extemporaneous preparations (N.B. bioavailability untested) were exclaimed to only be used if no alternative option is present.[174] In the long term and in order for patients to benefit from R&D, MA was explained to be necessary.[175] Furthermore, chances to overcome the shortage of drugs were firstly incentives and duties present for orphan or pediatric MPs and a supplementary indication (see 3.8 Criteria for simplified variation while assuring drug safety: Incentives and duties), secondly the much-discussed compulsive MA (not discussed for property right reasons) and finally this thesis identified the German standardized MA (§ 36 AMG Standardzulassung)[176]. Standardized MA was suggested as a way to overcome refusals of licensing by Zapf.[177] While forfeiting a patent and meeting formal requirements are preconditions, the MPs were indicated to be available cost effectively and at a high quality standard. Negative assessment reports could potentially suspend unsafe medications in the long term.

In absence of a systematic, cross-country research into the strategies to overcome situations when patients are requiring MPs missing an MA, legislation affecting nonlicensed drug use in the selected countries was identified in this chapter:

U.K. *"Except in accordance with a license [...] no person shall [...] (a) sell, supply or export any MP [...]"* (§ 7 (b) Medicines Act 1968) in the U.K. § 13 gave an exemption for *"the importation of a medicinal product where it is specially imported by or to the order of a doctor or dentist for administration to a particular patient of his"* and § 10 (extemporaneous products) from these requirements. The importation of MPs was seen to be subject to an obligation of notification by wholesalers in accordance with the Medicines for Human Use (Manufacturing, Wholesale Dealing and Miscellaneous Amendments) Regulations (SI 2005/2789) in the U.K. The importation was to proceed unless the MHRA informs the wholesaler within 28 days that it objects to importation. MHRA informs if there were concerns about the safety or quality of the product, or when an equivalent licensed MP was available and no 'special need' for the supply to an individual patient was apparent. Schedule 1 of the 1994/SI 3144 provided details on the exceptions for „named patient use". The MHRA also published a guidance note on the supply of unlicensed medicines.[178] Standard 12 of the Department of Health Medicines Management in the National Health Service (NHS) hospitals framework specified that guidelines should [...] be in place for unlicensed medicines use [...].[179] Examples of these guidelines are outlined in the following paragraph.

Off label and unlicensed use was managed variably from trust to trust within the NHS.$_{N.22}$ [180] [181] [182] [183] Extra quality assurance procedures on unlicensed products were present in secondary care;$_{N.21}$ the Royal College of Paediatrics and Child Health provided the model patient information leaflets (PILs) (not restricted to inpatient use).$_{N.24}$ Some trusts published internal request forms.[184] [185] [186] Others categorized unlicensed MPs or off label use of licensed MPs,[187] e.g., as a traffic light scheme.[188 189] The Liverpool Women's NHS Foundation Trust also published decision trees, PILs and a documentation system[190] as suggested by medical societies such as the RPSGB,[191] who issued legal considerations.[192] A list of MPs and established off label uses was enclosed in some guidelines[193] and the NHS Fife published an online database amounting to 246 unlicensed MPs on May 6th 2009.[194] Formalized collection of information on NDU was also conducted (a) in the Birmingham Hospital's Database to Manage Use of Unlicensed Medicines[195] and (b) nationwide in the BNF-C (British National Formulary for Children).[N.21] Table 9 summarizes the cited guidance's properties.

NHS TRUST \ CONTENT	Explanatory notes	Request form	Categorization	Decision tree	Legal considerations	List of approved medicines	PIL
FIFE	X	X	X*	-	X	-	-
GREENWICH	X	-	X	-	X	-	-
MORECAMBE	X	-	-	-	-	-	-
SOMERSET	X	-	-	-	-	-	-
PENNINE	X	-	X	-	-	X	-
YORKSHIRE	X	X	-	-	X	X	-
DUDLEY GROUP	X	X	-	-	-	-	-
SCOTTISH QUALITY GROUP	X	X	X	-	X	-	-
BRIGHTON AND HOVE	X	-	-	-	X	-	-
LOTHIAN	X	-	X*	-	X	-	-
LIVERPOOL	X	X	X	X	X	-	X
LONDON	X	X	X	-	-	X	-

Table 9 Details of selected British guidance (*traffic light scheme, x= present, –= absent)

CANADA MA was seen to be regulated in C.01.014 [Drug Identification Number (DIN)], with the importation of MPs being subject to C.01.014.1 FDR: "[...] in the case of a drug to be imported into Canada, the importer of the drug may make an application for a drug identification number (DIN) for that drug [...]". Once a drug has been approved, the Therapeutic Products Directorate issues a notice of compliance (NOC), which permits the manufacturer to market the drug in Canada. Several countries as we will see later, insist on an MA before importation of MPs.

The Special Access Program (SAP), originating from the emergency drug release program (EDRP), was seen to allow access to non-marketed drugs in Canada.[196] As early as 1996, Food and Drug Regulations (Sections C.08.010 [permission] and C.08.011 [dispensing] FDR) enabled access to unapproved drugs in cases of emergency. The Therapeutic Product Directorate was observed to handle the Special Access Requests (SAR); [197] [198] an application form of two pages was identified. The physician was documented to remain responsible for the (a) therapeutic decision, (b) proof of efficacy and (c) patient information.[199] A Special Access Management System (SAMS) was found to administer all dispensed products.[200] Health Canada was also discovered to encourage MAHs to perform open label studies with patients not meeting inclusion criteria of an RCT.[201] Drugs were recognized to be provided free of charge.[202] Temporary (restricted treatment period), emergency (urgent situation) and future uses (case by case) were shown to be distinguished.[203] Future use was found to require justification beyond the singular case.[204]

Compassionate use programs were in place for certain Canadian provinces or areas of supply; for example, the British Columbia Cancer Agency (BCCA) supported a compassionate access program (CAP). It enabled evidence-based treatment in unusual or uncommon clinical circumstances or during the implementation phase of an MP. A Tumour Group and Systemic Therapy Program was described to file CAPs on a case by case basis. It was found to uphold the following clinical goals: (a) best practice and safe application of anti-cancer agents, (b) evidence-based selection of MPs, (c) financial coverage and (d) report to a Provincial Systemic Therapy Drug Database. The applying physician was seen to have to support his request with references. If requests were shown to be frequent (> 5 requests), either a formal application to a Priority and Evaluation Committee of the BCCA was mandatory or a treatment strategy, protocol, Provincial Pre-Printed Order and patient information was to be presented. Periodically updated reports including publications, presentations and patient data were found to be solicited throughout the term of the program.

SWITZERLAND MPs were reported to have to be approved according to article 9 HMG and the VAM (Swiss Ordinance on Drugs). HCPs were shown to be allowed to import proprietary MPs on a small scale if authorized or exempt from authorization and a need to treat specific patients was evident. Article 10 HMG was observed to regulate the importation of MPs. The Swiss regulatory office was said to be allowed to license foreign drugs immediately in the case of a supply shortage and when the manufacturing process is true to the original$_{N.13}$ (Art. 9 Abs. 4 and Art 18 – 23 HMG as well as VAZV [Swiss Ordinance on the simplified approval of drugs][205]).[206 207] An applicant is charged 3,000 CHF (HGebV, Anhang I Abs. 2 Bst. k) at the time of this study. A list of admitted MPs was found published online.[208] As many as 23 temporary licenses were issued in 2005.[209] Extemporaneous formulation were seen to be regulated in article 9 (b) HMG. Furthermore, GMP rules were identified for small scale extemporaneous preparation in accordance with Swiss pharmacopoeia.$_{N.12}$ [210] Whenever MPs are judged to be unavailable in Switzerland, patients suffering from life threatening or serious disease may be treated after so-called 'special authorization' (Sonderbewilligung). This mechanism was shown to also be applicable if a product license is withdrawn or cancelled. Six preconditions were observed to be compulsory:

a) the disease to either be treated had to be fatal or lead to incapacitation,

b) a licensed, acceptable, alternative MP of Switzerland

    I. was to be unavailable or

    II. its risk/chance-ratios were judged to be poorer or

    III. it had not achieved satisfying therapeutic results

c) the intervention was to be

    I. an emergency or

    II. a last treatment option

d) the MP

    I. was found to be licensed in a third party country or

    II. had a license applied for.

    III. If neither is the case, solid scientific evidence from clinical trials and quality product information on efficacy, safety and quality of the drug was to be presented in the application

e) the MP was to be used in a single named patient

An opinion from a local IRB (institutional review board) was uncalled for. The authorization was found to be issued to a single physician who must then keep a record of all required data. He was also seen to be responsible for first documenting each case (history) and then issuing a report to Swissmedic when a therapy ends. Adverse drug reaction (ADR) reporting was observed to be subject to the customary system. The patient was to be informed about the special regulatory circumstances and was seen to have to give his or her consent for the pharmacotherapy prior to prescription. The physician was explained to have to ensure that his liability insurance covers harm that may result from such therapy. Swissmedic may set further preconditions. The request form[211 212] was to be forwarded by a licensed physician in primary care or a medical director in secondary care. Authorizations which were issued by the provinces before the HMG had come into force in 2002 remained valid until the expiration or ended in 2007. Statistics for 2008 reported: 1927 requests for special dispensation for human MPs, thereof 107 needlessly submitted (cases, where applications were withdrawn or special dispensation is not required by Art. 36 Abs. 3 of the Arzneimittelbewilligungsverordnung), 40 were denied and 1770 were approved.[213]

Further mechanisms for NDU identified in Switzerland were first parallel trials and second extended access[214]. A special authorization for a parallel trial was shown to be permissible for an investigator of a clinical trial or physician currently treating the patient. The authorization was seen to apply to patients who were not eligible to the corresponding clinical trial. Excluded patients could be treated "in parallel". The patient must suffer from a fatal disease or a disease causing incapacitation. Alternative MPs must be unavailable, second-rate or not achieve expected therapeutic results. Again, the permission was described to be reserved for emergencies and as a final treatment option. The MP was to either be licensed abroad or subject to clinical investigation in Switzerland. The patient was to be named and an opinion from the IRB is compulsory in this case. The sponsor was to provide a parallel investigation plan. The authorization was to be granted to a physician who holds the required data, keeps a patient's record and submits a report to the regulatory body. ADR reporting again was seen to apply to RCT rules. The patient was to give his informed consent to participation; the physician's liability insurance must be shown to cover the intervention's risks. A separate form was found for the parallel trial request.

Extended access to unlicensed MPs was seen to be possible in Switzerland if an application for product licensure has been filed and for patients who participated in the clinical trial, had a benefit and who would like to continue the treatment after notice of compliance to the MP. The MP's efficacy, safety and quality was to be proven. The investigator or physician currently treating the patient may apply for special authorization. The IRB must give its consent. In case of extended access, there need not be an emergency or absence of therapeutic alternatives (table 10). This procedure was also proven to have its separate request process. Applicants were charged CHF 200 per hour of processing at the time of the qualitative survey.

premise / NDU	IRB opinion	Drug status	Emergency/ last option	Alternatives
SPECIAL DISPENSATION	No	Licensed abroad/ NDA/ solid evidence	Must	unavailable
PARALLEL TRIAL	Yes	Licensed abroad/ RCT launched in Switzerland	Must	not available
EXTENDED ACCESS	Yes	NDA, continuous treatment of former subjects	Need not	May be available

Table 10 Three compassionate use mechanisms were identified in Switzerland

AUSTRIA § 7 AMG-Au (Austrian Drug Act) was seen to require MPs to be approved by the regulatory body. § 20 ABO (Ordinance on the Operation of Pharmacies) was found to regulate extemporaneous formulation. § 8 (a) N.2 AMG-Au was determined to exempt MPs from being licensed when supplied in response to the specifications of an authorized HCP for use by an individual patient suffering from a life threatening or serious disease who cannot be treated with available options according to the current state of knowledge. Demand for unlicensed MPs was said to be covered by import from European MSs.$_{N.17}$ However, an import was shown to require a notification for E.U. products or an authorization for products from third party countries and is only permissible if alternatives are not available in Austria (§ 2 AWEG [Austrian Medicines' Importation Act]).[215] An interview raised the ethical question of whether the delay of approximately two weeks for this permission is justifiable for life-saving products.$_{N.19}$

FRANCE MPs were found to need to receive a notice of compliance before marketing (article L5121-8 CSP) or importation (article L.5121 CSP). Extemporaneous dispensing was seen licid (article L5121-1-3 CSP). The ATU (autorisation temporaire d'utilisation, temporary use authorization) was seen to be a permission granted by the French regulatory body AFSSAPS.$_{N.34}$ It was shown to be issued only if no alternative French MP is suitable. A department within AFSSAPS was reported to assess requests. Electronic submission was said to be planned for the future.$_{N.37}$ The temporary use authorization was stated to be either patient specific (ATU nominative, ATU_N) or group based (ATU de cohorte, ATU_C). The ATU_N also was observed to serve as an authorization to import an MP. The temporary use authorization was considered to be an exceptional rule (L5121-12 CSP) and is applicable to the use of unlicensed MPs for the treatment, prevention or diagnosis of serious or rare disorders when no adequate therapeutic option is available. ATUs were shown to correspond to Art. 83 of Reg. 726/2004/EU and Art. 5 of Dir. 2001/83/EU if the MP is:

- Efficacy and safety were seen to have to be evident from clinical trials performed for licensing purposes. An NDA was required to have been filed or be filed within a given time frame (ATU_C, art. R5126-103), or

- If applicable, imported and was to be administered to a specific patient under the responsibility of the physician in charge. A benefit to the patient was to be visible from the scientific state of knowledge about the MP's efficacy and safety (ATU_N, art. R5126-104 CSP).

Legal use of an MP not approved in France was seen to only be permissible within the ATU framework. (a) Continued treatment at the end of a clinical trial, (b) off label use, (c) use of an MP that is licensed but not marketed and (d) extemporaneous MPs prepared in the dispensary were found to not qualify for ATU application. Use of an MP within a temporary use authorization was observed to not be equivalent to clinical investigation. Though clinical data were found to determine, whether a drug is made available on an ATU basis or must be subject to further investigation before temporary authorization. At an early point of drug development, participation in clinical trials was said to always have to be favored.$_{N.37}$

ATU_C was the key to allow unlicensed use of drugs at a late stage of clinical development in a group or sub-group of patients. The ATU application was to be issued by the licensee either at the same time as the NDA or shortly before. In the later case, the application must be filed soon. The dossier was to encompass the application for ATU_C including an explanatory statement (Art. L5121-12 CSP), the consent of the applicant to file the application pending a specified date, the conditions of dispensing and the expected number of patients eligible in France. Furthermore, the following were given to be added to the request for ATU_C: A copy of the NDA, a copy of the foreign license if the drug is licensed abroad, the

SmPC, the last PSUR and the data for the upcoming PSUR, a draft protocol for therapeutic use and synopsis of information (Protocole d'utilisation thérapeutique et de recueil d´informations), a draft of the SmPC, label and PIL, information on current clinical trials for the same indications including data on investigators and centers, the OMP designation (if applicable), any information on compassionate use outside of France and copies of scientific evaluations by EMEA, AFSSAPS or other European regulatory bodies. The 'Protocole d'utilisation thérapeutique et de recueil d´informations' was to be presented in the IMPD format containing the principles of an ATU, the SmPC, conditions for the drug application, prescription and dispensing, patient information, patient monitoring provisions, data collection obligations for physicians and the license, measures of pharmacovigilance, requirements for periodic reporting by the licensee and the periodic reports' dissemination. When filing its decision, the AFSSAPS takes into consideration quality, safety and efficacy for the indication, the draft Protocole d'utilisation thérapeutique et de recueil d´informations, draft SmPC, patient information, prescription as well as dispensing provisions and its significance compared to marketed drugs. An ATU_C was to be issued for a precise indication and remains valid for one year. Renewal is ideal two months before expiration. Re-submissions were necessary to include good reason, presentation of collected data, information on risk/chance ratios, the quantity of dispensed MPs and the number of patients treated (Art. L5121-12 CSP).

Patients were found to have to be informed about first the ATU, second the properties of the drug and finally monitoring in advance to treatment. Patients were to be provided the patient information approved by AFSSAPS and are also informed about data capture and data transfer to the licensee and AFSSAPS (Law Nr. 78-17 dated January 6th, 1978). The physician was obliged to inform the pharmacist in charge about details of the ATU; the physician must also secure drug monitoring and data capturing, inform the licensee and the pharmacist in charge about irregularities as well as reasons and fulfill his tasks in terms of pharmacovigilance (PhV).

The pharmacist was to confirm the compliance of the treatment protocol and data collection. He or she was seen responsible to dispense the medication. A physician requiring an ATU_C drug for a patient first was found to have to submit a request (Fiche de demande de protocole d'utilisation thérapeutique et de recueil d'informations) for the treatment protocol and data collection. He then was seen to have to send the entry-form via the pharmacist to the licensee, who validates it. If all criteria are met, the licensee was to provide the pharmacy with the product. Importation of an ATU_C drug was normal to require authorization by AFSSAPS.

Circulars by the licensee were found to inform HCPs, regional PhV centers and other drug safety institutions about ATUs. The licensee was shown to have to evaluate transmitted data; he also publishes periodic reports (rapports périodiques de synthèse). Reports were, at the time of this thesis, expected to include information on (a) the status of the product outside of France (i.e., NDA, NOC, and OMP designations), (b) current terms of the application (population, dose, criteria for administration, interactions with other MPs, etc.), (c) PhV and (d) recent results from clinical trials. The licensee was permitted to forward circulars to HCPs, regional PhV centers and other drug safety institutions only after validation by AFSSAPS.

An ATU_N authorization was found to be able to be modified, cancelled or withdrawn whenever circumstances, which have led to the authorization no longer apply. An ATU_N application was seen to be launched by the prescribing physician and passed on to the pharmacist who forwards the request to AFSSAPS. ATU_N MPs were found to only be dispensed by pharmacies in medical institutions. The physician was observed to hold the ATU_N. His ATU_N dossier was expected to convey information on the planned therapy, i.e., name of the MP, dose and duration of treatment, patient data (initials, gender and age) as well as the product's indication and reasons for the application. The application form was noted to consist of one page.

AFSSAPS and consulted experts were found to assess an ATU_N proposal by evaluating the drug's quality, safety and efficacy, its proposed indication as well as the absence of suitable, marketed alternative MPs. AFSSAPS also was seen to rely on a dossier which it requests from the licensee to-be. The dossier was observed to hold data on foreign SmPCs, information on quality, safety and efficacy (bibliography, investigators' brochure, and periodic safety reports) and a list of planned and completed clinical trials in France. The applicant for ATU_N was also seen to be required to forward treatment data to the regulatory body.

If an ATU_N is granted, the permit was observed to have to provide information on the name of the MP, contact data of the physician, the patient's initials, duration of the treatment and contact information of the hospital pharmacist. If applicable, it was found to have to also inclose a copy of a foreign SmPC or a notice by AFSSAPS on the drug's therapeutic use.

An ATU_N was seen to have to be rejected when (a) there is a therapeutic option available in France, (b) data does not provide evidence that the use of the MP would be beneficial to the patient or (c) an application for clinical trial was submitted. The evaluation process was found to take 24 to 48 hours if there has been previous assessment in other respects, processing time is determined by how long it takes to complete and review the dossier.

An ATU_N was given to be valid for a treatment period or a maximum of one year. If the treatment period was considered to exceed the given time frame, the application may be prolonged and further reasoning that justifies continued treatment (data on safety and efficacy) may be required.

The AFSSAPS was seen to both keep the physician up-to-date on an ATU_N and provide him or her with information about warnings, safety precautions, ADRs, foreign SmPCs or a synopsis of the properties of the MP, etc. In some cases, the AFSSAPS was found to may be request compliance with a "therapeutic use and data collection protocol" similar to the ATU_C. The physician was also shown to be required to (a) inform the patient about other physicians involved in treatment, (b) secure drug monitoring and pharmacovigilance, (c) inform the pharmacist in charge regularly and (d) provide AFSSAPS with any information required.

The following rules were found to apply to dispensing: if a distributor is present in France, pharmacists will use an ATU order form from AFSSAPS to request a drug; the pharmacist then dispenses the drug. If the MP is not available in France, it must be imported by the pharmacist. The ATU_N resembles an authorization for import. The pharmacist may stock products with long delivery periods. Stockpiling for cases of emergency (frequent in hospital settings) may also be approved by AFSSAPS and is subject to a separate import authorization (Art. R5121-108 to R5121-114 CSP). Any information the licensee was found to want to circulate must be validated by AFSSAPS beforehand. The two ATUs were found to share the goal of providing early access to innovative treatments, though each targets at a different point of research and development (table 11).

ATU / CHARACTERISTIC	Nominative	Cohort
PATIENT	named basis	group
APPLICANT		MAH
RESPONSIBILITIES	physician	commitment to submit an MA, follow up of patients and data collection according to a protocol for therapeutic use and data collection, periodic data reporting to AFSSAPS
SAFETY AND EFFICACY	presumed	highly presumed
MANDATORY	compassionate situations	SmPC, PIL, labelling
QUANTITIES	many drugs, few patients	few drugs, many patients

Table 11 Summary and comparison of ATU characteristics

ATU plays a major role in pediatrics: The AFSSAPS reported 251 pediatric hospital formulations in 2006 and 135 nominative ATUs for children, i.e., 22% of all ATU_N. Of 2081 clinical trials in 2002 in France, 222 (11%) were conducted in children, though children represent 22% of the French population.

U.S. Section 301 (21 USC § 331) FD&C Act was seen to prohibit the sale, stocking or supply of unlicensed MPs for trade in the U.S. Section 801 FD&C Act (21 USC 381) was found to regulate the importation of goods; Section 804 (21 USC 384) was observed to require an MA from an importer before a prescription drug is brought into the country. Individual import was to be tolerated on a small scale (Section 801(g) (1)). However, the FDA was discovered to be obliged to take measures when public health is endangered (Section 804(j) (1) (A)). Also, section 804(j) (1) (A) was given to exclude cases of individual use from handling by the FDA when no risk is evident. Section 804(j) (b) was recognized to enable the FDA to issue permissions for importation. Import from Canada was judged to be permissible according to Section 804(j) (2).

The Drug Shortage Program (DSP) of the Center for Drug Evaluation and Research (CDER) was seen to attempt to resolve problems relating to drug shortages in the U.S.[216] Emergency IND (eIND), single patient $IND_{N.9}$ and treatment IND (tIND) $protocol_{N.9}$ were found in place within the FDA. Special exception protocols,[217] treatment referral center protocols and group C protocols[218] were identified as National Cancer Institute (NCI) mechanisms for early access to NDU. Table 12 contrasts these mechanisms.

ASPECT / PROTOCOL	Institute	Request	Point of time	Regulation	Applicant
EMERGENCY IND		Subsequently			Physician
SINGLE PATIENT IND			RCT	21 CFR 312.36	Physician/ MAH
TREATMENT IND	FDA		Early stages of development	21 CFR 312.34 and 312.35	MAH/ physician
SPECIAL EXCEPTION			>Phase II and III ct	≙ eIND	Physician
TREATMENT REFERRAL CENTRE	CTEP[vi]		highly promising agents	~ simple multicenter ct	Patient/ physician
GROUP C	FDA/ NCI	In advance	Phase III ct	≙ tIND	CTEP/ (physician)

Table 12 Mechanisms for NDU in the U.S. (□ equal to, ~ similar to, > more than)

E.U. Art. 6 of Dir. 2001/83/EC was found to prohibit the sale, supply or stock-keeping of MPs without an MA. Art. 3 of Dir. 2001/83/EC was seen to exempt extemporaneous products from registration requirements. Art. 5 of Dir. 83/2001/EC was observed to exempt MPs supplied in response to a bona fide unsolicited order, formulated in accordance with the specifications of an authorized HCP and for use by an individual patient under the HCP's direct personal responsibility; this article has been associated with importation in the U.K., NDU in Austria, extemporaneous products by Blasius[219] and named patient use by Akbarian[220] and Schwarz[221] in the E.U.

A compassionate use concept was found to have been introduced at the E.U. level.$_{N.31}$ Article 83 of Reg. 726/2004/EU, the Guideline on Compassionate Use of Medicinal Products, pursuant to article 83 of Regulation (EC) No 726/2004 and article 5 of Dir. 83/2001/EU were stated to regulate compassionate use in Europe. By way of exemption, MSs were found to be able to make an MP for human use available for compassionate use if the MP is eligible for authorization via the

---

vi Cancer Therapy Evaluation Program

Centralized Procedure (CP, article 6 of Directive 2001/83/EC). When an MS was to envisage the need to make an MP available, the competent authority of that MS is to notify the EMEA indicating whether they consider a CHMP opinion on the conditions for compassionate use to be of interest. Compassionate use of MPs belonging to the "optional scope" shall only be reported to the EMEA if the eligibility for the CP has been confirmed by CHMP.

Companies were found to not be supposed to make contact EMEA directly to request a CHMP opinion, but may inform EMEA of compassionate use applications in an MS or of an ongoing application process for compassionate use at national level. CHMP opinions were seen to not be binding for the regulatory bodies[vii] of an MS. Justifications for the need of a compassionate use program were observed to have to be enclosed to demonstrate meeting of the criteria of article 83 (2). Any scientific data submitted was found to have to allow evaluation of the conditions for use of the MP in the target population. In terms of efficacy, the assumptions for compassionate use were shown to have to be based on mature phase III RCTs. Acceptable assumptions may, however, already rely on promising data observed in exploratory trials. In terms of safety, submission of all available data was seen to be encouraged.

GERMANY MPs were evidenced to have to receive MA before they are dispensed, stocked or supplied to patients in Germany (§ 21 AMG). Shipment of MPs requiring registration was found to only be permissible under § 73 AMG if the MP is (a) licensed in Germany and (b) imported from the E.U. or ETA by (c) an MAH, a wholesaler, a veterinary or a pharmacy or shipped to a patient by a pharmacy from the U.K., the Netherlands or a pharmacy in another country possessing a shipment permit. Shipment of licensed MPs from third party states was seen to be permissible for persons holding a shipment permit according to § 72 AMG. § 73 (c) was found to provide exemptions to the import of MPs not licensed in Germany. Medical products may be brought in in small amounts (no stock) for individual patients if first ordered by a pharmacy with an operating license and second licensed in their country of origin. Import from third party states was seen to require a valid prescription. Absence of identical E.U. products was found to be compulsory$_{N.43}$ (as shown in table 13).

[vii] Germany has three regulatory agencies for 1) drugs and medical devices, 2) sera and vaccines and 3) consumer protection and food safety handling veterinary drugs

ASPECT / ORIGIN	STATUS	PRESCRIPTION
E.U./EEA	OTC	Non-prescription
E.U./EEA	Rx	Prescription
THIRD PARTY COUNTRIES	OTC/Rx	prescription, absence of German alternative drugs

Table 13 Prescription requirements for import to Germany

According to § 18 ApoBetrO, the name of the MP, name and address of the manufacturer, quantity and formulation, name and address of the physician and patient, date of order and supply as well as the signature of the pharmacist in charge must be recorded. Multiple provisions including § 7 ApoBetrO, the EC-GMP Guidance, Guidance for the manufacture and analysis of unsterile extemporaneous products by the Federal Chamber of Pharmacists, the New Extemporaneous Formulary (Neues Rezeptur Formularium, NRF), a guidance for sanitation by the German Society for Dermatologic Pharmacy, the list of critical ingredients (Bedenkliche Rezepturarzneimittel) of the Drug Commission of the German Pharmaceutical Association (AMK), and the German and European Pharmacopeia all were judged to regulate extemporaneous preparation of MPs in terms of quality management.

Compassionate use was introduced in Germany by the 14th amendment of the AMG. Sect. 21 (b) N.6 AMG states that *"(b) an MA is not required for MPs which [...] 2. are made available under the provisions laid down in article 83 of Regulation (EC) N.726/2004 for (a) patients suffering from a disease leading to severe disability or (b) whose disease is life-threatening and who cannot be treated satisfactorily with an approved MP; procedural rules were stated to have to be determined in a legal regulation (ordinance) in accordance with section 80. [...]"* The German Federal Institute for Drugs and Medical Devices (BfArM) stated to currently not be authorized to make decisions on "compassionate use" programs on its website, for the reason that procedural rules according to sect. 80 were still being developed. Pharmaceutical companies, other persons or institutions were found to be able to refer to sect. 21 (b) N.6 AMG when conducting a "compassionate use" program. Reference may also be made to article 5 of Directive 2001/83/EC. BfArM was found to provide noncommittal recommendations:

- *"Existence of objective evidence that the patients suffer from a life-threatening disease or a disease leading to severe disability.*
- *Existence of objective evidence that there is no other satisfying treatment option with medicinal products approved in the European Community.*

- *Existence of objective evidence that a marketing authorization application has been submitted for the medicinal product or that clinical trials with this medicinal product are still ongoing.*
- *The "Guideline on Compassionate Use of Medicinal Products, Pursuant to Article 83 of Regulation (EC) No 726/2004 (Draft)" should be considered.*
- *Appropriate documents such as an investigator's brochure (IB) providing relevant non-clinical and clinical data proving safety and efficacy in the foreseen medical indication should be in place.*
- *Inclusion and exclusion criteria as well as withdrawal criteria for the compassionate use program should be in place.*
- *Provision for PhV measures should be arranged."*

"Recently, the German Ministry of Health proposed to exempt medicinal products available for compassionate use (article 83 EU 726/2004) from the general pharmacy-only requirement (§ 43 AMG), hence allowing direct supply from pharmaceutical manufacturers or wholesalers to hospitals or physicians (draft for amendment to the German Drug Act (AMG) as of 22 December 2008). The ABDA-Federal Union of German Associations of Pharmacists officially objected to this proposal" (personal correspondence Lutz Tisch, ABDA, Berlin, 22 January 2009).

JAPAN Authorization for marketing of MPs (jap. shōnin) was found to be granted by the Ministry of Health, Labor and Welfare (MHLW). No MP that is licensed was seen to be allowed to be manufactured, imported, stocked or supplied if its ingredients, properties or quality deviate from the regulatory provisions (art. 56 PAL). Article 22 PAL was shown to regulate extemporaneous formulations.

MPs were to be imported if a plant of the company is located in Japan, but when manufacture takes place abroad, an importation permit is mandatory and a local distributor is appointed. In April 2007, the Japanese Department of Health proposed a compassionate use system based on that of the EU and the U.S. for unlicensed MPs to treat serious illness in the absence of alternative options. Individual import was found to be feasible.

Table 14 contrasts the regulations affecting treatment of patients outside an MA or products requiring but missing a valid product license. In summary, importation of MPs was seen regulated in all nations; however, no harmonized rules were identified for the E.U. as a whole. Extemporaneous preparation was seen to be subject to pharmaceutical law in eight countries of investigations. In all countries but Japan, which plans to implement a strategy, there were conventions in place that allow for compassionate supply in theory. Off label use was never regulated by law.

NDU / COUNTRY	Registration requirement	Unlicensed Use		Compassionate use	
		Import	*Extemporaneous products*	*Named patient use*	*Expanded access*
GERMANY	§ 21 AMG	§ 73 (c) AMG, § 18 ApoBetrO	§ 7 ApoBetrO	unidentified	§ 21 (b) N.6 AMG
AUSTRIA	§ 7 AMG-Au	§ 2 AWEG	§ 20 ABO	§ 8 (a) N.2 AMG-Au	unidentified
SWITZERLAND	Art. 9 HMG, VAM	Art. 36 AMBV	Art. 9 Abs. 2 HMG	Art. 36, Abs. 3 bis 5 der AMBV	Art. 9 Abs. 4 HMG
FRANCE	Art. L5121-8 CSP	Art. L.5121 CSP	Art. L5121-1-3 CSP	Art. R5126-104 CSP	Art. R5126-103
U.K.	§§ 18 ff Medicines Act	MCA Guidance Note N.14. Feb 2000.	Schedule 1 of 1994/SI 3144	SI 2005 Nr. 2879	unidentified
E.U.	Art. 6 Dir. 2001/83/EC	unidentified	Art. 3 Dir. 2001/83/EC	Art. 5 of Dir. 83/2001/EC	Art. 83 of Reg. 726/2004/EC, Guideline on Compassionate Use of Medicinal Products, Pursuant to Article 83 of Regulation (EC) No 726/2004
U.S.	Section 301 (21 USC § 331) FD&C Act	Section 801 FD&C Act (21 USC 381), Section 804 (21 USC 384)	unidentified	unidentified	21 CFR 312.36, 21 CFR 312.34 and 312.35
CANADA	C.01.014 FDR	C.01.014.1. FDR	unidentified	Sections C.08.010 and C.08.011 FDR	
JAPAN	Art. 12-14 PAL	Art. 56 PAL	Article 22 PAL, PFSB/CND Notification N.0331004, March 31, 2005	unidentified	planned

Table 14 Synopsis of the regulations affecting nonlincensed drug use in selected industrial countries

3.3. Texts of law regulating nonlicensed drug use with regard to drug safety

Safety of and low-risk access to NDU has primarily been studied in pediatrics. In 2004, the EMEA reported harm to children in the course of off-label- and unlicensed use to the EC. Fewer adverse reactions were reported for children than for adults. Of the 820 serious ADRs that had been reported to the EMEA, 130 were fatal. Several studies (Schirm 2004, Ufer 2004, Horen 2002, Clarkson 2001, Turner 1999, Gill 1995) showed a higher incidence of ADRs in children. In pediatric inpatient care, twice as many ADRs were identified in comparison to adult settings. The relative risk for ADRs in outpatient pediatric care was reported to be 3.44 (95 percent confidence interval). The EMEA disapproved of SmPCs and PILs concerning pediatric information, especially with regard to a lack of recommendations for dosage. Dosing mistakes commonly were said to lead to medication errors in children. An accordingly large quantity of extemporaneous preparation was stated to be the result of absent pediatric formulations.

In terms of quality in patient care, harm to patients because of denied treatment versus ADR as a result of NDU was found to be unproven. Present studies were seen to also not give consistent evidence on whether ADRs occur more often during NDU or as frequently as with licensed MPs' use: Turner et al. and Horen et al. found that ADRs occurred at a higher rate during off label drug use.[222] [223] ADRs are more frequent in children (7%-20% in inpatient care, i.e., 38%-45% out of all ADRs occurring) because dosages are commonly matched to age and weight.[224] Choonara et al. could not support this conclusion in their review.[225] Table 32 is a synopsis of further studies presenting incidences of ADRs over a period of NDU.

ADR reporting and PhV in general was found to be regulated in pharmaceutical law and is often identical for licensed or INDs and nonlicensed drug use. INDs and compassionate use were seen to usually be subject to clinical trial provisions with regard to ADR reporting. Reporting practices for marketed products were observed to vary; mandatory systems are present in France, Italy and Sweden, and a voluntary reporting system e.g. in the U.K.[226] Any present foci were shown to turn to APIs as opposed to a drug's terms of use, e.g., thalidomide in Austria$_{N.17}$ or Japan, new APIs in the U.K. and vaccines in the U.S. (see table 15).

SCHEME / COUNTRY	Reporting
U.K.	Black Triangle Scheme
	Drug Safety Research Unit (DSRU)
	Yellow Card System
	Serious Adverse Blood Reactions and Events (SABRE)
GERMANY	Reporting of drug risks according to graduated plan procedure
	error reporting and learning system for office based physicians
FRANCE	Regional centres for PhV (CRPV)
EU	EUDRAvigilance[N.29]
	Council for International Organizations of Medical Sciences (CIOMS)
AUSTRIA	ADR Reporting
GERMANY	Arzneimittelsicherheit in der Psychiatrie (AMSP, Drug Safety in Psychiatry)
SWITZERLAND	Critical Incidents Reporting System (CIRS)
	Swiss Paediatric Surveillance Unit (SPSU)
	Regional centres for PhV Product defects and toxicologic centre
CANADA	Canadian Adverse Drug Reaction Monitoring Program (CADRMP)
U.S.	Adverse Event Reporting System (AERS)
	Kaiser Permanente National Patient Safety Program
	FDA MedWatch Program
	Vaccine Adverse Event Reporting System (VAERS)
JAPAN	Safety Management System for unapproved drugs (SMUD)
	Electronic ADR Reporting System

Table 15 Selected mechanisms of ADR reporting in surveyed countries

E.U. The European Risk Management Strategy (ERMS) was found to require applicants for MA to monitor off label use within the scope of the systematic implementation of risk management plans. Potential off label pediatric use of MPs in MSs was found to be discussed in NDAs. Off label use was seen to have to be covered by the commitment to PSURs. Reports on suspected adverse reactions after off label use, the potential of off label use (including pediatric off label use) and exposures that differed from those predicted were seen to have to be interpreted. The harm/benefit ratio was required to be evaluated in addition to a standard safety assessment. The possibility of introducing patient reporting in future to improve the overall reporting rate has been discussed. The reporting rate was said to be estimated to be low in the MS e.g. Belgium, and ADRs after off label use are thought to be reported more rarely than in licensed use.[N.33] The reporting mechanisms were judged to not function for unlicensed MPs; separate mechanisms were present for compassionate use due to the regulation of clinical trials (see 3.2 Investigations into supply shortages of drugs and the necessity as well as procedure of nonlicensed drug use). EudraVigilance was identified as a data processing network and management system for reporting and evaluating suspected ADRs during the development of MPs in the European Economic Area

(EEA) and following their MA. The CIOMS ADR Working Group (composed of representatives of seven multinational pharmaceutical manufacturers and six regulatory authorities) developed and implemented a standardized method for reporting post-NOC ADRs.

AUSTRIA was alike other MS suggested also to lack customized PhV for NDU. A pilot project in Salzburg named 'medicinal products seatbelt' ("Arzneimittelsicherheitsgurt") was stated to analyze drug interactions. Specific requirements for dispensing thalidomide formulations; contribute to drug safety in Austria. In all other respects, general rules for ADR reporting were seen to be valid. The Vienna Medical Association contemplated establishing an anonymous reporting scheme in the future. Together with Swiss, Hungarian and German hospitals, Austrian hospitals were found to participate in a program determining serious ADRs in inpatient psychiatry wards (AMSP, table 15). Until 2006, 45 sites monitored 166,073 patients. Case reports were to be evaluated by local review boards. Apart from this scheme, no reviews on safety issues during NDU were identified. In contrast to labeled use, the frequencies of ADRs in off label use were unavailable. The proportion of reports on ADRs after off label use was judged to be very low. According to the interviewees, reasons for this finding were at the time of this research an unreadiness to report ADRs on the part of physicians and patients. Readiness to report ADRs was said to be overall low and presumably decreases when using medical products in an off label way. All three strategies for drug safety monitoring in Austria were judged not to be custom-made to NDU.

SWITZERLAND CIRS was identified as an anonymous and international forum on critical incidents in anesthesiology. SPSU, an established hospital reporting system, was seen to monitor rare pediatric diseases. Regional centers for PhV as well as a product defects and toxicological center were found to collect ADR case reports. No separate obligations to report ADRs in NDU were acknowledged in Switzerland.$_{N.12}$

U.S. An Adverse Event Reporting System (AERS) was shown to be a computerized database supporting the FDA's post-marketing safety surveillance for approved MPs. It was reported to monitor new adverse events and medication errors. ADR reporting was seen to be voluntary for HCPs in the U.S.$_{N.8}$ If a manufacturer receives an adverse event report, he or she was said to be required to send the report to the FDA as specified by regulations (MedWatch, mandatory reporting).[N.4] Interdisciplinary teams at Kaiser Permanente National Patient Safety Program have been developing strategies to mitigate the risks of preventable adverse events.[N.9] The Vaccine Adverse Event Reporting System (VAERS) was identified as a program of the Centers for Disease Control and Prevention (CDC) and the Food and Drug Administration (FDA). VAERS was found to be a post-marketing safety surveillance program that collects information about adverse events after the administration of U.S. licensed vaccines. Experts put the overall reporting rate at one to ten percent.[N.5]

U.K. In the U.K., black triangle drugs were seen to be intensively monitored, in addition to new MPs and vaccines, in order to confirm the risk/chance profile of the MP. The U.K.'s spontaneous ADR reporting scheme, the Yellow Card Scheme,[N.26] was found to receive reports of ADRs from HCPs and patients. Clinicians were reported to tend to not report ADRs with off label use.[N.27] A Drug Safety Research Unit (DSRU) was found to perform prescription event monitoring on selected newly marketed drugs in general practice. Hospital blood banks, transfusion teams and other blood establishments were found to be able to report serious ADR and ADE relating to blood to the MHRA via SABRE. For compassionate use, a company was said to be able to draw up a contract with the prescriber to provide certain information in particular regarding safety.[N.27] In the qualitative survey the reporting rate was judged to be poor[N.24 N.21] and more reporting was demanded.[N.22 N.28] The quality of ADRs in children treated with antidepressants was criticized to justify end of treatment. A slight increase of ADR in unlicensed use over the past ten years was reported.[N.21]

GERMANY Reports from healthcare professionals about MPs' risks in accordance with the German graduated scheme procedure (Stufenplanverfahren) are required to be sent to the professional association, the MAH or the regulatory body in charge. There was evidence that off label use may not be reported at all, because the MP is not used according to the label because of the wording of law:[227] § 4 (13) AMG was said to distinguish ADR only when an MP is used according to the terms of the label. Use according to the label was taken to include obvious incorrect use, frequent incorrect use and acknowledged medical use.[228] For this reason and on one occasion, off label use that is not medically acknowledged was explained not to be subject to reporting requirements.

CANADA Mandatory ADR reports[N.2] were to be submitted to the Canadian ADR Monitoring Program (CADRMP). The Canada Vigilance Online Database was found to be called MedEffect. The reporting rate was estimated by polled experts to be 10%.N.2

JAPAN The Japanese PDMA has provided HCPs and medical institutions with an electronic ADR reporting system since April 2005. These reports by MAH have been published in an online database since January 2006. In 2005, the SMUD program was introduced in order to monitor and assess the medical use of thalidomide[i].

FRANCE The French drug surveillance (pharmacovigilance) system was found to be based on a network of 31 regional centers that enter ADR reports from health professionals into a common database. With respect to NDU, French physicians were seen to be obliged to keep records of patients treated under ATU permission and file reports with the AFSSAPS.

As a closing remark: Intensified monitoring of ADRs with nonlicensed drug use was not the specific aim of any mechanism. Some reporting forms (CIOMS form I, yellow card, Meldebogen für unerwünschte Arzneimittelwirkungen [BfArM, Germany]) permitted a comparison of terms of use of the MP for which an ADR was reported. Regulatory bodies, however, have not published such assessments in annual reports.

3.4. Regulations applying to health care professionals and law on supply and use of nonlicensed drugs

The supply and use of nonlicensed drugs was found to be subject to laws: Therapeutic freedom, emergency, duty of care, obligation of contract and objection to risky agents most commonly affect the practice of medicine.

In terms of NDU, MPs were able to, from a pharmaceutical law point of view, be provided to patients by pharmacists unless critical agents (§ 5 AMG in Germany, § 13 (d) ABO in Austria) are recognized. If the pharmacist was to have no reasonable concerns, he or she has the obligation to dispense the drug (§ 17 IV ApoBetrO in Germany, § 25 ABO in Austria).

Physicians were seen to be free to prescribe MPs as he or she feels necessary (§ 1 Abs. 2 BÄO [National Law on Physicians] in Germany,$_{N.37\ N.39\ N.41\ N.42\ N.44}$ Art 6 StGG in Austria$_{N.15\ N.19}$). Therapeutic freedom was found to be present for Britain$_{N.23\ N.26\ N.28}$ (Section 9 (a) of the Medicines Act 1968) and unlicensed and off label products may be legally dispensed by pharmacists (Section 10 of the Medicines Act 1968)$_{N.21}$ or administered by supplementary prescribers (Section 11 of the Medicines Act 1968).$_{N.24}$ It was observed to be in the realm of medicine to use an MP off label in Canada.$_{N.2}$ A physician in the U.S. was also judged to be free to prescribe an MP outside of its labeling,$_{N.8\ N.7\ N.6\ N.5\ N.4\ N.3}$ but should be able to defend its use in front of a jury of peers.$_{N.9}$ The right to prescribe medications in similar terms was also claimed to be present in Ireland$_{N.32}$ and Belgium.$_{N.33}$

A physician was even found to be obliged to treat a patient in a nonlicensed in the case of an emergency (§ 34 StGB in Germany, § 1306a ABGB [Austrian Civil Code] in Austria). However, he or she was seen to have to assure the current standard of care (§ 276 BGB in Germany, § 55 ÄG [Austrian National Law on Physicians] in Austria).

There was no evidence for prohibition of NDU for physicians and patients in health care law. A supply chain for MPs nevertheless involves MAH, wholesalers and pharmacists, whose actions may be restricted. Importation of MPs in such as it is relevant to unlicensed drug use was shown to be subject to restrictions (see 3.3 Texts of law regulating nonlicensed drug use with regard to drug safety).

3.5. Operating experience with provisions for nonlicensed drug use

Operating experiences with e.g. a temporary use program were taken as important indicators for the feasibility and acceptance of a solution. Operating experience was also assumed to illustrate what impact of an approach on the NDU difficulty. Different levels of knowledge of temporary use procedures among professionals became apparent and public training was found to be desirable.

U.K. According to expert N.22, a British regulation of compassionate use (describing patients, dosage and length of treatment) was in place. An investigation of the MHRA Guidance Note No.14 by the author of this work however, documented that the regulatory agency refers to the Guideline on compassionate use of medicinal products pursuant to Regulation (EC) 726/2004 for compassionate use. National legislation was not identified. The expert challenged the concept that illegitimate NDU can be regulated and believed that off label use cannot be regulated by law. In contrast findings in literature showed that the MHRA Guidance Note No.14 governs "the supply of unlicensed relevant medicinal products to individual patients" (see 3.3 Texts of law regulating nonlicensed drug use with regard to drug safety) and refers to off label use. The interviewee was aware of the Department of Health's "Medicines Management Framework and Standards for Better Health" but seemingly unaware of subsequent policies for the use of unlicensed (and off label use) medicines in U.K. NHS trusts. He disapproved of a federal indemnity fund for harmful consequences of NDU as suggested by the interviewer, because in his opinion "it makes a mockery of the licensing system".

The British interviewee N.23 (pediatric affiliation) believed NDU is necessary in the short term, but objected to NDU in the long term. He appreciated the financial incentives for MAHs and was confident in *"legislation introduced in Europe to finally improve the situation"*, referring to pediatric regulation (PedReg), although he was reserved on its success in pediatrics and allotted *"a couple of years"* to judge the success of the regulation. By January 26th, 2013, the Commission is to present to the European Parliament and Council a general report on its experience.[229] The first positive opinion on a pediatric formulation of powder and solvent for the oral suspension of losartane[i] potassium according to article 29 of the Pediatric Regulation (1901/2006) was given on October 23rd 2007 (see 3.8

Criteria for simplified variation while assuring drug safety: Incentives and duties).[230] The expert linked the therapeutic freedom of pediatricians and current best practices (see 3.4 Regulations applying to health care professionals and law on supply and use of nonlicensed drugs).

Respondent N.24 of the U.K., also in pediatrics, recognized the PedReg as a provision in place to decrease NDU and underlined that until the PedReg's arrival, an MP's label could easily have excluded children from pharmacotherapy. She criticized the MAH's disinclination to perform clinical trials in children. Up until the PedReg came into force, she explained, best empiric practice determined standards of pediatric care. She still was concerned about the lack of information on older drugs currently used off label and suspects that *"long-marketed drugs is the only area where the regulation perhaps is not as good as it could be"*. She was aware of provisions addressing older drugs (N.B. pediatric use MA [PUMA]) and believed this regulation aims to *"collect information on day to day use of off label drugs"*. The Task-force in Europe for Drug Development for the Young (TEDDY) is to set up a 'European Pediatric Drug Database' by exploring, validating and consolidating existing data sources containing information on MPs used in children (see 3.3 Texts of law regulating nonlicensed drug use with regard to drug safety).[231] The academic stated that NDU prescription, administration and dispensing were legal, but under the professional responsibility of a physician, nurse or pharmacist: A professional only *"uses unlicensed or off label medicines when there is no alternative"* (see 3.4 Regulations applying to health care professionals and law on supply and use of nonlicensed drugs).

A representative of U.K. general practitioners assumed that there is little legislation on NDU; expert N.25 pictured shortfalls in regulation. Health care planner N.26 however, recognized named patient use of the Medicines Act as a provision for NDU *"in individuals without identification"*. He described the provisions as "*modest*" and "*loose*". The expert acknowledged that (a) pediatricians may be too overloaded to notify each case of NDU, (b) regulation was developed in order to control MAHs (as opposed to physicians) and (c) the biggest NDU issue (children) is addressed by the new EU arrangements to promote better licensing. In spite of named patient use and in a liability suit, the physician would have to prove his cautious behavior (see 3.6 Liability for nonlicensed drug use); nevertheless, the interviewee did not express any desire to have extra primary legislation enacted. Despite named patient use, pharmaceutical manufacturers were seen not to be permitted to promote NDU. Regulation 3 of the Advertising Regulations confirmed that MPs without valid MA may not be advertised for medicinal purposes.[232] Also, material relating to products that do not hold U.K. MAs was found to be permitted to be displayed at international events provided that first a significant proportion of the attendees are from countries outside the U.K. where the product is licensed, and finally it is clearly and prominently indicated that the product is not licensed in the U.K.

A British industry associate N.27 assumed NDU is used as often as 15% in general practice and expects a future decrease with European legislation. He also stated that compassionate use is regulated through MHRA guidance, while believing off label use unregulated. He was familiar with a ban of advertising MPs to the public, as well as off label use to all addressees (see 3.7 Circumvention of drug approval: Law on advertising). He recognized the legality of pharmaceutical advertisement of licensed MPs and licensed uses to HCPs. A company was also found to be allowed to respond to a HCP's request for information about a NDU (see 3.7 Circumvention of drug approval: Law on advertising).

A hospital pharmacist$_{N.21}$ identified MPs that are made under section 10 of the 1968 Medicines Act, i.e., extemporaneous products, as "specials" and as an example of unlicensed use. He identified licensing and importation requirements as safety measures, but demanded safer practice. He did not think that goverment arrangements around using unlicensed MPs are adequate. In his opinion, all needed drugs should be available in the required formulations and licensed for essential indications, because bioavailability studies and standardization are absent for extemporaneous preparations. 'Specials' manufacturers, who are often assigned extemporaneous preparation in the U.K., are as per his statements, not responsible for clinical suitability; pharmacists are often unaware of their responsibility for a product's suitability (N.B.: plausibility check). He pointed out that there is a pediatric committee at the MHRA similar to the EMEA's PDCO. The Paediatric Medicines Expert Advisory Group of the Committee of the Safety of Medicines was found to advise on the safety, quality and efficacy of MPs for pediatric use, and on the implementation of the Department of Health's and MHRA's pediatric strategy, the recently implemented EU pediatric work sharing project, and the European regulation on MPs for pediatric use (see 3.3 Texts of law regulating nonlicensed drug use with regard to drug safety).[233] Therapeutic freedom, patient rights and dispensing were seen to remain unaffected by current legislation according to the interviewee's statements (see 3.4 Regulations applying to health care professionals and law on supply and use of nonlicensed drugs).

Regulatory expert N.28 did not "*think [compassionate use] has a very precise legal meaning in the English system*" and described it as a loose term assigned for reimbursement aspects. He understood off label use not as a problem but as a consequence of the lack of suitable MPs. The effort to include pediatric indications onto product licenses throughout the EU is, in his opinion, an attempt to reduce off label prescribing. He underlined that a prescriber must accept NDU risks but is free to prescribe MPs off-label, and that hence off label use is feasible (see 3.4 Regulations applying to health care professionals and law on supply and use of nonlicensed drugs). In his view, current rules on unlicensed use required no changes, but uncertainties needed clarification. MHRA has not undertaken specific measures to influence unlicensed use nor to the "*very small field*" of compassionate use. Legislation was in his mind, focused on the marketing of drugs and law derived from cases (N.B.: no case law was identified). Advertising of products without MA was seen to indeed be prohibited (see 3.7 Circumvention of drug approval: Law on advertising). The seven NDU provisions identified, were unequally known in the U.K. (table 16).

LAW / EXPERT	DH Med. Manag. Frame.	Guid. Note 14	Art. 83 Reg. EC 726/ 2004	E.U. Ped Reg	Sec. 10 Med. Act (NPU, specials)	Reg. 3 Med. Act (Advert.)	DH, MHRA Ped. Strateg.
22	Y	N	P	N	N	N	N
23	N	N	N	Y	N	N	N
24	N	N	N	Y	N	N	N
25	N	N	N	N	Y	Y	N
27	N	P	P	P	Y	N	N
21	N	N	N	Y	N	Y	Y
28	N	N	N	Y	Y	N	N

Table 16 Provisions familiar to the British (y=known, n=unknown, p=probably referred to)

CANADA Expert N.2 explained that in Canada, off label use is part of medical practice and that governors will in the future, analyze NDU as a result of the Progressive Licensing Framework, and hence identify areas for improvement. Progressive licensing will mean increased flexibility in the regulatory system to address particular medical needs or exceptional circumstances, such as rare diseases or compassionate use. This is confirmed by data by Yeates et al.[234] The polled expert saw minimal regulatory tools present to direct PhV in general. Although the SAP was reported to adopt the International Conference of

Harmonization (ICH) principles for ADR reporting, with regard to events that should be reported and associated timeframes.[235] Compassionate use requires previous authorization in Canada, as expert N.1 pointed out (see 3.2 Investigations into supply shortages of drugs and the necessity as well as procedure of nonlicensed drug use).

JAPAN In Japan, nothing more than on-label use is permitted, said interviewee N.12. It was found to have become possible to conduct clinical studies on unapproved drugs obtained by physicians and medical institutions or clinical studies on off label applications of approved drugs (MHLW Ordinance N.106 dated June 12, 2003, the revised GCP). With the broadening of the internet, cases of advertisement of unapproved drugs increased. One lecturer believed that a notification concerning the guidance and control of individual importers, including items related to drug advertising, has been issued (Notification N.0828014 of the PFSB dated August 28, 2002). Also, notifications for the guidance and control of personal import services as well as the appropriateness of advertising foreign drugs on the internet (Notification N.0828014 of PFSB dated August 28, 2002) were enacted.[236] The purpose of the notification was however, judged to be more likely to combat counterfeit drugs than to manage NDU.

SWITZERLAND Interviewee N.14 primarily distinguished between off-label, unlicensed and licensed use for Switzerland. Off label use is, according to him, not subject to legal provisions. Compassionate use requires prior authorization, which he thought, is necessary. Unlicensed use is prohibited; individual import (§ 36 of the Arzneimittel-Bewilligungsverordnung, Ordinance for the Authorization of Pharmaceuticals) is an exception from Swiss licensing requirements. The regulatory affairs manager did not regard use of products that do not require licensing as unlicensed use (also see 3.1 Terminology). A Swiss industry expert,$_{N.13}$ on the other hand, did assign individual import to the category of unlicensed use and said regulation there is similar to Germany. Extemporaneous preparation and analogous products manufactured by hospital pharmacies, he explained, are not subject to licensing but to the pharmacopeia and special GMP rules (N.B.: Ph.Helv. 10 and Suppl. 4 to Ph.Helv. 9). The Swiss drug act provides a rule for its regulatory agency to reflect on decisions filed by the EMEA, but data exchange is poor as per the expert's information. The association of Swiss MAHs "Interpharma" is proposing a memorandum of understanding to increase data exchange between regulatory agencies. Interpharma also participated in the design of an up-to-date database[237] by health insurance suppliers and leading oncologists for medically-acknowledged off label use in malignancy therapies; this database contains recommendations and detailed descriptions of indications. Affirmations were published; an extension of the database to other diseases is planned for the future (see 3.3 Texts of law regulating nonlicensed drug use with regard to drug safety). The industry associate demanded provisions for NDU, i.e., a requirement for peer review data on the safety, efficacy and quality of the product from RCTs or other research prior to off label use. There were plans to set up a clinical trial registry in Switzerland. Advertising to the public is prohibited with regard to prescription drugs, but circumvention of rules was observed by experts $_{N.15\ N.16}$. The industry associates suggested a lower level of evidence for OMPs. A published list of OMPs primarily serves commercial purposes, in the opinion of polled health care planners.

AUSTRIA In Austria, an attorney N.17 reported that consensus on NDU is easily found among Austrian peers; agreements remain undocumented. By drug law, the interviewee declared, a physician may have to treat a patient off label or with an unlicensed MP if licensed treatments fail (see 3.4 Regulations applying to health care professionals and law on supply and use of nonlicensed drugs). If an MP is available abroad, affluent patients are at any rate mobile enough to receive the treatment in a foreign country (N.B. health tourism). Reformulation of licensed MPs (e.g., into pediatric preparations) were regarded as extemporaneous products, which are regulated under the Austrian Drug Act. Off label use was not addressed in this context. The representative of the Vienna Medical Association was satisfied with Austrian legislation as it pertains to NDU, he is not aware of deficiencies in pharmaceutical law. Liability is subject to the Austrian Civil Code dated 1811. Continuing education is not restricted to in-label use in Austria. A representative of the Austrian pharmacist association N.19 called attention to the missing indication on a prescription; liability is however, indefinite in the case of harm and a pharmacist's knowledge about an off label use. The pharmacist must not fill a prescription that gives him or her cause for concern; the pharmacy will confer with the physician and keep a record if the physician insists on a medication. The expert was satisfied with provisions of the Arzneiwareneinfuhrgesetz (regulations on the importation of MPs) and explained that (a) imports from the EU are uncomplicated, (b) drugs from Germany arrived quickly (within hours) and (c) compounds from outside the E.U. were subject to prior permission. Within the scope of vocational and professional law, ADRs were found to have to be reported to AGES according to section 75 of the Austrian Medicines Act.

In Austria, a database for case reports on off label use of biologicals was said to be available to dermatologists and venereologists.[238] N.18 The Austrian Society for Dermatology and Venereology was informed to legal problems in 2007 and therefore restricted access to the data. An emergency law in the Austrian civil code was cited as support for NDU by an industry associate.$_{N.19}$ Unlicensed use is, in the interviewee's opinion, not regulated in Austria. The expressions used in 3.1 Terminology were not widespread, but circumscribed in Austrian legislation. Drugs were reported to only be legally dispensed, when licensed or if import is permitted. Section 7 AMG-Au was said to exempt drugs from this provision that are approved centrally or when importation is authorized according to section 5 of the importation regulations. Unlicensed use was stated to only be permissible in terms of importation and only if no licensed option is available in Austria; off label use was considered to be under a physician's personal responsibility. The Austrian Association of Pharmaceutical Industries (Pharmig) saw room for improvement in legislation on importation (i.e., its administrative costs and duration). Liability was observed to be subject to pharmaceutical, professional, civil and product liability law in Austria (see 3.4 Regulations applying to health care professionals and law on supply and use of nonlicensed drugs). Pharmaceutical advertisements were found to have to be compliant with the SmPC, excepting information in response to a physician' request for information about NDU to the MAH (see 3.7 Circumvention of drug approval: Law on advertising).

An executive of AGES$_{N.23}$ considered off label use lawful and under the direct responsibility of the physician only to treat life-threatening diseases. Section 8 of the AMG-Au matched the described rule: 1) (a) Proprietary MPs do not require MA, if [...] 2. A physician, dentist or veterinary authorized to practice medicine in Austria certifies that the proprietary MP is urgently needed to combat a fatal or serious disease and that licensed as well as available MPs can almost certainly not achieve the desired outcome. [...] AMG-Au.

France In France, MPs (a) without French MA, (b) to be used in a rare disease and (c) with no options of treatment in France were said to be available through the ATU program by law.$_{N.34}$ Article L.5121-12 of the French Public Health Code, emerging from law N.92-1729 of 8th December 1992, amended by law 96-452 of May 28th, 1996, provided the rules for (a) use of, (b) therapeutic purposes of and (c) exceptional measures for MPs without an MA in France.[239] Article 126a of Directive 2004/27/EC was said to be a promising opportunity to introduce a simplified procedure to authorize marketing of MPs. The interviewee also reported provisions dealing with pharmacovigilance: Decree N.95-278 of 13th March 1995 relative to PhV applies to MPs that are subject to ATU (article R.5144-3). Advertising must be in accordance with MA, said the expert. An MP with an ATU cannot be the subject of any advertising in accordance with article L.551-2 of the Public Health Code. French experts (industry, regulatory) were highly satisfied with the ATU procedure.$_{N.34,\ N.35}$

U.S. Compassionate use was an expression not to be found in U.S. regulation.$_{N.9}$ To obtain FDA approval for so-called "Single Patient-/Small Group Access", the sponsor should submit an IDE (Investigational Device Exemption) supplement requesting approval for a protocol deviation under section 812.35(a) 21CFR.[240] An IND authorization was seen to also be an authorization for shipment (N.B.:312.40 (c) 21CFR).$_{N.9}$ In the expert's opinion, the compassionate use process is tightly regulated: Consultation of the FDA and IRBs is compulsory. In this context, patient registries are only managed if required by the FDA or else set up by a sponsor or shared within a Patient Efficacy Group. The polled physician recognized the U.S.' efforts to stimulate research to increase pediatric information, as a provision that affects NDU. He also quoted the proposal to allow pharmaceutical companies to market an off label use of a drug (N.B.: by January 2009 finalized Guidance for Industry Good Reprint Practices for the Distribution of Medical Journal Articles and Medical or Scientific Reference Publications on Unapproved New Uses of Approved Drugs). The expert emphasized that, generally, marketing of off label use is illegal. In the finalized guidance, the FDA distinguishes promotional material from medical journal articles underlying specified criteria for acceptance and failure. The interviewee, however, criticized the guidance's vulnerability to publication biases, conflict of interests and ghost writing. The guidance addresses these issues by excluding scientific or medical reference publications from distribution that are written, edited, excerpted or published specifically for, or at the request of, a drug manufacturer. The polled expert's concern that "medical journals generally do not like negative studies" is not addressed in the guidance. He also brought up the complexity of cash flow; although the guidance demands disclosure of interests, sponsoring by a CME company may not reveal the subsequent funding from MAHs. The polled physician disapproved of direct consumer advertising, which, to his knowledge, is an interpretation of protected free speech and therefore a valued asset. On March 15, 2009 the Obama administration was reported to review and possibly change the FDA guidance on off-label marketing, which was approved in the final days of the Bush administration.[241]

Obligations of U.S. physicians were seen to include obtainment of patient's informed consent for use of different interventions. Patient briefing was found to include medications, potential complications and the reasons for suggesting a drug. These requirements were observed to be legally framed as the 'reasonable patient standard'. Compassionate use is done in the context of drug trials stated expert N.8 and is heavily regulated. The interviewee also associated provisions for pediatric studies with NDU, but believes these efforts to have subsided. He suggested caution with new drugs and pointed out that pediatric drugs have often been "*grandfathered in*". Monitoring and regulation of PhV is, according to his experience and compared to outpatient settings, tighter in inpatient care. Expert N.6 connected NDU to importation, which he described to be plentiful from Canada for reasons of cost. He suggested cooperation between regulators, industry, academia and parents to improve the pediatric situation; the pediatrician approved of FDAMA, FDAAA, BPCA and PREA. The interviewee (Dutch) and believes E.U. legislation to be more effective. Compassionate use, in his view, is primarily relevant in adults and is subject to reporting and record keeping requirements. The expert was uncomfortable with an obligation to inform parents about off label or unlicensed use in academic settings. He linked not only pediatrics but also rare disorders to NDU and was familiar with the Orphan Drug Regulation.

An FDA associate$_{N.5}$ explained that 'unapproved drugs' would be a term assigned to old drugs marketed before laws were in place, drugs which have been given time lines for applications but may currently still be marketed. She praised 150 label changes for approved or disapproved use in pediatric patients. In 1/5 of the changes, dosages were corrected and unique mechanisms of action or safety profiles in children were identified. Though in practice, prescriptions habits need not change (see 3.8 Criteria for simplified variation while assuring drug safety: Incentives and duties). She proposed an increase of pediatric labels by 20% and that E.U. legislation helps to increase the full number of pediatric drugs. U.S. expert 4 pointed out that the FDA only has the statutory authority to regulate drugs, but not dietary supplements (see 3.1 Terminology). He thought guidelines for off label use to be absent in the US. He considered a system to collect information on the consequences of using drugs off label to be useful. The legal implementation of such a system, in his opinion, bears a risk of marketing NDU. This concern was not unusual; in the U.S., Medicare expanded its coverage of drugs for cancer treatments not approved by the Food and Drug Administration by increasing the number of reference guides that the Centers for Medicare and Medicaid Services (CMS) rely on for determining which off label uses of cancer drugs to cover.[242] Coverage thereby is argued to open the market to NDU.

U.S. expert N.3 (pharmaceutical society) regarded the prescriber's ability to prescribe off label as a grey area. She felt that there is a demand for more information and regulatory guidance on NDU. Instead, scientific information and validity, in her opinion, are driven by standard of practice and care as well as the fluidity of research, which again are based on peer reviewed studies. She approved of the then-planned "FDA Guidance on Off label Use Publications" (see 3.7 Circumvention of drug approval: Law on advertising).

U.S. academic N.7 explained that therapeutic freedom is valid for any safe and effective purpose in line with a physician's professional judgment. Biomedical research, he pointed out, is regulated in the Belmont Report, written in reaction to the Tuskegee Institute experiment. It withheld penicillin from a cohort of black men with syphilis. "*It can be argued that the Belmont Report's three guiding principles of dignity, beneficence, and justice are ignored in allowing use of off-label, compassionate or unlicensed drugs. Patient dignity or autonomy is violated by physicians who knowingly use unproven drugs in uncontrolled experimentation on patients who are so desperate for a cure that they will reach for straws. The very suggestion that off-label use may make a difference is coercive suggestion. Beneficence requires that experimentation should contribute through the acquisition of knowledge to the future good of society. Uncontrolled experimentation cannot make such a claim. Justice in terms of the distribution of equal shares of benefits and costs is violated because off-label, compassionate or unlicensed drugs are largely available only to patients with financial means.*" The interviewee regarded NDU as liberally-regulated and connected to commercial interest instead of evidence-based medicine. He thought that U.S. law is unsystematic compared to German legislation. NDU in his opinion has the authority of law within the framework of the State Federal Vocational Rehabilitation Program and the Compassionate IND Program (see 3.3 Texts of law regulating nonlicensed drug use with regard to drug safety). He first addressed Whistle Blower Laws in context to NDU (see 3.7 Circumvention of drug approval: Law on advertising).

E.U. Interviewee N.31 stated that compassionate use has legally defined, implemented and frame-worked in 2005 by article 83 paragraph 1 of Regulation 726/2004/EC. It addresses products that are eligible for the CP (see 3.3 Texts of law regulating nonlicensed drug use with regard to drug safety). The pharmaceutical manufacturer's representative thought MPs, which have not received market authorization covered by law. She regarded patient treatment with foreign MPs as an ATU_N covered by many countries and considers ATU_N a successful process. She approved of the prior access to promising treatments under official control. She said NDU is affected by pediatric, OMP and new medicines' legislation as well as by the community code, in addition to the future provisions for clinical trials. She thought NDU a problem requiring case-by-case solutions. She reported discussions on making off label use official to be ongoing in the E.U. since 2008. National compassionate use procedures in her opinion are fast, short and cost-effective. The expert was unsure how successful the E.U. procedure is working (see 3.3 Texts of law regulating nonlicensed drug use with regard to drug safety). Legislators by her information, intentionally chose "superficial" rules because of being aware that patients needed NDU. Finally, she emphasized the problem of little legislation being present for physicians (see 3.4 Regulations applying to health care professionals and law on supply and use of nonlicensed drugs).

Expert N.32 illustrated legislation in Ireland as an example for an MSs' regulation on import of unlicensed MPs. Irish wholesalers were found to have to be authorized to import MPs on a named patient basis. Ordering of quantities only sufficient for one prescription was seen to be fixed. It is the wholesaler's obligation to report imports to the Irish Medicines Board. In case of concerns, the Irish Medicines Board can issue a recall to be followed-up by the wholesaler. This "paper trail" allows batch recalls. Preliminary notification was suggested in former times, but the Irish Pharmacists Union objected because of would-be delays in patient supply. Unlicensed MPs in Ireland also are not be advertised to public, consumers or HCPs. This provision extends to price lists. Absence of price lists was seen to complicate supply management in the U.K. Unlicensed MPs all are only available on prescription in Ireland.

Interviewee N.30, a representative of European physicians, could not name laws that affect NDU. Continuing education cannot be regulated with regard to NDU in his opinion. Unlike expert N.29, who named Compassionate Use Regulation for circumstances (a) after recruitment for a RCT is closed and (b) an NDA is or will be filed. She approved of a restrictive handling to avoid none-submission of NDA. She did not understand pediatric, age-based off label use as a classic example for off label use (see 3.1 Terminology). E.U. Interviewee 29 said MAH spokesmen sometimes look upon compassionate use as a new licensing strategy, which is incompatible with legislation. MAHs may conquer a market and then claim that an MA is crucial, because patients are stabilized on the drug. The Compassionate Use Regulation required application and data according to her information: When an MS envisages the need to make an MP available for compassionate use, as defined in paragraph (a) and (b) of article 83, the competent authority of that MS must notify the EMEA.[243] She welcomed transparency and the future possibility to arrive at conclusions for patients and physicians. This work however could identify no opinions on compassionate use as by September 11th 2008.[244] EU Regulation 1901 is meant to improve the situation in pediatrics and neonatology by means of incentives and funds, according to the regulator; off label use is supposed to be contained. Though she described the regulatory framework to generally only support the approved use of MPs, it is recognized that patients can circumstantially not be left without treatment. She listed new options to license advanced therapeutics [new medical products based on genes (gene therapy), cells (cell therapy) and tissues (tissue engineering)] conditionally or under exceptional circumstances in order to forestall off label and unlicensed use. Regulators approved expedited assessment and conditional approval in order to avoid off label use. She reported three compassionate uses, three conditional MAs and three exceptional circumstances in 2007, mainly with regard to OMPs. This report could not be verified by an inquest at the EMEA (see 3.4 Regulations applying to health care professionals and law on supply and use of nonlicensed drugs). Amendments to regulations on PhV in 2009 will, according to her information, provide further exceptions and open up the region to off label and unlicensed use. Liability is regulated in a different way in each MS, although all share compulsive duties for MAHs and sponsors, according to the poled regulatory associate. The interviewee pointed out that pediatricians have complained about failing to accomplish casualty insurance for RCTs. A transparency guideline was enacted by the EC primarily to gain information on drug pricing but also provided information about the difficulties of insurance for pediatric RCTs, as per the expert. The expert said that unlicensed use usually gets public attention only after an event occurs. She calls attention to patient reporting, which has been discussed in the past and is being discussed for future legislation.

Pediatrician and expert N.33 verified the absence of a legal definition for off label use in the E.U. He was aware of legislation for compassionate use and distinguished group and named patient use, pointing to France. The Belgian pointed out compliance with the compassionate use guidance and the possibility of requests for advice from the European authorities for group compassionate use. He did not distinguish between drugs eligible for the CP and others. He was not familiar with any compassionate use dossier yet having been handled at the European level as of June 2008. He proposed that the potential off label or unlicensed use addressed in PhV legislation did not mirror the practice of medicine.

GERMANY A German attorney (interviewee N.43) differentiated between legal definitions of off label use in social as opposed to pharmaceutical law. He believed that a generic company is liable for generic off label use, given that generic use in the unlicensed indication is common. He believed U.S. products of an MP that is licensed both in Germany and the U.S. should be 'licensed according to the model' though technically the 'pharmaceutical form' misses German informative texts. However, import to Germany is only permissible from outside the E.U. if a demand is current. In drug law, he said, Avastin® in wet AMD is an example of an extemporaneous preparation and not unlicensed use. He mentioned that compassionate use is a technical term that was present in the E.U. long before compassionate use was introduced to Germany. The interviewee called for a statutory order for compassionate use. Public liability for any future administrative procedure is feasible only in theory, said the lawyer. He addressed the problem of the pharmacy-only requirement and remuneration of pharmacists for compassionate dispensing. The German Ministry of Health proposed to exempt MPs available for compassionate use (article 83 EU 726/2004) from the pharmacy-only requirements (§ 43 AMG). The ABDA-Federal Union of German Associations of Pharmacists officially objected to this proposal (see 3.2 Investigations into supply shortages of drugs and the necessity as well as procedure of nonlicensed drug use). Expert N.43 criticized the imprecise nature of current law for patients and demands transparency. He suggested an application procedure but for reimbursement of NDU. Comparable procedures are already present for expensive therapies with single funding agencies.[245] In Germany, patient education and informed consent are subject to prevailing case law, according to his information. He did not think a register of off label use is permissible under present law.

Expert N.36 saw an unlegislated area regarding NDU. She thought individual treatment of a single patient is feasible in the scope of § 73 Sec. 3 AMG when first drugs are available (e.g. in the U.S.) and then in the case of emergency. To her knowledge, NDU in groups of patients is subject to compassionate use as amended in a draft by BfArM. She pointed out that off label use in RCTs can be covered by funding agencies nowadays (§ 35c SGB V) and that the project has made use of the rule.

Polled expert N.38 understood compassionate use to be practiced as a way to bridge patient supply until the MA is granted after a RCT ends with a positive outcome. Unlicensed use is, in his opinion, an expression of social law and refers to imported MPs. He objected to including the use of extemporaneous formulations into the definition of unlicensed use. He challenged the idea that compassionate use drugs should be covered by funding agencies or by the applicant for MA. The German Ministry of Health proposed that compassionate use drugs be provided free of charge, as enacted in the 15th amendment of the AMG (see 3.2 Investigations into supply shortages of drugs and the necessity as well as procedure of nonlicensed drug use). The interviewee thought compassionate use and import provisions to affect NDU, but saw no necessity for further pharmaceutical regulation. He expected the statutory order for compassionate use to first regulate care of former trial subjects and second duties for review boards. He supposed that a notification duty for physicians and a registry at the regulatory authority to be introduced.

Interviewee N.37 said what off-label- and compassionate use had ‘a state of therapeutic emergency’ in common. Compassionate use in her opinion is a “not legalized tradition of continuous supply of a drug after a RCT to patients until MA” (see 3.1 Terminology). The expert thought the G-BA and “expert groups for off label use at BfArM” did not have an impact on off label use. She believed unlicensed use to be an issue for criminal prosecution. BfArM’s recommendations for compassionate use are, in her opinion, for information only and without governmental liability. Since enactment of the GCP guideline, insurance for clinical trials has not been an issue anymore, said the DLH representative. When off label use occurs frequently, MAH are forced to act to the point of withdrawal of the MA, she explained.

Expert N.39 emphasized that a final statutory order is absent for compassionate use in Germany and points out France, stating that a French procedure has been in place for many years. Only noncommittal guidance is present at BfArM he confirmed and rules on EU level apply to MP eligible for the CP. He thought that there always will be off label use because either a treatment option is not economically feasible or expertise of the MAH is deficient for a new indication for an NDA. He saw room for improvement on behalf of the authorities in terms of time periods required to assess NDAs. He recognized PUMA i.e. ten years of marketing exclusivity for children's MPs in context with NDU. The industry associate was confident that medical guidance for NDU is available and did not demand changes. He approved of the off label expert groups, but regreted their small performance and achievements since starting.

Expert N.42 cited (a) compassionate use in the AMG, (b) off label expert groups and (c) national reimbursement guideline (AMR) as impacting NDU in addition to orphan and pediatric drug provisions. He criticized legal uncertainty. He approved of the G-BA procedure, though he thought more NDU should be assessed by the expert group's forces. Liability law was in his mind more complicated to regulate with regard to NDU; he believed that rules applying to compassionate use, expert groups and coverage of off label use in RCTs are crucial. Liability and reimbursement in his opinion are central aspects for the physician when treating patients off-label. Legislation is, in the contrary view of a polled expert N.44, currently sufficient.

Interviewee N.40 classified NDU in respect to social and drug law again. He put down compassionate use as an issue for MAHs, while unlicensed use is a concern for patients, physicians and funding agencies. He supported listing of the federal social court's off label criteria in a law to increase public transparency. This course of action was indeed taken in Austria (§ 8 AMG-Au). Both off label and unlicensed use are regulated less appropriately compared to compassionate use, says the German lawyer. The policy for unlicensed use, i.e., § 73 Sec. 3 AMG in his opinion is restrictive. He approved of such a "basic approach" because of quality criteria and PhV being guaranteed less as compared to off label use. He found liability to be well-regulated by the German civil code (BGB), AMG and case law. Potential for conflict remained to be present between physicians and funding agencies. The expert did not note any incentives for off label use. Though he suggested a clarification of the advertisement ban for off label use in legislation and a loosening of rules for post-authorization safety studies (PASS).

Country / *CRITERIA*	***Austria***	***U.K., Ireland[viii], France***	***Germany, Canada***	***Japan, U.S.***
PROVISION	*Duty to obtain a permit*	*Disclosure duty subject to prohibition*	*Prohibition subject to permission*	*prohibition*
PRO	Preventive, recording of all imports	Fast access, recording of all imports	Flexible, no delay	Drug safety
CON	Administrative expenses, time lag	Waiting periods delay fast access	No capturing, recall, DDL	enforcement

Table 17 Synopsis of expert's valuation of import regulation

Table 17 summarizes the assessment of import provisions; compassionate use programs were appreciated additionally but are discussed in 3.2 Investigations into supply shortages of drugs and the necessity as well as procedure of nonlicensed drug use. In summary, the narrated interview data illustrated deficiency of information and little transparency of applicable regulations.

[viii] Ireland was introduced by an EU-representative

3.6. Liability for nonlicensed drug use

Physicians prescribing in an off label manner may be found negligent and liable for harm by accusation of malpractice. Concerns have been raised regarding HCP's liability in the event of adverse outcomes associated with unlicensed drug prescription. It was necessary to distinguish off label from unlicensed and from compassionate use as it concerns questions to liability. MAHs, HCPs, wholesalers or sponsors of clinical trials were seen to possibly be held liable for harm caused by NDU. MAH, physicians and perhaps pharmacists may be found responsible for harm caused by an off label drug use. HCPs and MAHs were found to be at risk for criminal liability under acts of compassionate use.

Off label use By German civil law, MAHs were shown to be liable, independent of negligence for damage to health that is found to be not inconsequential and for harm that occurred while the MP was used as specified, including scientifically accepted as well as frequent or typical incorrect uses. Off label use was described to occasionally be scientifically accepted, e.g., misoprostol[i] in obstetrics.[246] If the MAH would not address the risks of a drug use being discussed in the PIL or if he expedites the drug use through supportive publication, he may be found liable for consequential harm and charged with § 823 ff. BGB in case of fault based liability. He was found to be prosecutable according to § 5 AMG in conjunction with § 95 Para.1 as early as he markets a risky product and is found responsible for actual homicide by § 211 ff. StGB and §§ 223 ff. StGB for bodily injury.[247] On the other hand, the acyclovir-case (30.5.1990 – 27 U 169/87) was frequently cited to give support for a circumstantial obligation to treat off label where an unlicensed treatment is considered to be state of the art.

Liability cannot only be accepted by MAH, but also by HCPs: In Germany, a physician's liability for medical malpractice was shown to originate from § 611 BGB (contractual relationship of physician and patient) and the law of torts §§ 823ff BGB. If a patient is killed or harmed by medication and the responsible pharmacist could have prevented the event, the pharmacist was judged to be found guilty of tortuous liability in Germany.[248] If a component is critical, the pharmacist was found to have to first refuse to dispense the MP and then inform the prescribing physician. To know of and judge off label drug use, however, pharmacists were required to have to know the diagnosis, which is usually not recorded on the prescription and any such effort challenges German data privacy laws. Liability was estimated to be improbable if the pharmacist meets his duty to demonstrate and explain an MP and maybe if the off label indication does not come to his attention and of course provided she or he did determine the patient's need for counseling. Partial liability for ADE was found to be possible if a pharmacist, knowing about a critical off label use, failed to obtain the physician's confirmation for the prescription.

In Austria, the extent of liability for use of an MP was found to be limited through § 15 AMG-Au and § 13 of the statutory instrument on SmPCs of proprietary MPs [Verordnung der Bundesministerin für AGS über die Fachinformation für Arzneispezialitäten]. Statutorily, absolute liability of an MAH for harm was seen to only be accepted if the MP was used according to its specifications. Off label use did not meet this criterion, but Austria often is observed to refer to German ruling.[N.17] Therefore, scientifically accepted as well as frequent or typical incorrect use could be regarded as 'use according to an MP's specifications' in Austrian courts. Austrian experts were unconcerned about liability for medical malpractice because it is regulated by ABGB 1811 and covered by professional liability insurance.[N.15] But what happens when an off label ADR justifies lawful damages that are not born by a professional insurance company? Austria planned to compensate the insolvent debtor's penalties (N.B. Japan already has such a fund in place) in the future. In Austria, product liability was shown to decrease if the claimant is jointly responsible (§ 11 Product Liability Act of Austria) and does not apply if the physician is found responsible. The physician was found to have a duty of care (§ 49 Abs 2 Nr. 2 physician's law of Austria) due to his special skills (§ 1299 ABGB). By § 1311 ABGB, a person was also seen to be responsible for any harm caused after breach of the related protective law.

Patient information was identified to play a superordinate role in Austria. The Supreme Court admitted a claim (Az. 6 Ob 54/04s) of a physician who had been treated with Novantron® (mitoxantrone[i]) by a specialist to treat multiple sclerosis. Mitoxantrone[i] had not been licensed for this indication at that time. The claimant sustained a myocardial syndrome. This ADR had been reported of in medical journals. The treating physician had not briefed her patient-colleague about the ADR and was found guilty. If a patient is not informed, consent has been judged to be missing or invalid and the treatment may be regarded as an unauthorized treatment (§§ 6, 88 und 110 StGB Austria). Informed consent was found to be dependent on a patient's individual judgment and discernment. Obtaining information and valid consent was necessary to require individual and comprehensive information as appropriate. The Austrian patient charters were found to constitute the legal framework for the right to appropriate medical counseling. On the other hand, the patient charter also was estimated to increase the patient's self-determination and personal responsibility in participating in a therapeutic decision. There were, however, exceptions to the physician's duty to inform patients: the therapeutic privilege, mortal peril and quitclaim. In all other circumstances, the patient was found to have to be fully informed about the diagnosis, treatment, risks and aftercare. The extent of information to be provided increased with both decreasing benefit and growing risks. Art. 7 Para. 2 of the patient charter addressed accepted methods and the state of science. A patient was for instance, seen to have to be referred to a different health care provider if the primary practice cannot offer accepted methods and provide the standard of care with regard to treatment. Damages for non-performance were found to be possible.

In the U.K., product liability was observed to be subject to the Consumer Protection Act of 1987. MAHs were judged to be liable for quality defects but are not responsible for harm as a result of unapproved use. British NHS trusts often were found to address liability issues in off label use guidance (see 3.3 Texts of law regulating nonlicensed drug use with regard to drug safety). Any liability associated with the use of approved, unlicensed MPs (or MPs used off-label) was shown to be, for example, accepted by an employing authority provided that best practice has been followed. The 'Policy for the Use of Unlicensed and Off Label Medicines' was seen to not be legally binding, but may be consulted in court, comparable to forecasted consultation of the British National Formulary for Children (BNF-C). The NHS Litigation Authority and the Medicines Protection Society were not aware of any claims as a consequence of NDU to date in the United Kingdom. The Bolam suit of 1957 (indirectly linked to NDU) recognized that a physician offends his duty of care when not acting according to the state of science as accepted by a jury of peers. Therefore, when refusing to provide nonlicensed care, a physician was proven to offend his duty of care when NDU is the state-of-the-art of science.

Patient information was also a major theme in U.K. legislation. According to section 2 § 12 Para. 4 of the Consumer Protection Act, a physician is responsible and found guilty if he fails to provide information that affects the validity of a patient's informed consent. The Northern Ireland Adverse Incident Centre was seen to take the perspective that use of a medicinal device outside of the recommendations of the MAH may influence risks of care, safety and liability. For these reasons, requirements for information were found to increase when treating a patient in a nonlicensed compared to a licensed way. Also, under the British Code of Ethics for Pharmacists, pharmacists were observed to have a duty of care when checking reasonability of a prescription. A pharmacist is obliged to object to risky medication. The attestation of a physician or an MAH's knowledge of off label use did not release the pharmacist from this responsibility. Over and above, British HCPs believed that the mutual trust of the patient in the physician should not be disturbed in the course of consultation.

By article L3131-3 CSP, French MAHs were not shown to be liable for harm that occurred when a drug was used in an unlicensed indication or in unapproved terms of use.

In Switzerland, liability for off label use of cytostatic preparations was found to be shared between physicians (for efficacy and safety-related harm) and pharmacists (for the extemporaneous formulation). But bear in mind: Extemporaneous formulations were assigned to the term unlicensed use in the U.K. and the Netherlands, or might even not be regarded as unlicensed at all, because they are exempted from licensing requirements. Pharmacists were generally found responsible for quality defects of extemporaneous products.

In summary, responsibility for harm in the wake of off label use was primarily shared between physicians and MAHs. Minor responsibility was shifted to pharmacists depending on the country's legal framework. An additional risk factor for unlicensed use was product quality, which was secured with off-label use. Latter products were unmanipulated and assumed to be licensed for other purposes. Quality was hence expected to be assured. Pharmaceutical companies, wholesalers and HCPs were discovered to be governed by laws with respect to liability for unlicensed use.

UNLICENSED USE Directive 85/374/EC was found to govern liability of defective products in the E.U. In Germany, an upper limit was seen to be fixed for civil penalties. § 88 AMG fixes a capital sum of € 600,000 or € 36,000 annually for a death, € 120 Mil. for a harmed person. And € 7.2 Mil. in case of death of or harm to multiple people. Absolute liability was found to not be applicable to MAHs of imported MPs imported on the basis of § 73 Abs. 3 AMG.[249] Wholesalers and HCPs may be found liable for harm that results from quality defects of an MP imported from a third party country. A physician could be liable by § 611 BGB and §§ 823ff BGB for harm secondary to unlicensed use; the physician was seen to have far-reaching duties of information when using unlicensed MPs. If a patient is harmed or killed because of a drug, and if this event could have been prevented by the pharmacist's accurate professionalism, claim for damages and compensation for immaterial damage (tortuous liability) towards the pharmacist was said to come into consideration.[250] If a drug is harmful, the pharmacist was judged to have to object to filling the prescription and he or she must inform the prescriber.[251] The pharmacist was seen to have an obligation to contract (§ 17 Abs 4 ApoBetrO); he or she brings the MP into circulation. He or she must object to bringing products into circulation that are risky (§ 5 Abs 1 AMG). This provision was found to have a higher level than therapeutic freedom. German community pharmacies were found to also dispense approximately 25 Mil. extemporaneous products per year, i.e., 1100 formulations per pharmacy annually. Extemporaneous ointments, capsules, powders and infusion lotions were seen to be common in dermatology, oncology and otolaryngology. Pharmacies could establish a quality management system or participate in inter-laboratory tests conducted by the central laboratory of German pharmacists (see table 18) to minimize the risks and the probability of liability.

Task / CATEGORY	Monograph	Assessment	Liability assumed	Inspection
PROPRIETARY MPs	MAH	BfArM, PEI, BVL	MAH	District Government
EXTEMPORANEOUS PREPARATIONS	New German Formulary	Central Laboratory of German Pharmacists	HCPs	Local health authority
	_HCP	No systematic testing		

Table 18 Quality control of extemporaneous products in North Rhine-Westphalia

In the U.K., the Bolton Primary Care Trust (PCT) Medicines Management Team placed the responsibility of obtaining informed consent from patients and caretakers as well as informing GPs about the melatonin's use onto the physician (see 3.3 Texts of law regulating nonlicensed drug use with regard to drug safety). Dispensing unlicensed products was shown to be prohibited according to the physicians' professional law. A British expert$_{N.24}$ reported that because of past manufacturing mistakes and errors, community pharmacies in the U.K. frequently refer extemporaneous preparations to 'specials' manufacturers; though pharmacists still remain liable for externally prepared specials. Extemporaneous preparation was reported to decline in British pharmacies. A second British expert$_{N.21}$ criticized that outsourcing of extemporaneous preparations bears new sources of error (see 3.5 Operating experience with provisions for nonlicensed drug use). He underlined that the pharmacist must guarantee the product's correct identity and its appropriateness for clinical use despite outsourcing. The PCT NHS Fife assigned documentation, briefing of physicians and obligations to preserve records of NDU to its pharmacists. The Bolton PCT Medicines Management Team referred employed pharmacists to follow through with the Royal Pharmaceutical Society of Great Britain's guidance on quality assurance measures for unlicensed MPs. Liability of a pharmacist for imported MPs and for extemporaneous products was found to derive from section 1 § 2 Consumer Protection Act (liability of businessmen for faulty products).

Placing MPs onto the market without an MA was found to generally be reciprocated with a fine. Pharmaceutical advertising of unlicensed MPs was prohibited in all researched countries (see 3.7 Circumvention of drug approval: Law on advertising). In France for example, MAHs were seen to be fined up to € 37,500 for advertising unlicensed use. Beyond marketing and if entered into the supply chains, HCPs are ultimately in charge for public health; French pharmacists for instance were observed to be forbidden to dispense unlicensed MPs by professional law.

Treatment providers were largely found to be responsible for harm resulting from unlicensed use and are thus liable for redress. Breach of abatement measures by wholesalers or MAHs were seen to probably cause both to be held responsible. Further rules were observed to be present for INDs used in clinical trials and compassionate use. MAHs, HCPs and sponsors were judged to be potentially liable for harm due to compassionate use.

Compassionate use In the E.U., MPs dispensed in accordance with art. 83 para. 7 of Regulation (EC) N.726/2004 were found to be without prejudice to civil or penal responsibility of a sponsor.

A French MAH, holder of a permission to import MPs or holder of an ATU (Art. L3131-3 CSP), was not seen to be liable for harm incurred during temporary authorization for use. Before a treatment within scope of the French ATU was to begin, patients were required to give their informed consent and receive the patient information validated by AFSSAPS. Furthermore, the hospital pharmacist was to be informed about the ATU treatment. Clinic pharmacists were obliged to fulfill duties with respect to the supply and monitoring of cohort ATUs. They were seen to have to contribute to the application process.

§ 611 BGB and §§ 823ff BGB were found to govern a physician's liability for compassionate use in Germany. He was seen to have to inform a patient about a considered compassionate drug use with accuracy similar to a participant's education about a clinical trial. In Germany, pharmacists were not said to be liable if the IND is supplied to the investigator directly as planned for the future.[252] If the product was to be supplied via a hospital pharmacy, the pharmacist would have to assay the MP. He would have been responsible for quality and expiry, which would both have to be inspected regularly (§ 12 ApoBetrO).[253]

The 'Patient's Charter for England dated 1997' was identified to accord the right of (a) access to treatment, (b) information and (c) drugs within the scope of compassionate use to patients. Confidentiality was seen to be addressed (relevant in terms of compassionate use because of compulsory reports to regulatory bodies). The guidance issued by the Sheffield Teaching Trust required physicians to provide sound scientific data, information and be experienced before using INDs in patients not participating in the corresponding trial, in order to avoid negligence.

The following aspects were confirmed to affect liability issues in NDU in summary: patient's informed consent, best practices, support from a jury of peers, MAHs' pharmaceutical advertisement, the physicians' duty of care, prohibition of risky active substances and the pharmacist' obligation to contract (table 19).

Duties / IN CHARGE	Responsibilities
PHYSICIAN	To obtain informed consent
	Perform best practices
	Assure support from a jury of peers
	Comply with duty of care
MAH	Act on provisions for pharmaceutical advertisement
	Do not place risky active substances on the market/ quality assurance
PHARMACIST	Fulfill obligation to contract

Table 19 Aspects with an impact on liability for NDU

The higher the assumed risk of a treatment, the more information must be conveyed to a patient. The physician was found to have to provide best practices at all times and should only refer to unapproved methods when licensed options fail, are inapplicable or exhausted. His or her approach should be estimated to receive support from a jury of peers and the measures taken should comply with duty of care requirements. Requirements to verify evidence for safety, efficacy and quality for an MP decreased with growing morbidity. The MAH must not infringe on provisions for pharmaceutical advertisement; else it may be found responsible for harm related to NDU. The MAH must not market risky products which, if they enter the supply chain, must not be dispensed by a pharmacist judging his expertise. If there is no reason to object, the pharmacist was found to be obliged to fill a prescription but assure the products' quality.

3.7. Circumvention of drug approval: Law on advertising

Off label decision-making was found to be vulnerable to marketing practices.[254] To a great extent, literature gave evidence for NDU marketing practices, including pharmaceutical advertising and sales representatives detailing off label use. Thought-leader's opinions, commentaries, case studies, abstracts, posters, compendia and using skilled sales representatives to solicit questions about off label use were described to be techniques by which companies covertly promote off label use.[255] Graves and Baker reported that "sales-representatives are generally limited to discussing on-label topics, industry-based drug information practitioners are not". Appropriately disclaimed off label information in response to an unsolicited inquiry was seen to be permissible.[256] Samples have been described to result in prescribing new drugs, often using NME for off label indications.[257] A study by Steinman et al. showed that while Gabapentin was approved by the U.S. Food and Drug Administration only for the adjunctive treatment of partial seizures, in 38% of sales visits (44/115) the "main message" involved at least one off label use.[258] Off label usage was confirmed to be rarely discouraged by manufacturers.[259] Information (not) found in published trials may cause overprescription for off-labels; data by Rising et al. comparing NDAs for NMEs to the FDA showed that trials with favorable outcomes were more likely to be published.[260] Selective publication of clinical trials has led experts to suggest a compulsion to publish predefined outcomes of clinical trials. Some authors even went to such lengths as to suggest a public or independent trials body staffed by methodologists and on an international scale. This publicly funded international infrastructure would conduct proposed studies in conjunction with clinical experts from around the world.[261] Radley et al. suggested more extensive post-marketing surveillance to identify non-evidence-based prescribing practices that lack FDA approval, and to research the potential influence of pharmaceutical marketing on off label use.[262] MAH are barred by the FDA from promoting off-label use, but they are using medical science liaisons (MSLs), often physicians and pharmacists, to discuss off-label uses. The number of MSLs has increased steadily, totaling 1,970 in 2008, up 48 percent from 1,335 in 2003.[263]

Off label drug promotion was generally shown to be illegal in all researched countries. However, handling of NDU information ranged from retrospect approaches in the U.S. to prospective management in the U.K. The British regulations were proven to allow the MHRA to require sight of advertising before it is issued. Self-regulation through Codes of Practice for MAHs, administered by trade associations, was a mean of checks and balances in terms of competition law (see table 20) was identified in Austria and Germany. In the U.S., whistleblowers were explained to report observed wrongdoings of employing MAH. Legal rights and safeguards for social security were reported to be in place for whistleblowers. This chapter looks at the laws governing drug information and pharmaceutical marketing in selected countries.

Feature / COUNTRY	Tool	Complainant(s)
GERMANY	Voluntary self-control for MAHs (Freiwillige Selbstkontrolle für die Arzneimittelindustrie e.V., FSA des VfA)	MAH
AUSTRIA	Code of behavior (Verhaltenscodex)	
U.K.	MHRA Independent Review Panel for Advertising (IRPA), Blue Guide	Patients, HCP, MAH
FRANCE	Advertisements to HCP must be notified to AFSSAPs within 8 days	n/a
EU	EFPIA Code of Practice on Relationships between MAHs and Patient Organizations	MAH
SWITZERLAND	seizure, safekeeping, destruction, prohibition of advertising materials by Swissmedic at the cost of the MAH	n/a
U.S.	FDA Risk communication advisory committee	MAH
CANADA	Pharmaceutical Advertisement Advisory Board (PAAB)	

Table 20 Measures to control pharmaceutical advertising in selected countries

Physicians regularly were seen to require and demand off label information on dosage, safety and effectiveness, e.g., for children. Advertising regulations and information duties were found to serve both purposes e.g., § 75 AMG and PharmRefPrV (sales representatives examination regulations) in Germany. In the U.S., court cases have gone to such lengths as to address the issue of whether FDA had interfered with drug manufacturers and physicians' freedom of speech to communicate information about off label drug use.[264] While some publications voluntarily started to disclose statements on discussions of off label use,[265] the FDA issued tolerant guidance for the distribution of medical and scientific information on off label drug uses, the action of which is believed to lessen incentives to submit supplementary approvals.[266] However, the guidance also was criticized to enable communication of incorrect off label use. A revised version of the Physician Payment Sunshine Act was seen to require drug manufacturers to disclose payments made to doctors that exceed $100 per year in the future. MAHs were found to be subject to penalties of up to $1 m for "knowingly failing" to disclose information.[267]

Fear of litigation, regulation, or judicial fines were thought to improved abidance: In France for instance, companies that use advertisements which do not comply with the product license were shown to be able to be fined up to € 37,500. Penalties to deter wrongdoing have however, been estimated to necessarily not yield the desired result. Several U.S. law suits have resolved allegations of improper off label marketing of drugs. Eli Lilly agreed to pay US$ 1.415 Billion in the U.S. on January 15th 2009 to resolve the allegations of off label promotion of Olanzapin[i] (Zyprexa®) as treatment for dementia and other conditions, causing false claims to federal insurance programs, none of which provided coverage. Eli Lilly pled guilty and had paid $36 m to settle allegations in the past; the company had marketed its drug Evista® (raloxifene[i]) for off label uses. In 2004, the case against Pfizer-Warner-Lambert resulted in the company being fined $240 m and ordered to pay $152 m in damages for promoting the off label use of gabapentin[i] (Neurontin®) in bipolar disorders and Lou Gehrigs-disease. Further cases of off label promotion in the U.S. were Sereno's somatropin[i] promoted to treat AIDS-related wasting, Schering's Intron-A® and Amgen's Enbrel®.[268] Bristol Myer Squibb, among other pharmaceutical companies, published a corporate integrity agreement also governing information policy about off label use.[269] Is it decent to then withhold information about effective treatments?

Full approval in multiple diseases was verified to be costly. The absence of an MA was found to not have to mean inefficacy. On the other hand, a 'narrow business incentive' choosing narrow indication strategically, but expecting wider range use was quoted in Ratner et al.'s paper as a cost saving regulatory strategy. He imposed the fundamental question on how approval can be made responsive to important drug use. For these and other reasons, lawmakers were expected to possibly reverse FDA guidelines on off label use.[270] Also, FDA was found to be undertaking efforts to reform MA of drugs in oncology to not be licensed by body part but by tissue. Tumors found in the head and neck region were seen to supposedly be licensed for all squamous cell carcinomas.[271]

The German advertising regulation (Heilmittelwerbegesetz, HWG) was seen to prohibit NDU marketing. Pharmaceutical advertising was found to not be routinely assessed as to the conformity with the regulations in Germany. Data on the number of breaches was absent. Data from surveillance authorities at community and state level or by courts on breaches of advertising regulations was inaccessible. Self-regulation through Codes of Practice for MAHs (FSA) reported 50 and 56 complaints in 2004 and 2005 of which two concern advertising regulation, but not NDU in specifically.

Generic off label use plays a special role in context of advertisement: The associations of MAHs, a study from Italy and the experts of the qualitative study also suggested that generics are as discussed in 3.1 Terminology, being advertised for nonlicensed indications by sales representatives. Table 6 illustrates legitimacy of generic substitution in selected countries.

Substitution / COUNTRY	**Generic**	**Therapeutic**[ix]	**Prescription of APIs**
GERMANY	Present	Emergency service, discount contract	Present
FRANCE	Present	Absent	n/a
U.K.	Present	Absent	Present
AUSTRIA	Absent	Absent	n/a

Table 21 Substitutability of medicinal products

Drug industry detailing was stated to promote off-label uses. Expert 8 remarked about detailing that many U.S. medical schools now will not allow a drug company representative into the hospital. Health care trainees were seen to also targeted in Germany (Novartis Studentenservice, Sanacorp Campus). In this context, the Federal Association of Pharmacists in Public Service (Bundesverband der Apotheker im Öffentlichen Dienst) (BApÖD) in their policy document of 2005 declared sales representatives and drug samples to be dispensable. To increase prescription of brand drugs, sales representatives were said to argue (a) against prescription of APIs and (b) that aut idem substitution offends therapeutic freedom. The association of national health care physicians of Bavaria (Kassenärztlichen Vereinigung Bayern) (KVB) also reported that generic manufacturers promote MPs for uses for which only brand products have received an MA, underlining absent legal responsibility.[272] KVB quoted Dierks et al., who did not regard

[ix] Dispensing of a therapeutic alternative instead of identical PIL without the prescriber's feedback

use of generics in brand indications as an off label use.

Generic manufacturers were found to be liable also for the brand's supplementary area of application (see 3.6 Liability for nonlicensed drug use). Generic off label use was also seen to occur in silico when indications are not taken into consideration in the search for cost-effective alternative products. In Germany, pharmacists were observed to be obligated to substitute discounted generics according to the patient's health care insurance (see table 21). Generic substitution was shown to be subject to § 129 Abs. 1 sentence 3 SGB V. A random aut-idem search with selected pharmacy software (Pharmatechnik®, ADG® or WinApo®) was proven to take into account the API and indications in ABDATA® pharma data service and the ATC code to level 5.[273] A search for Beloc ZOK® retrieved results for all metoprolole[i] products and ATC codes, though only results that show equal or more indications will be displayed in green font. MPs with fewer or no matching indications were seen to be displayed in grey and red, respectively, by the software. On the other hand, ifap® praxisCENTER for office-based physicians also displayed metoprolole[i] NOK Sandoz 95mg when a search for generics for Beloc Zok® 95 mg was performed, although the generic is solely licensed to treat hypertension and, e.g., not to prevent migraine.[x] In the strict sense, a physician would treat a patient off label using metoprolole[i] NOK Sandoz 95mg in the management of migraines. This detail was notable with respect to incentives for supplementary indications in off-patent products (e.g., orphan or pediatric drugs). On top of possible substitution to cheaper generics, pediatric and orphan incentives were judged to possibly become effectless through social law: Orphan or pediatric incentives may be repealed if MPs were found to be assigned the same fixed price group (Festbetragsgruppe) for reimbursement purposes by German social law,[274] not securing a return on investment for the MAH within the protection period. For these reasons, generic off label use was seen to not only be a result of marketing measures, but may also result from software, insurance contracts and drug information.

Alternatively, clinicians were said to rely on (industry-funded) expert recommendation. Polled physicians also stated that, as residents learn to use medications for use in a particular patient population, they may never be aware of the product not being studied or labeled in the indication.$_{N.5}$ Moreover only 10% of U.S. medical students were reported to be expected to have a mandated clinical pharma-

---

[x] Tested on July 23rd 2007

cology course before seeing patients. For this reason, there was more evidence to support an unawareness of NDU among physicians (see 3.5 Operating experience with provisions for nonlicensed drug use).$_{N.6}$

The British regulatory agency was found to have a complaint procedure in place for violation of MPs advertisement rules. The outcomes of investigations into complaints about advertising of MPs were proven to be published. An Advertising complaint form was evidenced to be available.[xi] Members of public, HCPs and pharmaceutical companies were shown to be allowed to issue a complaint. The MHRA's Review Panel for Advertising was seen to be state-run; administrative efforts for the complainant are small. The complaint was found to be subject to a transparent procedure. Committee members' interests are reconciled. The complainant's data was observed to not be published unless he or she is industry-affiliated.

The afore named memorandums of understanding and codes of conduct reported fewer complaints than federal bodies. From September 2005 to August 2006 the IRPA received 172 complaints and initiated 136 investigations.[275] The MHRA's Advertising Standards Unit also was found to routinely scrutinize medical journals, public magazines and the internet for the promotion of such complaints. Selectively, advertising was said to be checked prior to issue. On top of a review of advertising, the U.K.'s Royal College of Physicians (RCP) is expected to release a report on February 4th 2009 recommending that pharmaceutical companies stop giving gifts to physicians. The report predicts that forbidding drug companies to give even small gifts to physicians would rebalance the relationship between medicine and industry.[276]

Boundaries between advertising material and drug information often overlap. Both themes are assumed to affect patient information and consent. HCPs said they experience difficulties in obtaining information about NDU, which they required to educate and inform patients adequately. Expert N. 9 argued that physicians nowadays have to convince parents to allow their children to go into research treatment. Before, MPs had been used off label frequently without parents' knowledge, thus leaving parents to believe that treatment options were sufficient. He would welcome parents to be better informed about what medication constitutes off label use. Unswayed materials for patient education on NDU (see 3.3 Texts of law regulating nonlicensed drug use with regard to drug safety)

[xi] http://www.mhra.gov.uk/Howweregulate/Medicines/Advertisingofmedicines/Advertisinginvestigations/Advertisingcomplaintform/index.htm

were however found to be limited.

Information search was found to be challenging in terms of reliable supportive evidence for NDU. Publications addressed HCPs (e.g., Off label Drug Facts) or even patients (Patient's Guide to Off label Use of FDA approved drugs). Some literature was specific to an area of expertise such as pediatrics (Pädiatrische Dosistabellen and Kinderdosierungen von Phytopharmaka), then only accessible to hospital employees (Unlicensed Medicines Database Birmingham) or next registered customers (Off-label.co. U.K.). Single regulatory authorities, i.e., Health Canada and AFSSAPS, were seen to maintain private databases. Information platforms for pediatric and rare disorders were identified (see table 22).

Some institutions have passed into the "right sizing" off label technology as shown in 3.3 Texts of law regulating nonlicensed drug use with regard to drug safety. The Massachusetts General Hospital's IRB was reported to become involved when the use of a product is outside of published norms (off label with insufficient published supportive data).[277] Unfortunately, only patients transferred to such hospitals were found to benefit from regional procedures. In the U.K., 400 physician's offices were observed to contribute to the The General Practice Research Database (GPRD) by filing anonymous case reports. A comprehensive, national database such as the British GPRD but for NDU assessment reports was present in no research country.

A comparison of approaches to control pharmaceutical advertisement with regard to the impact onto prescribing patterns was found to be absent. Observations suggested that public training and continued education on regulatory issues, resolving the lack of enforcement of advertising regulation and an offer of independent, reviewed information might alter the impact of promotion on NDU.

NDU / COUNTRY	Pediatrics	Off label Use	Unlicensed Use	Compassionate Use	OMPs
U.K.	British National Formulary for Children		Birmingham Unlicensed Drugs Database; IDIS Pharma,[278] Fife UMP database	IDIS Pharma	Orpha.net,[279] National Organisation Rare Disorders Orphan Drug database[280]
CANADA	/	/	/	Special Access Management System, formally known as Emergency Drug Release Programme database	
SWITZERLAND	/	Off label Use in Onkology[281]	/	List of temporarily licensed medicines[282]	/
AUSTRIA	/	Biddbase[283]	/	/	/
FRANCE	/	/	IDIS Pharma	IDIS Pharma; non-public Autorisations temporaires d'utilisation database of Agence française de sécurité sanitaire des produits de santé	/
U.S.	/	Wolters Kluwer Facts & Comparisons: Off label Drug Facts (Loose-Leaf); The Guide to Off label Prescription Drugs: New Uses for FDA-Approved Prescription Drugs	/	Treatment INDs Allowed to Proceed[284]	List of Orphan Designations and Approvals[285]
EU	European Paediatric Medicines Database,[286] registry of pediatric studies within EudraCT, priority list	/	/	„up-to-date list" of compassionate use products (planned)	Orphan Drug List,[287] joint registry for orphan drugs
GERMANY	ZAK medicines for children database[288] pediatric dosages of herbal medicines	Tabulation of antipsychotic drugs licensed in Germany and their legitimate off label use;[289] supplemental medical directive appendix 9[290]	IDIS Pharma		Orphan-drugs by indication[291]

Table 22 Sources of information with impact on NDU (/= no findings)

3.8. Criteria for simplified variation while assuring drug safety: Incentives and duties

Many key opinion leaders in regulatory affairs emphasized that for the patients' benefit, research must result in an MA.[292] Incentives for MA have been passed in the E.U. and North America primarily to overcome supply shortage and NDU in pediatrics. Some variations to MA were found to be offered incentives: Well-established use, switch and significant, supplementary indications. Countries' efforts extended to patented and off-patent MPs with regard to the children's and rare disorder's fraction of NDU. Solutions, supportive measures and programs that have been introduced to encourage pediatric and OMP development were multiple. The work sharing project, committal non-clinical testing in juvenile animals and amendments to ICH E11 (guideline on clinical trials in children) were seen to be EU programs supportive of pediatric R&D. Further measures on an EU level included guidelines on pharmacokinetics in pediatric population and on trials in small populations, and an addendum on pediatric oncology. A reflection paper on pediatric formulations, concept papers on brain/lung and heart/liver immaturity, and a discussion paper on liver immaturity have highlighted pediatric problems in the EU. The European Organization for research and treatment of cancer (EORTC) was seen to engage itself with regard to NDU. An initiative to capture dosages and formulations in Swiss hospital pharmacies in co-operation with London's School of Pharmacy was another example for cross-country research activities in the E.U.

In Germany, § 25 Sec. 7a AMG eased pediatric RCT for future MPs, while pediatric dosage tables and the ZAK database for medicines for children were found to be sources of information for child medications already available today. In France, Réseau d'Investigations Pédiatriques des Produits Santé (RIPPS), a French society for pediatric oncology (SFOP), French acute Lymphoblastic leukaemia group (FRALLE), Société Française de Pédiatrie (SFP) and Institut National de la Santé et de la Recherche Médicale (INSERM) were identified to be organizations working on NDU. A Medicines for Children Research Network was seen to co-ordinate pediatric research activities in the U.K. U.K. physicians were reported to refer to the BNF-C for pediatric information. PILs by Royal College of Pediatrics and Child Health (RCPCH), continuing education in pediatric pharmacy by NPPG (Neonatal Pediatric Pharmacists Group) and networking were found to help pharmacists overcome the obstacles of NDU in Great Britain. Updating of SmPCs, improving transparency of pediatric information, and a call for pediatric studies were found to be Swiss measures to surmount NDU. Simplified approval, improvement of circumstances for the development of formulations for children, and a list of essential medicines for children shall direct pediatric research activities in Switzerland. The pediatric rule and exclusivity program, FDAMA, BPCA, PREA and FDAAA have been passed to increase pediatric NDA. The Children's Oncology Group was judged to be an example for an U.S. association that exchanges information with other institutions to secure best care for pediatric cancer patients. In Japan, the period for renewal of pediatric MA was extended from six to ten years. These mechanisms are choosy to pediatrics. Selectivity of the regulatory tools may be responsible for a future success, but was also judged to disregard areas of NDU outside pediatrics or rare disorders.

Further specific approaches to decrease NDU and drug supply shortages aimed at OMPs. As with NDU or age classes (pediatrics or geriatrics), rare disorders were also seen not to be characterized homogenously. They were distinguishable from "neglected diseases", which occur frequently but in countries with little purchasing power (e.g., Dengue Fever in developing countries) and therefore do not trigger commercial research interests. Furthermore the expression "ultra orphan diseases" was found to describe disorders that occur in fewer than 10,000 patients. All expressions jointly were observed to describe disorders with few therapeutic options available. Criteria for OMP designation and more regulatory incentives and duties are addressed among other incentives and duties affecting NDU.

E.U.: Protecting and exempting children from participation in clinical trials has caused drugs not to be tested in children. Beginning in 1990, the WHO undertook efforts to eventually reduce child mortality by two thirds in children aged one to five years by 2015; these efforts include improvement of the medical treatment of children (e.g., EML for children).

In the EU, incentives and duties were introduced to enhance commercial research and the development of children's medicines. All NDAs were found to be required to provide a pediatric investigation plan (PIP). By July 30th 2008, 218 applications were subject to review for waivers or deferrals. Bonuses were also seen to be granted for negative outcomes, if transferred into the PIL and SmPC. The PIP compulsion was initiated to require companies to acquire pediatric expertise. Waiver or deferral of a manufacturer's research duties was made possible with drugs that are not important for the pediatric population. An example for deferral was a product-related decision on clopidogrel[i] that shall be available in liquid form. It is planned to be studied in five RCTs (bioequivalence, pharmacokinetics, efficacy and safety, open label study and pharmacodynamics) for the treatment of thromboembolic events in children. The pharmaceutical company received a deferral with the aim of not delaying licensing for adults. Class waivers were to be feasible with conditions not relevant to pediatric patients, e.g., erectile dysfunction. Patented drugs may receive an extra six months of marketing exclusivity for all indications for pediatric data. Four MAH were applying for a so-called pediatric use MA (PUMA) by June 30th, 2008.[293] On October 23rd 2008 the CHMP recommended to license a pediatric formulation of losartane[i]– the first positive opinion subsequent to a PIP.[294] An annual directory of all MAHs that receive bonuses is planned. Pediatric formulations of off-patent substances were governed to be able to acquire ten years of data protection, a PUMA. OMPs licensed for use in children in the EU may gain another two years of protection. Scientific consultation of the EMEA was found to be free of charge on pediatric matters.

An E.U. Pediatric Committee (PDCO) (see table 26) was formed to file decisions on the appropriateness and nature of clinical trials in children. The PDCO was initially assigned the task of suggesting a symbol for pediatric MPs. The committee, however, came to the conclusions that such a symbol was not recommendable because its drawbacks outweigh its benefits. On January 26th 2007, the Guideline on conduct of pharmacovigilance for medicines used by the pediatric population (EMEA/CHMP/PhVWP/235910/2005) came into effect, providing guidance on risk surveillance of medicines for children. An EU pediatric network was established to link pediatric research projects of the E.U. Pediatric trials can be funded by financial resources (MICE, Medicines Investigation for the Children of Europe) within the scope of the seventh framework project. A work-sharing project was organized to tie all MSs together committing them to collect pediatric data, which were transferred to the EMEA by January 26th 2009. In 2013 and 2017 a field report and an analysis of the pediatric regulation are due.

In the E.U., OMPs were decided to be given ten years of exclusivity, scientific advice, and reduction of fees, and may be funded research in the EU. OMPs must be designated first and can then be authorized for marketing as an OMP. Criteria for designation were developed to include either certain incidence rates or a predicted low return on investment and no satisfactory alternative or significant benefit in comparison to licensed MPs. Until 2001, the EMEA's Committee on OMPs (COMP) had announced 52 applications out of a received 131. While

22 applications were withdrawn, 73 applications received a positive and one a negative opinion. By 2001 52 OMPs were licensed.[295] On one occasion, on August 3rd 2001, two OMPs received approval for the same diagnosis (EU/1/01/188/001-003 and EU/1/01/189/001). Both OMPs were licensed to treat Fabry disease (Agalsidase[i]-Beta [Fabrazyme®] and -Alpha [Replagal®]) in the EU.

Free-of-charge scientific advice through so-called Protocol Assistance was tailored to be granted to MPs that have been assigned the OMP status in the EU. Conditional approval thus was made achievable. Research into rare disorders was ever since encouraged. A rare diseases task force was formed to advance the development of research strategies. The fifth framework for research, technological development and demonstration (FP5) funded 47 projects on rare diseases. The European Organisation for Orphan Disorders (EurOrDis) planned to introduce a service to answer questions on rare diseases.

Art. 9 of the EU Orphan Medical Products Regulation demanded that MSs provide national incentives in the E.U. Between 1983 and 2006 all researched countries, except for Canada, additionally met measures to combat shortages of OMPs. Multiple criteria for the frequency of occurrence resulted from the individual legal definitions (see table 23).

Details / COUNTRY	**Coming into effect**	**Legislation**	**Rate** [less than x patients/year]	**Incidence** [per 10.000 residents]	**Frequency** [out of x residents]
GERMANY					
AUSTRIA					
U.K.					
FRANCE					
E.U.	1999	Orphan Drug Regulation			
SWITZERLAND	2000	Art. 9 Sec. 4 HMG	230.000	5	2.000
U.S.	1983	Orphan Drug Act	200.000	7.5	1.500
JAPAN	1993	Orphan Drug Law	50.000	4	2.400

Table 23 Provisions for orphan drug designation

The effect of the above-named differences on regulatory practice was found to be unknown. No discussion on heterogeneous acknowledgement of an OMP status across countries has been observed in the literature. MPs to treat rare disorders were seen to hypothetically underlie regular provisions in some while being subject to simplified requirements in other countries (see table 24). Accordingly, MPs to treat disorders occurring fewer than 7.5 and more than 5 times in 10,000 residents were found to be considered OMPs in the U.S. but need not be granted this status in Japan or the E.U. Drugs to treat conditions that are diagnosed fewer than 5, but more than 4 times in 10,000 residents, were seen to be OMPs in the E.U. and U.S. but not in Japan. Inconsistency in patient supply was already found to be known in the E.U. despite uniform legislation (see 3.2 Investigations into supply shortages of drugs and the necessity as well as procedure of nonlicensed drug use). It was unknown whether this outlook discourages pharmaceutical companies from performing research or cause the drug to be licensed and only be available in the U.S. or whether regulatory agencies mutually recognize statuses.

Country / Incidence	E.U.	U.S.	Japan
7.5<X>5 per 10.000 inhabitants	No	Yes	No
5<X>4 per 10.000 inhabitants	Yes		No
<4 per 10.000 inhabitants	Yes		
>7.5 per 10.000 inhabitants	No		

Table 24 Orphan drugs status in comparison

In the E.U., non-selective incentives to encourage R&D were found to include expedited assessment, conditional approval, approval under exceptional circumstances (thereinafter discussed) and facilitations for investigator initiated trials (IITs). IITs were seen to mirror real practice and true patient supply, but NDUs must always not be subject to IITs. The sponsor of an IIT was observed to have to be a nonprofit organization, though pharmaceutical companies may contribute to sponsorship. A sponsor was obliged to supervise the study's design, procedure, documentation and reports. Germany introduced facilitations for PhV in IITs (a saving of minimum £ 2,000 for EudraVigilance training) and health care insurances may cover off label use (§ 35c SGBV) in RCT; stakeholders additionally called for a waiver of fees and coverage of liability insurance by national reimbursement companies.

Patents were judged to be the most efficacious incentive for drug development, affecting product extension strongly. Research into a treatment was only assessed to be promising if patents are granted. A patent was found to last up to 20 years (European Patent treaty of 1973, § 16 PatG of Germany) starting on the day on which the patent is registered (see figure 8). Several constellations causing a drug to be on the market exclusively were seen to be possible:

1. The patent protection period outlasts data protection period or market exclusivity
   a. Generic marketing may only start after the patent expires
2. The data protection period or market exclusivity outlast patent protection
   a. Reference to the originator's data may only be made after the data protection period has ended; marketing is legal after the marketing exclusivity expires
   b. After patent terms end, a company may conduct its own developmental and clinical research into the efficacy and safety without making reference to the original research in an NDA

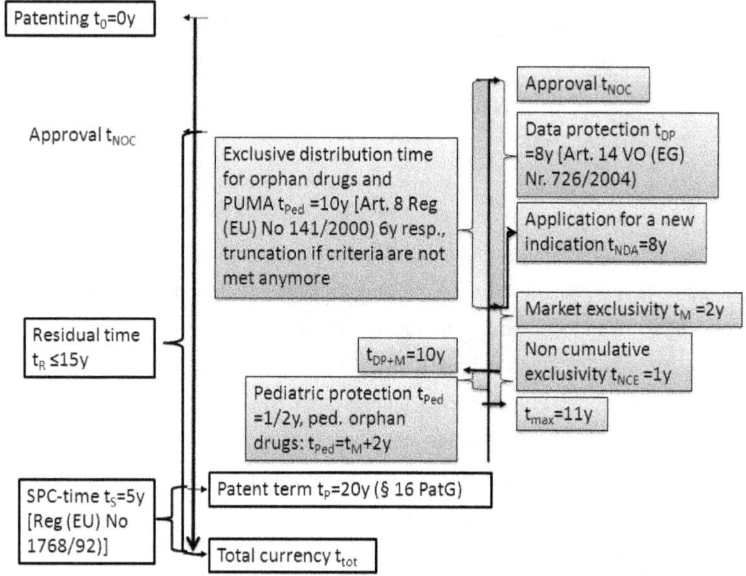

Figure 8 Timelines for mechanisms of market exclusivity in the E.U.

GERMANY Problems in pediatric drug supply were found to include (a) over- as well as under-dosage specific to each API, and (b) child maturity as seen with the Grey syndrome of newborns in response to the application of Chloramphenicol. Toxicity of adult drugs in children was not possible to be extrapolated from body weight, height or body surface. Growth can then either cause over-proportional metabolism or hyper-elimination of adult MPs in babies and infants.[296] Age-appropriate MPs for children were found to be essential. Although dosage schemes have been developed at the university hospitals of Gottingen and Hamburg in

2005 e.g., for sotalol[i],[297] no licensed pediatric formulation was yet available by September 2008. As seen also in 3.7 Circumvention of drug approval: Law on advertising, it was judged to be possible that social regulation adds to the lack of interest in R&D: The joint national committee (G-BA) assigned a pediatric antibiotic drinking straw to the same fixed price group for reimbursement by public funding agencies like other antibiotic formulations. Although an antibiotic drinking straw could have hypothetically been eligible to pediatric incentives if these had already been in place, fixed prices discourage the development of pediatric formulations of off-patent APIs. A PUMA was therefore estimated to not be sufficient to encourage development of new children's MPs with off-patent APIs in Germany. By German social law, generic substitution was also seen to be permissible even if the dispensed product has fewer indications than the prescribed item (see 3.7 Circumvention of drug approval: Law on advertising). Pharmacists are obliged to substitute an MP if the aut-idem box is not ticked on the prescription form.[298] This compulsion may also affect incentives of pharmaceutical law such as PUMA because in spite of data exclusivity for off-patent pediatric or orphan products, there may not be a return on investment due to generic dispensing (see 3.7 Circumvention of drug approval: Law on advertising). Substitution was found to require the pharmaceutical formulation of the drug to be identical to the prescribed item. Pharmaceutical companies were therefore prompted to develop pioneering formulations and dosages that are not divisible from MPs for adults in order to circumvent substitution and extemporaneous preparation.

The compulsion to set up a commission to improve drug safety for children and adolescents at the BfArM was put through in the 12th amendment to the AMG (§ 25 Sec. 7a AMG). The commission for drugs for children and adolescents (Kommission für Arzneimittel für Kinder und Jugendliche, KAKJ) was formed to advise the regulatory body on questions relating to pediatric approvals. Scientific efforts to improve child health care were seen to be present in the department for clinical pharmacy at the Heinrich Heine University of Dusseldorf in Germany. 'In silico' simulation creating physiology based pharmacokinetic (PBPK) models was found to be studied as a tool to prevent medication errors. The PK-SIM® software was reported to imitate a whole body model and can calculate personalized dosages.

Experts identified increasing insurance premiums as a difficulty with regard to pediatric studies, leading to cancellation of RCTs in children: § 3 Sec. 3 AMG-KostV was identified to address the option to reduce fees by up to three quarters in response to an application showing that (a) the applicant cannot expect an economic benefit related to regulatory and development costs and, (b) if marketing of the drug for a specific indication has an impact on public health or (c) if the diagnosis is rare or the target population small. Further incentives were seen to be present in Germany in terms of scientific advice on pediatric drugs.

Orphan therapeutic needs were observed to be partially meet by means of extemporaneous preparation (see 3.2 Investigations into supply shortages of drugs and the necessity as well as procedure of nonlicensed drug use) in Germany: Monographs were proven to be present in the NRF e.g. 15.17 Cysteamin[i]-hydrochloride eye drops 0.15 % or 0.5 % for the treatment of cystinosis (incidence 1:60,000 to 1:100,000) or 22.3 % 3,4-Diaminopyridin[i] capsules 5 or 10 mg to treat Lambert-Eaton-Myasthenia syndrome (LEMS, 1:100,000).[299] The German federal government has discussed expedited approval for drugs with a great therapeutic impact, fewer administrative requirements for applications for relevant MPs and a research program for rare disorders.[300]

Other than the mechanisms mentioned above, a number of regulatory tools were confirmed not focus on specific conditions. The options of variation, extension and NDAs in Germany are summarized in figure 9. § 24b AMG was found to govern the licensure of generic pharmaceutics and data protection periods in Germany with regard to applications referring to data of the originator (§ 22 Sec. 2 Sent. 1 N.2 and 3, Sec. 3c and § 23 Sec. 1). According to § 24 Sec. 1 Sent. 2 N.2 – 4, a generic applicant was seen to be able to refer to the originator's data if the drug has been licensed for a minimum of eight years (also see other E.U. MS). A generic product that was licensed in accordance with this provision may only be marketed ten years after the originator had been granted approval. This rule was evidenced to be known as: eight years of data protection plus two years of exclusive marketing (8 + 2). The period was found to be possibly extended by a single year if the MAH applies for an MA for one or more supplementary indications (see figure 9). These indications were found to have to provide significant clinical benefit in comparison to established pharmacotherapies, as appraised through scientific assessment by the regulatory agency. This additional non-cumulative exclusiveness of one year was verified to amount to a total period of 8 + 2 + 1 years of market exclusiveness.

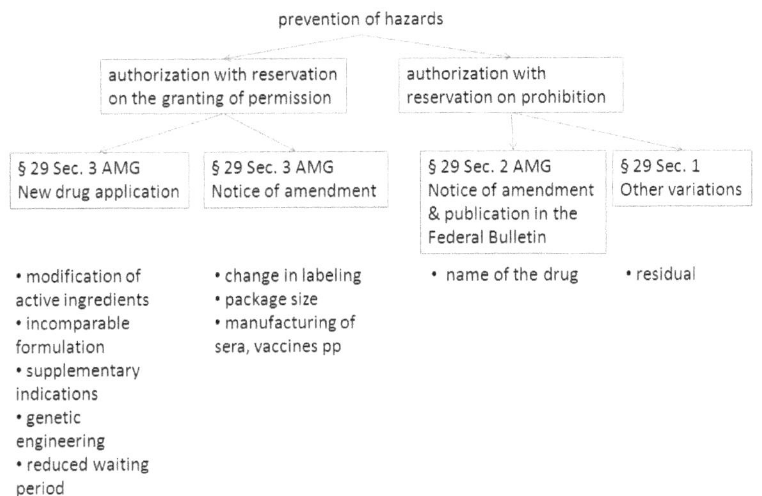

Figure 9 Types of variations and properties in addition to details and examples[301]

In Germany, MAHs have suggested further approaches for the faster availability of innovative MPs by means of improved co-operation between regulatory agencies in a policy paper. The task force 'Regulatory Affairs and Health Policy' of biotechnological industry organization (BIO) Germany called for reduction of application fees, e.g., for an MA or for a permit to conduct clinical trials. Remission of fees and charges were seen to be in place for advice on development as it relates to pediatric quality, safety and efficacy.

Both non-commercial IITs were found to be subject to fees in accordance with § 33 Sec. 1 AMG. Legal facilitations were identified to be present in terms of coverage for standard treatment (§ 35c SGB V) and labeling for open-label trials (§ 5 N.8 GCP-V). IITs were to be exempt from EudraVigilance; ADR reporting is carried out by BfArM. Additionally, Clinical Study Support Cores (CSSCs) have been set up at university hospitals. CSSCs have been assigned the task of unburdening physicians from administrative duties and were formed to provide frame contracts for insurances, standard wording for patient information and contract templates for agreements between the principal investigator, the university's office of administration, investigators and the sponsor. CSSCs were also established to provide advice on RCTs, preliminary assays and to interact with research networks in Germany.

One final regulatory strategy was proven to be unique to Germany: standardized MA according to article 36 AMG. An applicant was shown to refer to a previously existing monograph without presenting documentation to the BfArM. Monographs were seen to include analytical test requirements and templates for PILs. Compliance with the monograph was found to be controlled by the local inspection authority. Standardized MA was identified to be the pre-emptive development of a drug model by the regulatory agency, historically introduced to combat post-licensing. In the past, 279 monographs have been published. The procedure was given as follows: An MP may be suggested to the expert advisory board, which forwards the proposal to the German Ministry of Health, which then drafts an ordinance. External experts and the BfArM first conduct research and development and then draft the monograph which is then presented to specialist audience. Secondly, the expert advisory board reassesses the draft and shows it to a specialist audience after public comment. Lastly, the finalized ordinance is presented to the Federal Assembly for enactment. Well-established APIs were found to currently be eligible for standardized MA.[302]

Lastly, BfArM was seen to publish harmonized specimen texts for informative labels (i.e., SmPCs and PILs) taking into account the originator's labels and relevant, state of the art and recent scientific information (see 3.1 Terminology).

AUSTRIA As of October 2007, Austria had not granted reduced fees to pediatric or OMP development. Variations were found to cause high monitoring and administrative expenses in Austria, whereas restrictions can be added to a label easily and inexpensively. This detail was judged to be important for off label use, because contraindications may be effortlessly imposed and hypothetically lessen treatment options. As an E.U. MS, Austrian marketing exclusivity was also observed to be extended to eleven years (§ 10 Sec. 3 und 6 N.2 AMG-Au). An MAH was obliged to provide data for significant indications as assessed by a scientific assessment of the federal office for safety in health care (Bundesamt für Sicherheit im Gesundheitswesen) within eight years after licensure in order to achieve this extended protection period (§ 24 AMG-Au). The European joint term for this recurrent mechanism was seen to be Art. 14 Sec. 11 of regulation (EC) N.726/2004.

SWITZERLAND Information on the use of MPs in children was being collected in Swiss hospitals in cooperation with the London School of Pharmacy. To date, Swissmedic published three diploma theses on pediatric drug safety identifying insufficiencies in SmPCs with regard to drug use in children. An essential children's medicines list was issued by the agency. The protection period for an MP may be lengthened by five years if a new drug development involves pediatric formulations or dosages.

Art. 17 Sec. 2 VAM was found to authorize an additional protection period of three years for original MPs that are licensed for new indications, dosages, and formulations or are to be given via a new route of application to humans in Switzerland. Article 13 HMG was seen to simplify variation to MA as to the current state of knowledge for applicants in Switzerland by considering results that have been subject to granted MA in other countries with similar regulatory criteria.

FRANCE The French Comité d'orientation pédiatrique (COP) was founded in 2000 and advises AFSSAPS on questions of MPs for children, extemporaneous formulations, hospital preparations, a list of essential medicines for children and the implementation of the E.U. pediatric regulations. Different schemes were identified to support pediatric research.

In France, 20% of all "médicaments orphelins" were seen to be accessed early via the temporary use authorization. A total of 23 out of 34 OMPs that received approval via the central procedure had already been dispensed to patients in France. Exceptional approval was confirmed to be permissible in accordance with L5121-9 CSP. The applicant was found to be able to make reference to well-established use and extemporaneous products. Waivers for fees, inexpensive scientific advice, reduced taxes and price fixing within 15 days were shown to be feasible with OMPs. Several initiatives were grouped and now jointly build a single platform for information on rare diseases. In 2004, a national plan for rare disorders supplying financial support was enacted.

In France, extemporaneous preparations by hospital pharmacies were estimated to close supply gaps. Hospital pharmacists were obliged to notify the regulatory agency about new extemporaneous formulations and report on the quality and number of extemporaneous products to the agency every two years. All data was found to be entered into a public database. Forty preparations are then identified and classified with regard to licensed alternatives or ATUs. Essential formulations are to be standardized.

U.K. The U.K.'s Department of Health and MHRA was found to pursue a pediatric strategy that encourages MAHs to (a) seek supplementary licensing of pediatric line extensions, (b) improve the research environment for RCTs in children (U.K. Medicines for Children Research Network) and (c) improve access to pediatric drug information (BNF-C, British National Formulary for Children) for HCPs. Priority lists of essential extemporaneous products and desired proprietary MPs were identified on the MHRA web page. The Commission on Human Medicines (CHM) Expert Advisory Group on Pediatric Medicines (PMEAG), established in 2006, replaced the Committee on Safety of Medicines (CSM) Pediatric Medicines Working Group (PMWG). PMEAG advises the CHM on MPs for pediatric use and on the implementation of (a) the pediatric strategy, (b) the E.U. pediatric work sharing project, and (c) the European regulation of medicines for pediatric use (Regulation (EC) No 1901/2006). Small U.K. entities, such as groups of hospital pharmacists and physicians, were seen to practice networking to collect pediatric information or else rely on good medical practices. Medicines for Children (RCPCH Publications Ltd) and the British National Formulary were seen to form the basis for BNF-C. Its predecessor 'Medicines for Children' has been formerly translated into at least one foreign language (Italian).

COSTS / NECESSITY	Fee
FULL DOCUMENTATION	€ 232,000,-
TYPE I & II VARIATIONS	€ 5,800,- and € 69,600,- respectively
SCIENTIFIC ADVICE	Up to € 69,600,-

Table 25 Regulatory fees in the U.K.[303]

Table 25 illustrates the costs of different types of variations for the U.K. Scientific advice on pediatric questions was found to be at no cost in the U.K. No application fees for new pediatric formulations or indications were identified. Also, variations to adult dosages for pediatric purposes were seen to be implemented at no costs. If the annual return on investment was rated to be low, e.g., in pediatric patients or rare disorders, a further reduction of fees was seen to be permissible.

Despite low cost MA, future MPs for children need not be inexpensive. Expirience with OMPs showed price explosions. Cost explosions for licensed OMPs such as nitrogen monoxide, which had previously been used (as biological active substances) in the U.K. were condemned by physicians.

The Council Regulation EEC N.1768/92 and Patent Protection Act were shown to contain British protection rights. Supplementary protection certificates, market exclusivity and additional exclusiveness (8 + 2 + 1) were found to be achievable. Interestingly, the U.K. has a statute that was found to oblige manufacturers to guarantee a drug's supply via wholesalers, importers or specials' manufacturers if marketing of an MP is stopped.

ASPECT / COUNTRY	Committee	Pediatric protection (variation)
E.U.	Pediatric Committee (PDCO)	½ year
U.K.	Expert Advisory Group on Pediatric Medicines (PMEAG)	
FRANCE	Comité d'orientation pédiatrique (COP)	
USA	Pediatric Review Committee (PReC)	
CANADA	Office of Pediatric Initiatives	
GERMANY	Kommission für Arzneimittel für Kinder und Jugendliche (KAKJ)	
SWITZERLAND	absent	5 years

Table 26 Selected countries' pediatric commissions and supplementary protection

U.S. In addition to pediatric research units, several legal instruments have advanced pediatric drug development in the U.S.: BPCA (Best Pharmaceuticals for Children Act), FDAMA (Food and Drug Administration Modernization Act of 1997), FDAAA (FDA Amendments Act) and PREA (Pediatric Research Equity Act). As early as 2001, Pediatric Exclusivity was introduced to the U.S. A Pediatric Review Committee (PReC) was founded in 2007 (see table 26). As of August 18th 2008, the program had already led to the approval of 16 pediatric formulations. Furthermore, 149 label changes recommended or opposed a drug's use in children. Applications for 853 CTs were submitted to the FDA, leading to 301 pediatric drug applications; of these, 155 drugs managed an extension of the market exclusivity period. Physician and expert N.5 declared that the number of MPs licensed for use in children since the 1980s has risen from 20% to 30%. However, she criticized the poor regulatory knowledge of physicians. This was found to be a possible explanation for the increase in prescription rates despite negative outcome to the pediatric information: In the U.S., a clinical trial[304] targeting the extension of patent-produced data showed that carvedilole[305] [306] was not suitable for patients younger than 18 years. Nonetheless, there was a 9% increase in off label use among 12.4 prescriptions within 12 months.[307] But as seen in 3.7 Circumvention of drug approval: Law on advertising, announcement of discouraging research findings by drug detailers is unlikely. Such label changes were judged to not be sufficiently made known. HCPs do not reexamine SmPCs regularly.

In the U.S., RCTs with regard to licensing of OMPs were seen to receive a 50% tax reduction. US$ 200,000 and US$ 350,000 respectively, can be granted to phase I and II OMP RCTs for a total period of three years in the U.S. No licensure fees are charged. The period of marketing exclusivity was found to be seven years for OMPs, five years for new APIs, three years for others, six months for pediatrics and 180 days for patent challenge.

Conditional approval (Section 506(b) (21 USC 356 FD&C Act), expedited assessment (21 CFR 601 Subpart E) and exceptional circumstances for these requirements (Section 506 (21 USC 356 FD&C Act) were identified in the U.S. The U.S. was also found to give a five-year period of data protection to the pioneer applicant for an NCE and a three-year data exclusivity period for new indications.

CANADA There were no duties identified with regard to pediatric trials, but MAHs are advised to follow the ICH-Guideline E11 on the subject of pediatric investigations. Data protection was found to be extended by six months in return for pediatric trials within five years after NOC. Pediatric protection was not found to, protect from me-too products e.g. valsartane[i] from competing with AT II antagonists loosing patent protection.

The RCTs grants program of the Canadian Institute of Health Research was seen to provide aid to clinical trials on drugs with expired patents. An Institute for Human Development, Child and Youth Health was found to fund research on child pharmacotherapy. Application fees were observed to be reduced for drugs that are expected to achieve a low return on investment. Tax incentives were shown to be present for conducting RCTs. The Biomarker Initiative of the Ontario Cancer Research Network was known to provide funding for biomarker analysis in drug development in order to better understand efficacy in specific patients and hence demonstrate efficacy in subpopulations.

Canadian patent law was judged to be similar to the regulations in other industrial countries; forced licensing has been restricted. It previously allowed the use of a patent without a patentee's permission if a compensation of 4% of the sales revenue was paid. Nowadays, generic manufacturers may only prepare an application preceding the patent's expiry. Health Canada issues the NOC as recently as the patent has ended.

Use patents for off-patent APIs were seen to not protect patentees infinitely. An appeal by Lundbeck against the application of an MP containing citalopram for the unpatented indication of depression was dismissed by a Canadian court: The law court did not agree that the approval should be prohibited due to an excepted, law-violating off label use. Expected off label use was found to not support claims on use patents.

Market exclusivity was seen to be granted for eight years in Canada. An applicant may refer to the originator's data after a period of six years. Variations were verified to cost less than half of what an NDA costs. Priority assessment of NDAs and variations of MPs was proven to be first possible for the treatment, prevention or diagnosis of serious or fatal diseases or diseases affecting quality of life and then applyed to disorders where there is no MP marketed yet, or finally to new drug significantly improving tolerance in comparison to old MPs. Survival rates and the probability of health impairment without effective treatment were seen to be referred to in order to determine seriousness of disorders. HIV/AIDS, Alzheimer's disease, amyotrophic lateral sclerosis, angina pectoris, myocardial insufficiency and malignant neoplasms were judged to be serious diseases. The MAH was found to have to apply for expedited assessment before submitting the NDA. Conditional approval of MPs and prescription monitoring to ensure data-driven development of relevant MPs was being discussed in Canada.

JAPAN reported time problems in supply with innovative drugs. By 2009, processing of 80% of NDA shall take less than one year in Japan. Since April 2005, scientific advice is offered to MAHs. Conditional approval for early marketing was evidenced to be permissible, provided that further RCTs are guaranteed. Simplified licensing was confirmed to be present for variations to indications sought by medical associations. Parts of or entire RCTs may not be necessary if a dossier is filed that has been submitted to a comparable licensing authority or publications in an international, medical journal are enclosed.

In Japan, the data exclusivity period was found to vary from four years (new indications, formulations, dosages, or compositions) to six years (new chemical entity or composition, or formulation for a new route of administration) to ten years (OMPs or new drugs requiring pharmaco-epidemiological data).[308]

Ultimately, 14 pharmaceutical bills affect NDU in eight countries and the E.U. (table 27).

MA / COUNTRY	Conditional approval	Expedited assessment	Exceptional circumstances	Temporary approval
GERMANY	§ 28 Sec. 3 AMG	Art. 14 VO (EG) N.726/2004	Art. 14 Sec. 8 VO (EG) N.726/2004	Unidentified
AUSTRIA	Art. 14 Sec. 7 VO (EG) N.726/2004			n/a
U.K.				
E.U.				
FRANCE			Article L5121-9 CSP	Unidentified
SWITZERLAND	Art. 14 HMG	Art. 5 VAM	Unidentified	Art 9 Sec. 4 HMG
CANADA	Unidentified	Priority Review of Drug Submissions – Policy	Unidentified	Unidentified
U.S.	Section 506(b) (21 USC 356 FD&C Act	21 CFR 601 Subpart E	Section 506 (21 USC 356 FD&C Act	Unidentified
JAPAN	Present	Present	Unidentified	Unidentified

Table 27 Marketing authorization clauses with an impact on NDU

4. Discussion

OUTLINE The emphasis of the present comparison of the impact of nonlicensed drug use (NDU) lies on aspects of (a) terminology for NDU, (b) supply, necessity and inevitability of NDU, (c) pharmaceutical promotion of NDU, (d) legal obligations and (e) policies related to NDU. Best solutions are postulated after prioritizing patient safety and medical attendance over realization of profit and after weighing the advantages and disadvantages of approaches. Appraisal by other authors, who choose to assign different weighting, may lead to different conclusions.

LIMITATIONS In this study, triangulation is used to assess the impact of NDU on health care legislation. This investigation comes to the following main conclusions: The impact of NDU on health care law is varying. A standard definition for NDUs is advisable in all countries as well as short term management and long term solutions. This study is representative for the current situation in eight countries and the E.U. The study period limits validity of the results. Underrepresentation is addressed sufficiently by triangulation.

Off-label use is interpreted to first refer to a breach of no more than an medicinal product's (MP's) indication or second to medically ordered drug use that is not listed in the label and finally to any use, which is eligible to variation, extension or an NDA. Seven types of off-label use are categorized. Unlicensed use is incomprehensible and associated to drug importation in Japan, extemporaneous products in the Netherlands and use of biological active substances (BAS) as MPs in the U.K. E.U. legislation provides definitions for compassionate use, distinguishing between use in (a) cohorts, in the following 'expanded access', and (b) named patient use in individuals.

The regulatory points of time and product identities form a common pattern of understanding of NDU: Off-label use is best related to proprietary MPs, used post- marketing authorization (MA) and pre-variation. Compassionate use happens peri-randomized control trial (RCT) as well as pre-notice of compliance (NOC) and is linked to investigational new drugs (active treatment) in groups and individuals. The product identity of unlicensed MPs often is 'imported', 'BAS' or 'extemporaneous products', which are being put to use pre-RCT relating to the country of drug use. The term 'off-label use' is often defined as a breach of preset indication. In literature however, use by another route of administration or by physicians without additional qualifications is also termed 'off–label'. Therefore 'use outside the terms of indication' does not emerge to be an appropriate description. 'Use outside the terms of a PIL' is a model that excludes dosage-based and population-based off-label use from the definition, because a PIL may very well allow a physician to alter e.g. a dose or may not describe the target population in detail. Off-label use defined as 'the use of a proprietary MP in a way, requiring a variation to the MA, extension of the MA or a new MA, describes all seven off-label-classes and takes the aforementioned regulatory point of time into account.

Interestingly, importations, BAS (both eligible to MA) and extemporaneous products (exempted from MA), are assigned to the concept of 'unlicensed use'. There is a discrepancy between the U.K., Ireland and the Netherlands and German-speaking countries as to whether to solely judge 'unlicensed use' by presence or absence of a product license or take into account registration requirements. There is no explanation for the discrepancy; pharmaceutical law in all countries exempts extemporaneous products from licensing requirements. If a country plans to consider extemporaneous products when assessing NDU, definition must be comprehensive. In consequence, an all-encompassing definition must consider that an unlicensed product fulfils medicine criteria, though it does not need an MA or if requiring an MA, then has neither an MA nor CTA in the country at the time.

There is no need to define 'compassionate use'. Definitions are available in the E.U., the U.S. and Canada. Japan is planning to adopt a compassionate use system. The mediocre level of recognition of the meaning among experts in the survey suggests further quantitative research to measure the true level of awareness among peers. If surveys confirm false or no knowledge of the term, public training and continues medical education will be necessary.

Investigations into the supply of MPs give evidence of a circumstantial need for nonlicensed drug uses. On top of a situational necessity for NDU, physicians are commonly awarded therapeutic freedom e.g. in Austria or Germany and are therefore entitled to NDU. Legislation of many countries also imposes a duty of care on physicians, irrespective of medicines' marketing statuses and hence an obligation to perform best practice irrespective of MA. However, evidence can also be found illustrating practice of unsupported, non-indicated off-label use and non-standard, irrational NDU.

Therapeutic need and patient protection are particularly relevant to the discussion of NDU. There is mutual agreement that safe and efficacious MPs shall be accessible to patients in need of treatment (first quarter of figure 10). A disproportionate harm-benefit ratio may be accepted for salvage therapy of severe diseases with no treatment options (fourth quarter). Patients must not be treated with inefficacious MPs (second and third quarter).

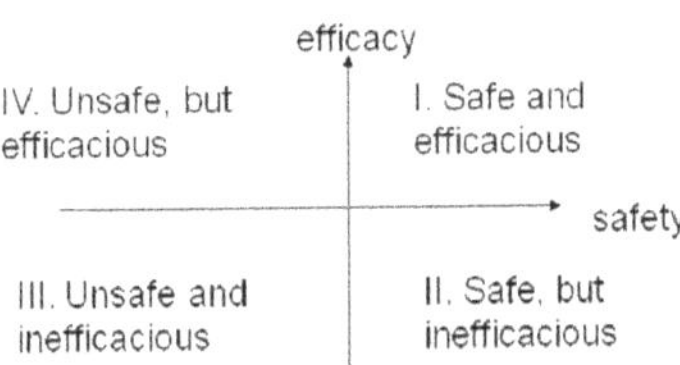

Figure 10 Coordinate plan of favored and unwanted NDU

Early access to unmarketed MPs is possible in a controlled way in some industrial countries. Different systems to manage unlicensed and compassionate use are present in Ireland, the U.K., France, Canada and the U.S. Wherever nonlicensed use is subject to regulatory requirements, safety mechanisms are expanded as well. Batch recalls, "Dear HCP"-letters or notices to doctors are possible for MPs imported to Ireland or compassionate use products in France. Market surveillance of nonlicensed drug use in other countries relies on ADR reporting and good practice. Whenever temporary use authorizations are adopted successfully, access to treatment also is on equal terms for all patients and not dependant on the individual commitment of patients or physicians as seen in Austria.

E.U. and German temporary use authorizations are offered in principle, but not implemented successfully and therefore unsought. Effective solutions for the short term management of nonlicensed drug use can be obtained from U.K., France, Canada and the U.S. This qualitative analysis finds a high acceptance of systems in the U.K. and France.

Four centralized methods of resolution are to be conceptualized for the short term management of nonlicensed drug use: (a) prohibition i.e. off-label use in Japan, (b) permission e.g. for compassionate use in France, (c) notification (for example imported MPs in the U.K.) and (d) administration of data (for instance extemporaneous products in France).

Japan's prohibition policy for off-label use is unsusceptible to marketing, explicit and bears low costs. Unfortunately, breaches are observed, patient's needs remain unidentified and therapeutic requirements may not be met. 'Obligations to obtain permits' allow a check by a second instance and can contribute to drug safety. However, time-lags and conflicts of interest must be avoided to assure prompt patient supply and independent filing of decisions. 'Obligations to obtain permits' affect physician's therapeutic freedom, but they may be suitable for expanded access programs by MAH. 'Notification' guarantees an immediate supply while an intervention is possible if necessary. This approach may be suitable for named patient use and drug importation. Data capturing is advantageous to identify essential medicines and publish lists. Given this, a hypothesis is postulated that data capturing from electronic health records, modeled on the GPRD, DSRU and IMS Health or French hospital pharmacies reporting extemporaneous products to Afssaps can be used to review off-label use. In general, management of nonlicensed drug use is welcomed in short the term, but experts call for full MAs in the long term. Therefore long term solutions are discussed later.

Liability for ADE in consequence of nonlicensed drug use is shared between MAH and HCPs. MAH are found liable for harm if they violate advertisement law as seen in the U.S. Physicians are found guilty for ADRs as a result of nonlicensed drug use as shown in Austria if they fail to acquire valid informed consent from the patient. In Germany, physicians are also found responsible for the course of the disease when denying a state of the art off-label treatment. Although no court trials have been held against pharmacists, experts judge them to be held responsible for harm resulting from quality defects of dispensed, unlicensed or compassionate use products. In this context, British experts assume that a pharmacist's best care and attention must always be dedicated to advising the patient properly, to conferring with the physician or even not filling a risky prescription.

Different solutions for claims costs are available: Experts in the U.K. argue that professional indemnity insurances cover nonlicensed drug use if a treatment is standard of care. In Austria, an expert proposed to introduce a fund to cover patient claims in case of a declaration of inability to pay. Funds to cover patient claims are criticized, because the low risk for patients and physicians is feared to lead to an incautious exposure to NDU. In Japan, injuries as a result of off-label use are not covered by public health insurances thereby increasing claims costs.

This approach is also questionable for ethical reasons. It was seen that aforementioned temporary use procedures and derivatively negative assessment reports can give legal certainty and define the liability. Wherever reasonable, permanent "legalization" of NDU or negative assessment reports would provide legal certainty.

There is isolated data by different authors concerning inappropriate detailing about off-label use and compassionate use as a pre-launch marketing strategy e.g. in Italy and for instance in Germany respectively. Trials held in U.S. courts give evidence for illegal advertising of off-label use. Pharmaceutical law in the U.K. explicitly demands that health care professionals (HCPs) are pointed to missing MA at conferences in the U.K. and in medical journals; lists of foreign MPs available via wholesalers are prohibited. On the other hand, information needs are expressed by HCPs. Information demand is also apparent when looking at the plentiful, non-commercial and commercial databases and publications, which are offered across the world as sources for information about off-label use, unlicensed MPs, pediatric drugs or OMPs.

One can identify three core approaches to control drug commercials: German and Austrian codes of conduct, U.S. whistle blower laws and British preliminary assessment. Additional research is necessary to better determine (a) the true dimension of NDU marketing ubiquitously and (b) which attempts are most effective to control inappropriate marketing of nonlicensed drug use.

Variations or extensions of MA and new drug application (NDA) for non-patentable agents often are not cost-effective. In the E.U., the long-term change of off-label use to in-label use is only rewarded on for occasions with non-cumulative market exclusivity for a relevant new indication or NDA for non-patentable agents only in pediatric and rare conditions.

Potentially, amendment of templates by the competent authority offer a way to authorize an off-label use in the long term provided that sound scientific proof is available for its efficacy and safety. Compassionate use MPs meeting safety and efficacy requirements must be followed by full NDA. MA for unlicensed MPs however, is only sought by MAHs for new chemical or biological entities, pediatric and OMPs. Research into other off-patent MPs is unprofitable. Furthermore, price increases for formerly unlicensed children's MPs or OMPs are subject to criticism. Only one country is able to issue an MA, in spite of missing incentives, which also allows price competition: Germany's unique[xii] procedure the 'standard MA' is the development of a drug monograph by BfArM. All applicants for the standard MA must refer to the standard MA monograph. Currently, general sales list medicines are preferred for a standardized MA; suggestions for monographs may be made to an expert advisory board. Latter rules must be amended to allow a data-driven development of essential medicines. Negative assessment reports could suspend inadequate drug uses. Figure 11 depicts a possible model of NDU processing.

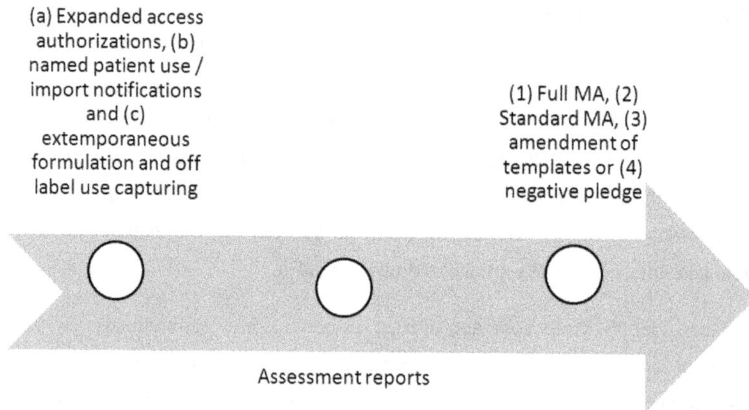

Figure 11 Three-step approach to the authentication of NDU

Conclusion and Outlook Nonlicensed drug use has lead to miscellaneous concept formulations. The NDU classes identified give support for first, an off-license understanding of off-label use, next a perception of unlicensed-use to also include preparations not eligible to MA and finally a distinction between expanded access in groups of patients and named patient use in individuals as compassionate uses. Temporary approval settles responsibilities in the short term and in the long term, MA incur liabilities. With regard to inappropriate advertising and at this stage, it can only be marked that further research into actual marketing practice and control procedures is advisable.

In the short term, an ATUc procedure is suitable for expanded access compassionate use, as experience in France displays that early access to innovative drugs proves itself. A procedure similar to ATU_N for named patient use and importation will improve equal access for all patients and assure

[xii] A second nation, Switzerland, is considering introducing the standard MA in near future.

pharmacovigilance. The procedure must not call for permission, but for notification as to not violate physicians' therapeutic freedom. Data capturing is a short term solution to collect information about essential extemporaneous products as seen in France and off-label use from electronic health records. In the long term, compassionate use results in full MA or non-admission. If an NDA is unprofitable for an essential unlicensed MP, the German standard MA may provide a key solution to authentication. Scientific sound off-label use could be recognized officially by amendment of templates. Negative assessment reports could dispose of inadequate treatments.

<table>
<tr><th>NDU</th><th colspan="2">Compassionate use</th><th colspan="2">Unlicensed-Use</th><th rowspan="2">Off-label Use</th></tr>
<tr><th>TERM</th><th>Expanded access</th><th>Named-Patient Use</th><th>Imported medicines</th><th>Extemporaneous products</th></tr>
<tr><td>SHORT</td><td>Permit procedure</td><td colspan="2">Notification (subject to prohibition)</td><td colspan="2">Data capturing</td></tr>
<tr><td rowspan="2">LONG</td><td colspan="2">Full MA</td><td colspan="2">Standardized MA</td><td>Data driven templates</td></tr>
<tr><td colspan="5">Or negative pledge</td></tr>
</table>

Table 28 Model management assumption

A new data set on solutions is to be presented, which could be used to develop a system to manage NDU (table 28) in the future. The relevance of this system is eloquently shown by the observation that NDU is inevitable in specific medical situations.

In summary, the data demonstrate that the impact of NDU on health care law is most pronounced. NDU is a major factor in the development of temporary use authorizations. Temporary use authorizations assure that special medical needs are met by providing early access to medications while securing pharmacovigilance. A suggestion for the long term management of supply shortage in medical areas, providing for incentives and duties, emanates from NDU: Temporary use provisions and data capturing may be used to identify essential medicines and channel research and drug development into the authentication of efficacious and safe NDU. The next stage of work will involve a pilot study into the feasibility and acceptance of the short term solutions.

5. Preliminary publications and presentations

Plate, V. et al. "Reducing Off label use in paediatrics by improving drug information: Comparative study of approvals of children's medicines since 2001 and a database for approved children's medicines." In . DIA 19th Annual EuroMeeting. Wien, 2007. *Drug Information Journal:* P-273.

Plate, V. et al. "Online-Informationen zu Arzneimitteln für Kinder." *Deutsches Ärzteblatt*, N.12 (2007): 764–65.

Lewinski, D., V. Plate, S. Wind, C. Belgardt, and H. G. Schweim. "Risk Management in German Community Pharmacies: Safety-relevant Problems in Self-Medication." In vol. 30. International Society of Pharmacovigilance (ISOP) 7th Annual Meeting. Bournemouth, October 24, 2007. *Drug Safety:* 975.

Plate, V. "Entwicklung eines neuen Arzneimittels: Arzneistoffforschung, Galenische Entwicklung, Klinische Studien, Originalpräparat - Generikum." Fachkraft für Entwicklung und Herstellung von Arzneimitteln, Dokumentationen, Verfahrenstechnik, Prüfmethoden, Qualitätsrichtlinien und Zulassung (IHK).

Blasius, H., V. Plate, Behles C., and H. G. Schweim. "Nicht-zugelassene Arzneimittelanwendungen in Japan." Bonn, July 15, 2008.

Plate, V. et al. "Comparative survey of off-label, unlicensed and compassionate use in selected industrial countries – impact on drug regulation." In October 11, 2008. *Abstractband Deutsche Pharmazeutische Gesellschaft (DPhG) Annual Meeting:* 306.

Plate, V. "Computer-Aided Qualitative Data Analysis: Comparison of the impact of off-label, unlicensed and compassionate use on drug law in selected industrial countries (Project "Off-Label")." Doktoranden-Vortragstag. Bonn: Rheinische Friedrich-Wilhelms-Universität Bonn, April 04, 2008; available from http://home.arcor.de/janna-schweim/3-Plate.pdf; Internet; accessed February 16, 2008.

Plate, V. et al. "Nicht zugelassene Arzneimittel: Maßnahmen zur Minimierung der Risiken: Unlicensed use of drugs: measures to minimize risks." Dtsch med Wochenschr 134 (2009): 944–48.

Plate, V. "Medikamentensicherheit. Medikamentenhandel im Internet: Sicherheit gewährleisten. - Ein Balanceakt zwischen Schattenwirtschaft, organisiertem Verbrechen und regulärer Ökonomie." Goslar: St. Jakobushaus. Katholische Akademie, October 16, 2008.

Plate, V. et al. "Wohin treibt der Off-Label-Use?". *Arzneimittel und Recht*, N.5 (2008): 195–203.

Plate, V. "Impact of Off-label, Compassionate and Unlicensed Use on Health Care Law in preselected countries: mock thesis defense." Pharmazeutisches Institut, Lehrstuhl für Drug Regulatory Affairs, Prof. H. G. Schweim. 2. Doktorandentagung. Bonn: Rheinische Friedrich-Wilhelms-Universität Bonn, April 25, 2009; available from http://www.harald-g-schweim.de/Plate-2009.pdf; Internet; accessed May 22, 2009.

Plate, V. et al. "Intraartikuläre Hyaluronsäure, Glucocorticoide und Lokalanaesthetika, eine retrospektive Analyse." Bonn, September 29, 2009.

Lewinski, D. Wind S., C. Belgardt, V. Plate, C. Behles, and H. G. Schweim. "Prevalence and safety-relevance of drug-related problems in German community pharmacies: Drug-Related Problems in Community Pharmacies." Bonn, June 05, 2009.

Appendix

Feature / Number	Country	Institution
1.		Coverage
2.	Canada	Regulatory
3.		Society
4.		Academia
5.		Regulatory
6.		Academia
7.		Academia
8.		Academia
9.	U.S.	Academia
10.		
11.		Academia
12.	Japan	Academia
13.		MAH
14.		Regulatory
15.		
16.	Switzerland	Coverage
17.		Society
18.		Coverage
19.		Society
20.		Academia
21.		
22.		MAH
23.	Austria	Regulatory
24.		Academia
25.		Society
26.		Academia
27.		Academia
28.		Society
29.		HTA
30.		MAH
31.	GB	Regulatory
32.		Regulatory
33.		Society
34.		MAH
35.		Society
36.	E.U.	Regulatory
37.		Regulatory
38.	France	MAH
39.		Society
40.		Coverage
41.		Coverage
42.		MAH
43.		Academia
44.		Academia
45.		MAH
46.		Academia
47.	Germany	Academia

Table 29 Participants by country and institution

Number	Date (dd.mm.yy)	Time (hh:mm) CET	Length [min]	Interviewer [initials]	Mode
1.	06.12.2008	08:00 am	44	VP	Telephone
2.	02.01.2008	03:00 pm	35	VP	Telephone
3.	12.12.2008	08:00 am	58	VP	Telephone
4.	10.04.2008	02:00 pm	60	VP	Telephone
5.	28.04.2008	03:00 pm	47	VP	Telephone
6.	30.04.2008	04:00 pm	39	VP	Telephone
7.	25.04.2008	03:00 pm	89	VP	Telephone
8.	02.05.2008	06:00 pm	60	VP	Telephone
9.	05.05.2008	02:00 pm	65	VP	Telephone
10.	29.01.2008	03:00 pm	53	VP	Group
11.	11.04.2008	09:00 am	37	VP	Telephone
12.	12.12.2007	09:00 am	150	CB	One-to-one
13.	13.02.2008	02:00 pm	42	CB	Telephone
14.	13.12.2007	02:00 pm	120	CB	One-to-one
15.	26.03.2007	02:00 pm	60	CB&VP	Group
16.	26.03.2007	11:00 am	30	VP	Group
17.	28.03.2007	09:00 am	60	CB&VP	Group
18.	08.11.2006	09:15 am	9	VP	Telephone
19.	26.03.2007	09:00 am	180	CB	Group
20.	13.09.2006	07:00 pm	10	VP	Telephone
21.	29.11.2007	03:00 pm	60	VP	Telephone
22.	21.11.2007	03:00 pm	60	VP	Telephone
23.	05.12.2007	11:00 am	20	VP	Telephone
24.	14.12.2007	09:00 am	47	VP	Telephone
25.	12.12.2007	04:00 pm	21	VP	Telephone
26.	08.01.2008	04:00 pm	29	VP	Telephone
27.	22.11.2007	02:00 pm	30	VP	Telephone
28.	22.10.2007	01:00 pm	30	VP	One-to-one
29.	18.02.2008	11:00 am	60	VP	One-to-one
30.	19.03.2008	02:00 pm	14	VP	Telephone
31.	16.05.2008	09:30 am	50	VP	Telephone
32.	14.04.2008	03:00 pm	45	VP	Telephone
33.	16.06.2008	04:00 pm	54	VP	One-to-one
34.	11.03.2008	10:00 am	54	VP	Telephone
35.	16.04.2008	03:00 pm	25	VP	Telephone
36.	11.04.2008	03:00 pm	90	PN&VP	Group
37.	16.04.2008	04:00 pm	95	PN&VP	Group, Telephone
38.	16.04.2008	10:00 am	40	VP	One-to-one
39.	16.04.2008	04:00 pm	31	VP	Telephone
40.	13.05.2008	03:30 pm	67	VP	One-to-one
41.	06.05.2008	11:00 am	48	VP	Telephone
42.	24.04.2008	04:30 pm	120	PN&VP	Group
43.	15.05.2008	05:00 pm	120	PN&VP	Group
44.	28.04.2008	05:30 pm	45	PN	One-to-one

Table 30 Details of expert interviews

NDU / COUNTRY	Off label use			Compassionate use			Unlicensed use		
	Legislation	*Literature*	*query*	*Legislation*	*Literature*	*query*	*Legislation*	*Literature*	*query*
GERMANY		Ol, [309] nri, [310] oolu[311]	Ol, $_{N.43,N.38,N.39}$ nri$_{N.42}$		Npu/ inp[314]	Ea$_{,N.43}$ pl$_{,N.43}$ pct$_{,N.36}$		ep[315]	imp$_{N.36}$
AUSTRIA		nri[316]	nri$_{N.19,}$		pe[317]	Npu/Imp/ pl$_{N.19}$		u	a$_{N.19}$
FRANCE		Ol, [318] oolu, [319]	Ol$_{,N.34}$ oolu$_{N.35}$		U	Pl$_{,N.34}$ ea/ npu$_{N.34,N.35}$		u	A$_{N.34,N.35}$
U.K.	u	Ol, [320 321 322 323 324] oolu, [325 326] nri [327 328]	Ol, $_{N.22,N.23,N.21,N.28}$ nri$_{N.25,N.27}$		pl[329]	Pe/pl/pct/eas$_{,N.22}$ a, $_{N.23,N.25}$	u	Ep/pl/imp[330], pe/inp[331]	nri$_{,N.25}$ ep$_{,N.22}$ imp$_{,N.24}$ pl$_{N.28}$
E.U.	ol[332]	Oolu/ ol[333]	Nri$_{,N.29,N.31,N.32}$ oolu$_{N.33}$	Ea/pl,[312] npu[313]	Ea[334]	Ea/npu$_{,N.33}$ pe/inp$_{,N.31}$ pe/pl/ pct$_{N.29}$	~~Ep~~/imp[335]	ep[336]	oolu$_{,N.31}$ a$_{,N.32}$ pl$_{,N.30}$ imp$_{,N.29,N.33}$
SWITZERLAND		ol[337338339]	Ol$_{N.12}$		pl[340]	Npu$_{N.12}$		Off label use[341]	Imp$_{N.12}$
U.S.		oolu[342]	Oolu$_{,N.9,N.3,N.7}$ nri$_{N.5}$		Inp, npu[343]	pl$_{,N.9}$ pct$_{,N.8}$ inp$_{,N.5}$ off-label$_{N.3}$		u	A$_{,N.9}$ imp$_{,N.8}$ off-label use$_{,N.6,N.5,N.4,N.3,N.7}$
CANADA		ol[344]	Nri$_{N.1}$		u	Pct/pe/npu$_{N.1}$		u	A$_{N.1}$
JAPAN	u	ol[345]	Nri$_{N.11}$	u	U	A$_{N.11}$	u	u	Op/pct/pl/imp$_{N.11}$

Table 31 Definitions to NDU by source and country abbreviated according to the predefined categories (cancelled= excluded, pl= pre-licensing, pct= post-clinical-trial/ pre-NDA, pe= post-enrollment, imp= imported MP, inp= investigational new product, u= undefined, ol= off-license, oolu=out of label use, nri= not registered indications, npu= named patient use, ea= expanded access, a= absent)

CITATION	Result
GILL AM ET AL.: ADVERSE DRUG REACTIONS IN A PAEDIATRIC INTENSIVE CARE UNIT. ACTA PAEDIATRICA; 84 (D); 438-41	One-third of the ADRs were due to drugs used outside their product license.
JONVILLE-BÉRA AP ET AL.: ARE INCORRECTLY USED DRUGS MORE FREQUENTLY INVOLVED IN ADVERSE DRUG REACTIONS? A PROSPECTIVE STUDY. 2005, EUROPEAN JOURNAL OF CLINICAL PHARMACOLOGY 61(3):231-6	Of 642 drugs, 169 (26%) were incorrectly used in 81 patients (44.5%), ADRs involved at least one "incorrectly" used drug. These included 10% (64 of 642) drug interactions, 7.3% (47 of 642) off-license indications, 5% (32 of 642) inadequate dosage, 3% (20 of 642) incorrect duration of treatment and 1% (6 of 642) contraindications. "Correctly" used drugs appeared to be less often the cause of ADRs than "incorrectly" used drugs (59.4% versus 75%, P=0.0001).
LADEWSKI LA ET AL.: DISSEMINATION OF INFORMATION ON POTENTIALLY FATAL ADVERSE DRUG REACTIONS FOR CANCER DRUGS FROM 2000 TO 2002: FIRST RESULTS FROM THE RESEARCH ON ADVERSE DRUG EVENTS AND REPORTS PROJECT. 2003, JOURNAL OF CLINICAL ONCOLOGY 21(20):3859-66	Twenty-five serious ADRs associated with 22 oncology drugs were identified after approval. ADRs were described in articles in medical journals (17 ADRs), PIL revisions (18 ADRs), and Dear Doctor letters (12 ADRs). Five of the seven ADRs lacking PI changes occurred with off label use.
MCQUEEN KD, MILTON JD: MULTICENTER POSTMARKETING SURVEILLANCE OF ONDANSETRON THERAPY IN PEDIATRIC-PATIENTS. 1994, THE ANNALS OF PHARMACOTHERAPY 28(1):85-92	Surveys from 197 of the 210 patients enrolled were complete for evaluation. Ondansetron was used to treat chemotherapy-induced emesis in 88% of the patients and 12% received it for various other indications. Ondansetron dosing was off label in 15% and 73% prior to and after an emetogenic exposure, respectively. Possible ondansetron-associated adverse reactions were similar to those of previous reports for all patients, although some recorded reactions are not currently included in package labeling.
NEUBERT A ET AL.: THE IMPACT OF UNLICENSED AND OFF LABEL DRUG USE ON ADVERSE DRUG REACTIONS IN PAEDIATRIC PATIENTS. 2004, DRUG SAFETY 27(13):1059-67	A total of 178 patients were included in the study and 740 drug prescriptions were given to 156 patients (median three prescriptions per patient). In 198 cases (27.7% of all prescriptions) drugs were used in either an unlicensed (n = 3) or off label (n = 195) manner. A total of 46 ADRs were observed in 31 patients (17.4%). Patients receiving at least one unlicensed or off label drug prescription during hospitalization (n = 92) experienced an ADR significantly more frequently (n = 26 patients) than patients receiving only licensed drugs (n = 64.5 patients). ADRs were associated with 29 (5.6%) of the 517 licensed drug prescriptions and with 12

	(6.1%) of the 198 unlicensed or off label drug prescriptions. The majority of ADRs caused by unlicensed and off label drug use were recognized by the attending physician. However, statistical analysis revealed no significant difference in the number of licensed and unlicensed/off label drug prescriptions causing ADRs.
RODRIGUEZ W ET AL.: ADVERSE DRUG EVENTS IN CHILDREN: THE U.S. FOOD AND DRUG ADMINISTRATION PERSPECTIVE. 2001, CURRENT THERAPEUTIC RESEARCH - CLINICAL AND EXPERIMENTAL 62(10):711-23	Of the first 16 products that were subsequently studied in children, 6 (37.5%) had significant changes in labeling that had an impact on safety or efficacy. Situations in which proposed dosing could have led to overdosing or under dosing and in which adverse events, previously not described, could be expected were identified.
SCHIRM E ET AL.: REPORTED ADVERSE DRUG REACTIONS AND THEIR DETERMINANTS IN DUTCH CHILDREN OUTSIDE THE HOSPITAL. 2004, PHARMACOEPIDEMIOLOGY & DRUG SAFETY 13(3): 159-65	The main findings were that ADRs were disproportionately more often reported on systemic drugs (OR 3.0; [95%CI: 1.9-4.8]), new drugs (2.4; [1.6-2.7]), anti-infective drugs (1.7; [1.1-2.7]) and nervous system drugs (2.1; [1.3-3.5]), whereas unlicensed drugs (0.1; [0.0-0.4]), frequently used drugs (0.3; [0.2-0.5]) and dermatological drugs (0.1; [0.0-0.4]) were less likely to be associated with a reported ADR. Overall, the proportion of off label prescriptions did not differ between drugs with a suspected ADR and drugs used by children in a general population.
TURNER S ET AL.: ADVERSE DRUG REACTIONS TO UNLICENSED AND OFF LABEL DRUGS ON PAEDIATRIC WARDS: A PROSPECTIVE STUDY. ACTA PAEDIATR. 1999 SEP;88(9):965-8.	ADR: 3.9% in 2881 licensed drugs, 6% out of 1574 unlicensed or off label drugs
UFER M. ET AL.: ADVERSE DRUG REACTIONS AND OFF LABEL PRESCRIBING FOR PAEDIATRIC OUTPATIENTS: A ONE-YEAR SURVEY OF SPONTANEOUS REPORTS IN SWEDEN. 2004, PHARMACOEPIDEMIOLOGY & DRUG SAFETY 13(3): 147-52	The average proportion of off label drug prescribing amounted to 42.4%. It was more frequently associated with serious than non-serious ADRs and mostly due to a non-approved age or dose. The most common clinical manifestations were psychiatric disorders and mucocutaneous inflammatory reactions.
VALICENTI-MCDERMOTT, MR, DEMB H: CLINICAL EFFECTS AND ADVERSE REACTIONS OF OFF LABEL USE OF ARIPIPRAZOLE IN CHILDREN AND ADOLESCENTS WITH DEVELOPMENTAL DISABILITIES. 2006, JOURNAL OF CHILD AND ADOLESCENT PSYCHOPHARMACOLOGY 16(5):549-60	Side effects were reported in 16 (50%), with the most frequent being sleepiness (n = 6).

Table 32 Summary of studies on the frequency of ADRs during NDU

Project description

„Comparative survey of off-label, unlicensed and compassionate use in selected industrial countries"

I. Research question

About 25% to 90% inpatient and 13% to 70% outpatient prescriptions are not within the terms of the medicines' marketing authorization (off label use) or include medicines prescribed without a marketing authorization (unlicensed use). The meaning and consequences of off-label, unlicensed and compassionate use of medicines in outpatient and inpatient care has not yet been subject to research in Germany. A comprehensive, cross-national appraisal including Germany and relevant industrial countries is not available up until now. Information on off label use is poorly or inaccessible for both physicians and pharmacists.

Recommendations on off label use are produced heterogeneously and do not meet the standards of evidence-based medicine. An expert group was founded in Germany in 2002 whose responsibility is to decide in which situations medicines can be applied, despite the fact that they are not approved for an indication or the treatment of a severe disease.

Reasonable off label use is supposed to be reimbursed and should be supported on the basis of earlier theories. The group experienced that assessment is very complicated and only few results were achieved. However, since there is an unequivocal therapeutic need in certain medical disciplines (or even a statutory commitment) for the described application in individual cases, despite the risks to patients of prescription freedom on behalf of physicians, data for evidence-based decisions is crucial.

The aim of this and subsequent projects is to improve drug therapy by introducing a rational, scientifically founded application of medicines outside the terms of (or even without) a marketing authorization. A special objective of the project is to compare regulations or practices in foreign countries in depth with the situation in Germany. There are three stages to the project:

A. Pre-stage:
This stage includes the literature research, analysis and documentation of the international and scientific existing state analysis as preliminary and legwork for the German groups. As a part of the complete pre-stage part of the project, all documentation of the international and scientific status of off-label, unlicensed and compassionate use will be made available for public (project years one and two).

B. Recommended action:
Check sheets and other tools are developed for support of concerned physicians and pharmacists regarding their decisions and documentation (project year three).

C. Support to the decision maker:
The continuing support of the work of future decision makers (e.g., off label committee) and prescriber/applicant/patient/pharmacists by supplying data

according to A. and B. (from 2008 onward) is a key issue. A decision on this part will be made in 2007.

II. Initial stage

Definition

The quality of drug therapy in Germany is assured under the German drug act (circulation safety) and the same is assured for national health care by the social security code (benefit and cost effectiveness). Nevertheless, both inpatient and outpatient consumer health care in Germany is affected by applications that have not been approved by one of these entities. This problematic use of medicines is characterized by the terms 'off label use', 'unlicensed use' and 'compassionate use'.

Off label use is the use of medicines outside the terms of the application for a marketing authorization and is neither verified nor approved by the authorities. This definition can include the drug's use for another indication, but also with a different dose, interval of application, route of administration and even type of use (such as single or combined therapy) or for specific patient's features (e.g., age, co-morbidity).

Unlicensed use is the use of medicines without a marketing authorization.

Compassionate use is widely understood to be the accepted use of a medicine either outside its license or before it is licensed by authorities for compassionate reasons.

All terms are used heterogeneously according to the national legal status or the academic use, as well as to individual levels of awareness and assessment. Since these medicines or their specific use have not undergone testing regarding efficacy, quality and risks, both cost -effectiveness and safety of such drug therapy are not guaranteed. Thus the German social security code largely abandons own rules on how to secure quality, notwithstanding other services; it is bound compulsorily to the German drug act and obliged to the drug act's criteria concerning the quality, efficacy and safety of a drug. If a medicine for which proof of quality, efficacy and safety has not been provided is used, its cost-effectiveness and benefit cannot be assumed. However, absence of benefit of such a medicine can also not be assumed merely because the formal authorization process has not been performed with the available scientific data. Therefore, uncertainty regarding reimbursement arises, which again undoubtedly influences the quality of consumer health care. Statements regarding this issue were only made in distinct sectors and are usually not based on empirical studies. The problem of co-operation between regulatory agencies and reimbursement through the social security system in order to best use financial resources as well as supply the country with medicines is also present in foreign countries.

The circumvention of the German drug act due to off-label, unlicensed and compassionate use is all the more difficult if the origin of the act is considered. This act is inseparably linked to the thalidomide scandal; it was enacted to protect patients from serious harm by unavoidable risks of medicines.[xiii] [xiv] The drug act demands exceptionally high requirements from the pharmaceutical industry for proof of efficacy and safety through clinical trials. The specification 'use in compliance with the label' by both SPC and PIL as a core element of consumer protection is negated when regulatory status and therapeutic efficacy grow apart.

Recent papers are calling to attention the presence of significant circumvention of these legal mechanisms of protection. The dimension of off-label and unlicensed use varies depending on patients and the supply area.[xv] Bücheler et al. discovered in their study that 13.2% out of a total of 1,74 Mio. prescriptions in the first quarter of the year written by all pediatric physicians, general practitioners and internal specialists at the expense of an insurance company in 1999 (i.e., 210,528 out of 1,59 Mio.) were off-label; in certain disciplines this percentage was even up to 64%.[xvi] Schirm et al. found a rate of 22.7% with extreme deviation in pediatric outpatient care in the Netherlands. Another survey by Conroy et al. suggests that off label use is even more common in specialized pediatric care. Their results show that on average among all institutions (46% of which were German institutions) in 41% of all cases patients did not receive prescriptions in accordance with the marketing authorization.[xvii]

Further European and foreign studies verify this observation. Schirm et al. detected both off label use and unlicensed use in 22.7% and O'Donell at al. in 58% of all child prescriptions.[xviii] [xix] The situation is even more dramatic in pediatric oncology. Conroy et al. found out that all children had at least one drug prescribed out of terms of the particular marketing authorization.[xx] This fraction is equal to 90% in neonatal care.[xxi] The German Ministry for Health estimates rates of 70-80% for off label use in oncology care in Germany.[xxii] Off label use and unlicensed use are explained to be due to the fact that use in compliance with the label of used medicines as regulated in a marketing authorization often does not

---

[xiii] *Amtliche Begründung zum Gesetz zur Neuordnung des Arzneimittelrechts.* A. Allgemeiner Teil, August 24, 1976.

[xiv] "Ausschußbericht zum Gesetz zur Neuordnung des Arzneimittelrechts: II. Allgemeiner Teil; 1. Die Mängel des geltenden Rechts." 24. 8. 1976.

[xv] Schirm, E. "Risk Factors for Unlicensed and Off-Label Drug Use in Children Outside the Hospital." *Pediatrics* 111, no. 2 (2003): 291–95.

[xvi] Bücheler, R. "„Off-label "Verschreibung von Arzneimitteln in der ambulanten Versorgung von Kindern und Jugendlichen." *Deutsche Medizinische Wochenschrift* 127, no. 48 (2002): 2551.

[xvii] Conroy, S. et al. "Survey of unlicensed and off label drug use in paediatric wards in European countries." *BMJ* 320, no. 7227 (2000): 79–82.

[xviii] Schirm, E. "Unlicensed and off label drug use by children in the community: cross sectional study." *BMJ* 324, no. 7349 (2002): 1312.

[xix] O'Donnell, C. P. F. et al. "Unlicensed and Off-Label Drug Use in an Australian Neonatal Intensive Care Unit." *Pediatrics* 110, no. 5 (2002): e52.

[xx] Conroy, S. et al. "Unlicensed and off label drug use in acute lymphoblastic leukaemia and other malignancies in children." *Annals of Oncology* 14, no. 1 (2003): 42.

[xxi] Anonymus. "Arzneimittelzulassung und Therapiefreiheit: Anmerkungen des wissenschaftlichen Arbeitskreises der DGAI zum nichtbestimmungsgemäßen Gebrauch zugelassener Medikamente in der Anästhesie." Deutsche Gesellschaft zum Studium des Schmerzes e.V., 03.2001; available from http://www.kinderschmerz.org/?action=download&id=5; Internet, accessed February 12, 2009.

[xxii] Deutscher Bundestag. *Antwort der Bundesregierung auf die Kleine Anfrage der Abgeordneten.* 14/9274 (Drucksache). Bundesregierung, June 24, 2002.

comply with substantial care or state-of-the-art of medical science.[xxiii] [xxiv] [xxv] This statement corresponds to publications abroad.[xxvi] Governmental and academic facilities both publish lists and comments on reasonable and reviewed off label use.[xxvii] [xxviii]

Reasons for the unevaluated use of medicines are numerous.

The planning, transaction, evaluation and assessment of studies necessary in order to receive an approval require a lot of time. On the other hand, physicians and patients have a desire to employ medicines that have achieved first positive results in clinical trials as soon as possible in order to make use of the best possible practice. However, comprehensive proof of efficacy and safety is often not available for use of medicines beyond marketing authorization.

Furthermore, the first approval of a medicine is often a model marketing authorization for which studies were performed in a small group of patients not including all possible applicants. From a point of view of patient supply, all desired therapeutic capabilities of an active agent may not be covered by a marketing authorization.

Moreover, not all scientific information may exist in order to employ pharmacotherapy on a rational basis. The causes for the existence of only a few clinical trials are of an economic, ethical, scientific and practical nature.[xxix] There is, for instance, a missing incentive for studies in groups of patients with an expected narrow market. Even if some incentives are currently being provided, the limited nature of the capacities for the management of clinical trials and

---

[xxiii] Weißbach, L., and E. A. Boedefeld. "Off-Label-Verordnungen in der Onkologie." *Bundesgesundheitsblatt, Gesundheitsforschung, Gesundheitsschutz* 46, no. 6 (2003): 462–66.
[xxiv] Fritze, J., and M. Schmauß. "Off-Label-Use in der Psychopharmakotherapie." *Nervenarzt* 73, no. 8 (2002): 796–99.
[xxv] See footnote xxi
[xxvi] Department of Health and Human Services. "Patient Access to New Therapeutic Agents for Pediatric Cancer: Report to Congress." 12.2003.
[xxvii] *Federal Register* 68, no. 13: 2789.
[xxviii] Fritze, J., and M. Schmauß. "Off-Label-Use in der Psychopharmakotherapie." *Psychoneuro* 28, no. 8 (2002): 431–39.
[xxix] Budetti, P. P. "Ensuring Safe and Effective Medications for Children." *JAMA* 290, no. 7 (2003): 950–51.

biometric problems will still make studying all possible patients impossible.[xxx] [xxxi] [xxxii]

One possibility to encourage the pharmaceutical industry to perform more clinical trials is to offer incentives. This method is applied in the U.S. by means of the pediatric exclusivity provision. Pharmaceutical companies that begin specific research in children may be granted a six-month extended patent protection for the complete medicine. Due to combined regulations requiring manufacturers to assess the safety and effectiveness of new drugs and biological products in pediatric patients, which allows the FDA to request additional trials for the treatment of children for specific marketing authorizations, clinical trials in children have increased. Analogous incentives have already submitted to the parliament and council and are also now subject to approval by the EC.[xxxiii] Extended terms of copyright for product development, financial support for relevant research and simplified terms of approval are also regarded as positive incentives. In this way, the pharmaceutical companies are supposed to plan specific research for indications or groups of patients during the development of an active agent for which costs are currently not affordable during the data protection period. An approach such as the European regulation for medicines against rare disorders was successful and led to many accepted applications. Whether drug therapy can be improved and to what extent will have to be assessed after introduction of these regulations. Foreign experience in countries that have already provided incentives should also be assembled and assessed regarding their impact for Germany. A further method will be to review to what extent common off-label, unlicensed and compassionate uses are in accordance with the current state of scientific knowledge and are based on trial data.

In Germany, the Department for Health started a group of experts in 2002 with the function of assessing which cases of medicines for treatment of severe disease may be applied, with these medicines not being approved under the drug act for that disease. Based on these results, off label or unlicensed use should be reimbursed, permitted and encouraged, and a marketing authorization supported. For supplying quality medicines, the following question is also relevant: 'To what extent does off-label, compassionate, and unlicensed use endanger patients because they are denied effective therapies, and to what extent does danger patients because unexpected adverse reactions occur?' Studies are evaluating the quality of pharmacotherapy on an off-label, unlicensed or compassionate use basis, especially investigating to what extent therapeutic decisions are based on scientific findings and whether therapeutic results justifying use are rare.

[xxx] Enterprise Directorate-General, "Better Medicines for Children - Proposed regulatory actions on Paediatric medicinal products," press statement, February 28, 2002; available from http://ec.europa.eu/enterprise/pharmaceuticals/pharmacos/docs/doc2002/feb/cd_pediatrics_en.pdf; Internet, accessed February 17, 2009.

[xxxi] FDA. "Best Pharmaceutical for Children Act." 115 Stat 1408; available from FDA Best Pharmaceutical for Children Act, PubLNo. 107-109, 115 Stat 1408 (2002); Internet, accessed February 17, 2009.

[xxxii] European Medicines Agency. "Status Report on the Implementation of the European Parliament and Council Regulation on Orphan Medicinal Products: EMEA/7381/01." 08.04.2002.

[xxxiii] Commission of the European Communities. "Proposal for a Regulation of the European Parliament and of the Council on medicinal products for paediatric use and amending Regulation (EEC) No 1768/92, Directive 2001/83/EC and Regulation (EC) No 726/2004: Final Proposal." (COM (2004) 599); available from http://eur-lex.europa.eu/LexUriServ/LexUriServ.do?uri=COM:2004:0599:FIN:EN:PDF; Internet, accessed February 17, 2009.

Off-label, unlicensed and compassionate uses do not generally affect the quality of a pharmacotherapy supply. In individual cases there may well be medical reasons justifying a departure from use in accordance with the marketing authorization. A physician might even be obliged to prescribe off label or unlicensed (as in the acyclovir case) and may be liable for failing to render assistance.[xxxiv]

A Canadian study on the use of immunoglobulins found rates of 53% off label use in adults and 38% in children, but analysis showed that a rate of 89% use was justified.[xxxv]

The question of whether adverse drug reactions occur more often has not been answered. Turner et al. and Horen et al. recorded an increase in adverse reactions. Choonara et al. could not confirm this effect in their review.[xxxvi] [xxxvii] [xxxviii]

The quality of pharmacotherapy is not limited to its efficacy and safety, but also includes financial security in the case of aftermath of harm from medicines, such as that which the German drug act grants under § 84. However, this security is limited to when the drug is used conventionally. In such cases liability may pass to the physician. This situation may burden the patient with his claims under private law against the physician.[xxxix]

The patient must be informed that he is meant to be treated outside the approved indication, that this use is not conventional use and that the pharmaceutical company is not liable for possible harm (but instead the physician is). He must be informed on what basis of which scientific experience the physician chooses the treatment and of the risks existing for him.

The extent to which these requirements are fulfilled abroad is unknown.

III. Organizational implementation of the project

The Ministry for Heath and Social Security (Bundesministerium für Gesundheit und Soziale Sicherheit, BMGS) granted Prof. Dr. Harald Schweim, Department for Drug Regulatory Affairs, University of Bonn funds for three years. The furnishing of an opinion and the laying out of a library on off-label, unlicensed and compassionate use, especially the comparative study of off-label, compassionate, and unlicensed use in selected industrial countries (member states of the E.U. and the International Conference on Harmonization of principles, ICH) are required by the contract. The assessment especially

---

[xxxiv] Higher Regional Court Cologne 27 U 169/89. May 30, 1990.

[xxxv] Hanna, K. et al. "Intravenous immune globulin use in Canada." *The Canadian journal of clinical pharmacology* 10, no. 1 (2003): 11–16.

[xxxvi] Turner, S. et al. "Adverse drug reactions to unlicensed and off-label drugs on paediatric wards: a prospective study." *Acta Paediatrica* 88, no. 9 (1999): 965–68.

[xxxvii] Horen, B. et al. "Adverse drug reactions and off-label drug use in paediatric outpatients." *British journal of clinical pharmacology* 54, no. 6 (2002): 665–70.

[xxxviii] Choonara, I., and S. Conroy. "Unlicensed and Off-Label Drug Use in Children: Implications for Safety." *Drug Safety* 25, no. 1 (2002): 1–5.

[xxxix] Kloesel, A., and Cyran W. *Arzneimittelrecht. Kommentar: Kommentar zu § 5 AMG Absatz 2 Nr. 20 „Medizinische Wissenschaft".* Edited by Deutscher Apotheker Verlag. Stuttgart: DAV.

considers the different groups in society such as children and people suffering from rare diseases.

The following tasks will have to be performed:

In the first and second years of the project:

- Review the literature concerning methodological papers and studies on off-label, unlicensed and compassionate use
- Request used methods in studies of scientific institutions
- Analyze the offer of information
- Search for information concerning organizational and institutional methods of resolution in the field of off-label, unlicensed and compassionate use.
- Requests to scientific institutions concerning their methods of resolution
- Analyze, compare and document regulations or constitutions under drug and social law in the named countries with reference to the reimbursement of unapproved medicines in addition to the research and analysis of studies on the consequences for medical service
- Research the demand and/or consumption of unapproved medicines in the named countries and a comparative presentation of the facts
- Research the consequences of off-label, unlicensed and compassionate on drug safety
- Analyze the information/data acquired
- Issue an opinion and a document of all information

In the third year:

- Issue a recommendation for action as part of the opinion on off-label, compassionate, and unlicensed use in Germany and taking into account means available

(From 2008 under reserve of examination in 2007):

- Support decision-making unit in the development of finances of off-label, compassionate, and unlicensed use and taking into account means available

Contact:

Vanessa Plate

Rhein. Friedr.-Wilh.-Univ. Bonn
Pharm. Institut
Drug Regulatory Affairs
c/o IZMB
Raum 106b
Kirschallee 1

53115 Bonn

Tel: +49 (0)228 736726

Fax: +49 (0)228 739414

dra@uni-bonn.de
www.dra.uni-bonn.de

CONFIDENTIALITY NOTICE

The content of this description is confidential to the ordinary receiver to which it was given and may also be privileged. If you are not the addressee you may not copy, forward, disclose or otherwise use it or any part of it in any form whatsoever. If you have received this document in error please inform the author of this document.

Expert interview TOPIC GUIDE within the report

"Comparative study of off-label, unlicensed and compassionate drug use in selected industrial countries"

Questions refer to medicinal products for humans. The opinion of the respondent or his/her deputy is centered in the interview.

__Questions:__

1. Determination of terms

a. What is understood by off label use in [country]?

b. What is meant by compassionate use in [country]?

c. Please, define the meaning of unlicensed use in [country] for me.

2. Reasons for off-label, compassionate- and unlicensed use

a. Which considerable reasons may be responsible for off-label, compassionate- and unlicensed use in [country]?

b. What provisions affect off-label, compassionate- and unlicensed use in [country]?

3. Functional implementation

a. What influences the feasibility of off-label, compassionate- and unlicensed use in [country]?

b. What improvements regarding a more efficient use of off-label, compassionate- and unlicensed use do you know?

4. Relevance

a. To what degree is using drugs off-label, compassionate or unlicensed a relevant problem in

- medical science,
- ethics,
- liability law,
- social justice and/or
- insurance industry

E.g., in quantity or drug safety in [country]?

b. Which problems of off-label, compassionate or unlicensed use do you face in your field of work in [country]?

5. Necessity

To what extent is off-label, compassionate- and unlicensed use necessary in order to secure health care provision in [country]?

6. Adequacy

Are off-label, compassionate- and unlicensed use medically, ethically, concerning liability and social law adequate in their current practiced form in [country]? Please give reasons for your opinion.

7. Regulation

Are there any laws which affect off-label, compassionate- and unlicensed use in [country] or should there be? Please outline in detail.

8. Liability policies

Are product liability and liability for medical malpractice in [country] satisfactorily regulated for

- Patients, family members or parents,
- Authorities,

- Health care providers,
- insurance suppliers,
- Pharmaceutical industry or
- Others?

Please give reasons for your opinion.

9. Scientific analysis

a. In which way is scientific analysis of knowledge gained when using medicines off-label, compassionate- and unlicensed in [country] guaranteed?

b. Would you support a national database which was supplied with off-label, compassionate- and unlicensed use case reports from health care providers? Explain why.

10. Pharmacovigilance

To which extent are concerns of Pharmacovigilance being met sufficiently in [country]?

11. Scientific information/training

To what extent is off-label, compassionate- and unlicensed use affected by laws and rules controlling scientific information/training in [country]?

Comments:

The following questions refer to public and private health insurance.

12. Ruling

Is using drugs off-label, compassionate- and unlicensed well-regulated in [country] social and insurance law? Please give reasons for your opinion.

13. Transparency of law

Is law in [country] apparent for:

- Patients, family members, parents,
- Authorities,
- Health care providers,
- Insurance companies,
- Pharmaceutical industry or
- Others? Please give reasons for your opinion.

14. Reality of health care provision

Do social law and insurance law respectively influence the quality of health care provision in [country]? Please give reasons for your opinion.

15. References

Which Preambles, documents on the discussions on laws, commentary on laws, commentary on the medicines act /social law, official reasons, directory of decisions or further contact persons in [country] can you recommend us?

Drug Regulatory Affairs

Rheinische Friedrich-Wilhelms-Universität Bonn

Vanessa Plate
Pharmazeutisches Institut
Drug Regulatory Affairs
c/o IZMB, Raum 106b
Kirschallee 1
53115 Bonn

Tel: 0228/73-67 26
Fax: 0228/73-94 14
Cell: 0170/1548-373

dra@uni-bonn.de
www.dra.uni-bonn.de

An
[Adresse einfügen]

Dear Madam or Sir,

The research group "Drug Regulatory Affairs" of the Department of Pharmacy at the Rhein. Friedr.-Wilh.-University of Bonn is currently preparing a report for the German Ministry of Health addressing pharmaceutical and social law in European and industrial countries regulating off-label, compassionate, and unlicensed use of medications. Please find the project description attached.

Selected informational publications and literature on the subject of off-label, compassionate, and unlicensed use of medicinal products identifies you as an expert in this discipline.

We would like to interview you on the topics off-label, compassionate, and unlicensed use emphasizing pharmaceutical and social law. Please find the interview topic guide attached to this message.

We are looking forward to meeting you between 1st of December and 15th of December if you agree to share your points of view and experience.

Yours sincerely,

Vanessa Plate

Attachments:

1. Project description
2. Questionnaire

Expertenrating

Gutachter: ______________________________

Berufsbezeichnung: ______________________________

Tätigkeitsfeld: ______________________________

Einstufung der Inhaltsvalidität des teilstandardisierten Interviewleitfadens für eine Expertenbefragung im Rahmen des Gutachten „Vergleichende Untersuchung des Off-Label, unlicensed und Compassionateuse in ausgewählten Industriestaaten":

- **Hoch**
- **Befriedigend**
- **Niedrig** (Bitte um Angabe hinsichtlich der Verbesserung des Interviews)

Plausibilitätsüberlegungen:

____

____

____

____

____

____

____

Ort, Datum Unterschrift

______________________ ________________

Bibliography

*All Sentences were retrieved from Juris – Rechtsinformationen.

---

[1] Higgins, LC. et al "Off-label Rx. Insurers starting to balk." *Med World News,* 29 (20), October 24, 1988, 22-4; 26; 31-2.
[2] Van der Ven, K. "Die Pille wird 50. Entwicklung der oralen Kontrazeption und heutige Indikation." AEKNO. Uni Club Bonn, February 04, 2009.
[3] Flannery, EJ. et al "Should it be easier or harder to use unapproved drugs and devices?". *Hastings Center Report, The* 16, no. 1 (1986): 17–23.
[4] Franklin, W. and Lowell, FC. "Sounding board. Unapproved drugs in the practice of medicine." *The NEJM* 292, no. 20 (1975): 1075–77.
[5] Bücheler, R. et al "Off label prescribing to children in primary care in Germany: retrospective cohort study." *BMJ* 324, no. 7349 (2002): 1311.
[6] Schütz, H. et al "Verwendung von Misoprostol in der Geburtshilfe–Eine bundesweite Erhebung." *Geburtshilfe und Frauenheilkunde* 67, no. 5 (2007): 541.
[7] Conroy, S. et al. "Survey of unlicensed and off label drug use in paediatric wards in European countries." *BMJ* 320, no. 7227 (2000): 79–82.
[8] Plate, V. et al. "Vergleichende Untersuchung des Off-Label-Use, Unlicensed-Use und Compassionate-Use in ausgewaehlten Industriestaaten: Endbericht zum Forschungsprojekt." (Analyse). Bonn, December 31, 2008.
[9] Krüßen, H. et al. "Arzneimittelimporte gemaeß § 73 Abs. 3- Was, wie viel und mit welchen Konsequenzen?". *DAZ* 145, no. 29 (2005): 54.
[10] Deutscher Bundestag. *Antwort der Bundesregierung auf die Kleine Anfrage der Abgeordneten.* (Drucksache),14/9274. Bundesregierung, June 24, 2002.
[11] Anonymus. "Arzneimittelzulassung und Therapiefreiheit: Anmerkungen des wissenschaftlichen Arbeitskreises der DGAI zum nichtbestimmungsgemaeßen Gebrauch zugelassener Medikamente in der Anaesthesie." Deutsche Gesellschaft zum Studium des Schmerzes e.V., 03.2001; available from http://www.kinderschmerz.org/?action=download&id=5; Internet, accessed February 12, 2009.
[12] Assion, HJ. et al "Off-label prescribing in a german psychiatric hospital." *Pharmacopsychiatry,* 40, no. 1 (2007): 30–36.
[13] Lauktien, G. "BtM-Rezeptausgabe, -auswertung und Substitutionsregister: Auswertung von BtM-Rezepten (Beispiel-Methylphenidat)." BfArM. Bonn: BfArM, May 28, 2003; available from http://www.bfarm.de/nn_1232318/SharedDocs/Publikationen/DE/BfArM/publ/praesent/dialog__2001-2005/dialog-030528/lauktien,templateId=raw,property=publicationFile.pdf/lauktien.pdf; Internet; accessed February 13, 2009.
[14] Blasius, H. et al "Die arzneimittel- und sozialrechtliche Stellung des Off-Label-Use, Unlicensed-Use und Compassionate-Use in Frankreich." Bonn, 07.2008.
[15] European Medicines Agency. "Guideline on Compassionate Use of Medicinal Products, pursuant to Article 83 of Regulation (EC) No. 726/2004." (2007): 1–8. EUR-Lex Official Journal; available from www.emea.europa.eu/pdfs/human/euleg/2717006enfin.pdf; Internet, accessed February 12, 2009.
[16] da Rocha Dias, S. Public register of CHMP opinions on products for compassionate use in the EU. E-Mail to V. Plate. London. September 11, 2008.
[17] Blasius, H. et al "Off-Label-, Unlicensed- und Compassionate-Use in der europaeischen Regelungen und den Festlegungen der ICH unter besonderer Berücksichtigung der arzneimittel- und sozialrechtlichen Regelungen." Remagen, 03.2008. (Projektbericht)
[18] "European Medicines Agency consulting on a draft guideline on pharmacovigilance for medicines used in children," press statement, August 12, 2005; available from http://www.emea.europa.eu/pdfs/human/press/pr/26213505en.pdf; Internet, accessed February 12, 2009.
[19] Jōhōblog, "Unapproved anticancers in Japan: latest progress," press statement, July 29, 2005; available from http://jouhoublog.jouhoukoukai.com/?m=200507; Internet, accessed 10.2008.
[20] Wilton, LV. et al. "The use of newly marketed drugs in children and adolescents prescribed in general practice." *Pharmacoepidemiology and Drug Safety* 8, no. S1 (1999): S37-S45.
[21] Wilton, LV and Shakir, SA. "A Post-Marketing Surveillance Study of Formoterol (Foradil(R)): Its Use in General Practice in England." *Drug Safety* 25, no. 3 (2002): 213–23.

[22] Robinson, A. Notifications for named patient prescriptions to MHRA in the U.K. for 2002 till now. E-Mail to V. Plate. London. January 25, 2008.
[23] Conroy, S. et al "Unlicensed and off label drug use in acute lymphoblastic leukaemia and other malignancies in children." *Annals of Oncology* 14, no. 1 (2003): 42.
[24] See endnote 7
[25] See endnote 14
[26] See endnote 8
[27] Thouvenel, C. et al. "Autorisation de mise sur le marché et information pédiatrique pour les médicaments de chimiothérapie des cancers: état des lieux et propositions." *Archives de pédiatrie*, no. 7 (2002): 685–93.
[28] Autret-Leca, E. et al. "Particularité de l'évaluation des médicaments en pédiatrie et son application à la prescription en pédiatrie." *Paediatrica*, no. 7 (2002): 685–93.
[29] Autret-Leca, E. and Jonville-Béra, AP. "Besoin d'essais cliniques chez l'Enfant et aspects éthiques." SFP-Congrès. Cassis, 10.2003; available from http://www.sftox.com/congres/sft2003/posters/Elisabeth_Autret.pdf; Internet; accessed February 13, 2009.
[30] Sommelet, D. et al "L'enfant et l'adolescent: un enjeu de société, une priorité du système de santé." *Archives de pédiatrie* 14, no. 8 (2007): 1011.
[31] Erickson, SH. et al "The use of drugs for unlabeled indications." *JAMA* 243, no. 15 (1980): 1543.
[32] Thompson, DF. and Heflin, NR. "Frequency and appropriateness of drug prescribing for unlabeled uses in pediatric patients." *Am J Health Syst Pharm*, no. 44 (1987): 792–94.
[33] Rayburn, WF. and Turnbull, GL. "Off-label drug prescribing on a state university obstetric service." *Journal of reproductive medicine*, no. 40 (1995): 186–88.
[34] Radley, D. C. et al. "Off-label Prescribing Among Office-Based Physicians." *Archives of internal medicine* 166, no. 9 (2006): 1021.
[35] Behles, C. et al. "Die arzneimittel- und sozialrechtliche Stellung des Off-Label-, Unlicensed-Use und Compassionate-Use in den USA." Bonn, 07.2006.
[36] U.S. General Accounting Office Washington, D. C. *Off-label drugs: reimbursement policies constrain physicians in their choice of cancer therapies.* GAO/PEMD-91-14 (report), 1991.
[37] Cote, C. J. et al. "Is the 'therapeutic orphan' about to be adopted?". *Pediatrics* 98, no. 1 (1996): 118.
[38] Committee on Drugs. "Unapproved Uses of Approved Drugs: The Physician, the Package Insert, and the Food and Drug Administration: Subject Review." In vol. 98. American Academy of Pediatrics, 1996. *Pediatrics:* 143–45.
[39] Convington & Burling. *Proposed Rules Regarding Requirements for Expanded Access to Investigational Drugs and Charging for Investigational Drugs* 17.03.2009, March 17, 2009; available from http://209.85.129.132/search?q=cache:rquSAj054FYJ:www.linexlegal.com/content.php%3Fcontent_id%3D40607+%22Emergency+INDs+per+year%22&cd=2&hl=en&ct=clnk&gl=uk; Internet.
[40] See endnote 8
[41] Health Canada. *Special Access Programme Issue Identification Paper* Health Canada, 2007, May 06, 2009; available from http://www.hc-sc.gc.ca/dhp-mps/acces/sap_pas_ident-eng.php; Internet.
[42] Weiss, E. et al. "Off-Label Use of Antipsychotic Drugs." *Journal of clinical psychopharmacology* 20, no. 6 (2000): 695.
[43] Kurz, R. et al. *Ethik in der paediatrischen Forschung: Grundsatzpapier der Ethik-Arbeitsgruppe der Österreichischen Gesellschaft für Kinder- und Jugendheilkunde* 2001; available from http://www.meduni-graz.at/ethikkommission/Forum/Download/Files/Paediatr.pdf; Internet; accessed February 13, 2009.
[44] Müllner, M. et al. "AGES Österreichische Agentur für Gesundheit and Ernaehrungsischerheit GmbH: Health. Nutrition, Safety. Our concern." AGES: AGES, May 15, 2007; available from http://www.ages.at/uploads/media/MA1_4llner_WS_Industrie_150507.pdf; Internet; accessed May 06, 2009.
[45] Ibid.
[46] "Geschaeftsbericht 2002." Bern: Schweizerisches Heilmittelinstitut, 2002; available from http://www.swissmedic.ch/org/00064/00066/00323/index.html?lan; Internet, accessed May 06, 2009.
[47] Scheurer, G. et al. "Arzneimittelsicherheit in der Paediatrie." Diplomarbeit, Universitaet Basel, Basel, 2003.

[48] Blöchliger, M. et al. "Arzneimittelsicherheit in der Paediatrie." Diplomarbeit, Universitaet Basel, Bern, 2005.
[49] Schirm, E. et al. "Unlicensed and off label drug use by children in the community: cross sectional study." *BMJ* 324, no. 7349 (2002): 1312.
[50] Schirm, E. et al. "Risk Factors for Unlicensed and Off-Label Drug Use in Children Outside the Hospital." *Pediatrics* 111, no. 2 (2003): 291.
[51] O'Donnell, CPF. et al. "Unlicensed and Off-Label Drug Use in an Australian Neonatal Intensive Care Unit." *Pediatrics* 110, no. 5 (2002).
[52] See endnote 8
[53] Mays, N., and Pope, C. "Assessing quality in qualitative research." *BMJ* 320, no. 7226 (2000): 50.
[54] Walji, R. et al. "Herbal product related adverse events- Pharmacies vs. health food stores." In vol. 30. ISoP, October 21, 2007. *Drug Safety:* 948.
[55] Teng, L. et al. "Views and behaviours towards effectiveness and safety of chinese herbal meidicne (CHM) – Qualitative interviews with CHM shop employees in London." In vol. 30. ISoP, October 21, 2007. *Drug Safety:* 937.
[56] Knight, C., and Wilkinson, J. "Independent Safety Evaluation for all Newly licensed Medicines – an in-depth study of expert opinion within industry and society." In vol. 30. ISoP, October 21, 2007. *Drug Safety:* 935.
[57] Oosterhuis, I. et al. "Lareb intensive monitoring – an interim analysis." In vol. 30. ISoP, October 21, 2007. *Drug Safety:* 960.
[58] Bennett, A. et al. "The Agenda: The development of qualitative methods." *Qualitative methods* 1, no. 1 (2003): 14.
[59] Chi, MTH. "Quantifying Qualitative Analysis of Verbal Data: A Practical Guide." *The journal of the learning sciences* 6, no. 3 (1997): 271.
[60] Hernandez, M. and Davis, C. "Review Team Leader Training Manual." University of South Florida, 02.2004; available from http://rtckids.fmhi.usf.edu/rtcpubs/SOCPR/ReviewTeamLeader.pdf; Internet, accessed February 13, 2009.
[61] de Ruyter, K. and Scholl, N. "Positioning qualitative market research: reflections from theory and practice." *Qualitative market research* 1, no. 1 (1998): 7.
[62] Lorenzen, M. et al. "The land of confusion? High school students and their use of the World Wide Web for research." *Research strategies* 18, no. 2 (2001): 151.
[63] Mlcakova, A. and Whitley, EA. "Configuring peer-to-peer software: an empirical study of how users react to the regulatory features of software." *European Journal of Information Systems* 13, no. 2 (2004): 95.
[64] Hay, I. et al. *Qualitative research methods in human geography.* 2. ed. South Melbourne, Vic.: Oxford Univ. Press, 2005.
[65] Robert Wood Johnson Foundation. *Semi-structured Interviews* Robert Wood Johnson Foundation; available from http://www.qualres.org/HomeSemi-3629.html; Internet; accessed February 13, 2009.
[66] University of the West of England. *Research Observatory* University of the West of England; available from http://ro.uwe.ac.uk/RenderPages/RenderLearningObject.aspx?Context=7&Area=1&Room=3&Constellation=25&LearningObject=113; Internet; accessed February 13, 2009.
[67] Sturges, JE. and Hanrahan, KJ. "Comparing telephone and face-to-face qualitative interviewing-a research note." *Qualitative Research* 4, no. I (2004): 107–18.
[68] Bauer, MW. and Gaskell, G. "Qualitative Researching with Text, Image and Sound." *SAGE* (2000): 38–57.
[69] Guest, G. et al. "How Many Interviews Are Enough?: An Experiment with Data Saturation and Variability." *Field methods* 18, no. 1 (2006): 59.
[70] Ibid.
[71] Chew-Graham, CA. et al. "Qualitative research and the problem of judgement: lessons from interviewing fellow professionals." *Family Practice* 19, no. 3 (2002): 285.
[72] Silverman, M. et al. "Strategies for Increasing the Rigor of Qualitative Methods in Evaluation of Health Care Programs." *Evaluation review* 14, no. 1 (1990): 57.
[73] Hopf, G. et al. "Bevacizumab-Ranibizumab." In *Hess. AErztebl.,* vol. 2 (2008), 227.
[74] See endnote 72
[75] Miller, PR. et al. "Inpatient diagnostic assessments: 1. Accuracy of structured vs. unstructured interviews." *Psychiatry Research* 105, no. 3 (2001): 255.

[76] See endnote 65
[77] Webb, C. et al. "Feminist research: definitions, methodology, methods and evaluation." *Journal of advanced nursing* 18, no. 3 (1993): 416.
[78] Hsieh, HF. et al. "Three Approaches to Qualitative Content Analysis." *Qualitative health research* 15, no. 9 (2005): 1277.
[79] Whittemore, R. et al. "Validity in Qualitative Research." *Qualitative health research* 11, no. 4 (2001): 522.
[80] Stiles, WB. et al. "Quality control in qualitative research." *Clinical Psychology Review* 13, no. 6 (1993): 593.
[81] Onwuegbuzie, AJ. and Daniel, GD. *Typology of Analytical and Interpretational Errors in Quantitative and Qualitative Educational Research* 2003, February 16, 2009; available from http://cie.asu.edu/volume6/number2/; Internet.
[82] Madill, A. et al. "Objectivity and reliability in qualitative analysis: Realist, contextualist and radical constructionist epistemologies." *British Journal of Psychology* 91, no. 1 (2000): 1.
[83] Neubert, A. et al. "The impact of unlicensed and off-label drug use on adverse drug reactions in paediatric patients." *Drug Safety* 27, no. 13 (2004): 1059–67.
[84] Ruiz-Casado, A. et al. "Ecteinascidin in heavily pretreated advanced sarcoma patients as a compassionate basis." In vol. 21, 2002: (abstr 1631); available from http://www.asco.org/portal/site/ASCO/menuitem.34d60f5624ba07fd506fe310ee37a01d/?abstractID=1631&confID=16&index=y&vmview=abst_detail_view; Internet, accessed February 12, 2009.
[85] See endnote 5
[86] Perucca, E. et al. "Should widespread compassionate use before registration be allowed? A contrary view." In vol. 1995: 217; available from http://www3.interscience.wiley.com/cgi-bin/fulltext/119235258/PDFSTART; Internet, accessed February 12, 2009.
[87] Schweim, HG. "Projektantrag „Vergleichende Untersuchung des Off-label-, Unlicensed- und Compassionate-use in ausgewaehlten Industriestaaten"." Bonn: Rheinische Friedrich-Wilhelms-Universitaet, 12.12.04.
[88] Choonara, I. and Conroy, S. "Unlicensed and Off-Label Drug Use in Children: Implications for Safety." *Drug Safety* 25, no. 1 (2002): 1–5.
[89] Schroeder-Printzen, J. and Tadayon, A. "Die Zulaessigkeit des Off-label use nach der Entscheidung des BSG vom 19.3.2002." *Sgb*, no. 12 (2002): 664.
[90] "Food and Drug Act: FD&C Act." In *21 U.S.C. 321,* Section 201. Amended Through December 31, 2004
[91] Storz, G. *VFA-Positionspapier: Zulassungsüberschreitender Einsatz von Medikamenten bei schweren Erkrankungen* VfA, 2009, April 02, 2009; available from http://www.vfa.de/download/SHOW/de/presse/positionen/offlabeluse.html/offlabeluse.pdf; Internet; accessed May 06, 2009.
[92] Dierks, C. et al. "Gesetzliche Rahmenbedingungen und die Leistungsgrenzen der GKV für die Arzneimitteltherapie." In *Glaeske, G. and Dierks, C. "Off-Label-Use Weichenstellung nach dem BSG Urteil 2002""*, 56.
[93] Franken, A. "Zwischen Haftung und Mitverantwortung: Wo liegt die Bestimmung eines Arzneimittels?". *Arzneimittel&Recht*, no. 4 (2006): 156–58.
[94] Anynomus. *Themen- Arzneimittelinformation: Bewertung aus der Praxis für die Praxis* ABDA, 02.08.2007, August 02, 2007; available from http://www.abda.de/810.html; Internet
[95] Kraemer, M. *BPI-Positionspapier Orphan Drugs: Compassionate use, wirtschaftliche Anreize, Erstattungsfaehigkeit* Berlin, Heidelberg: BPI, 2005, October 21, 2004; available from http://www.bpi.de/UserFiles/File/bpi/publikationen/BPI-OrphanDrugs.pdf; Internet; accessed May 06, 2009.
[96] Nies, P. *Gemeinsamer Bundesausschuss - Fragen und Antworten zum "Off-Label-Use"* G-BA, 01.04.2009, April 01, 2009; available from http://www.g-ba.de/institution/sys/faq/78/; Internet; accessed May 06, 2009.
[97] BfArM. *BfArM Off-Label (Expertengruppen): Die Expertengruppen Off-Label - Anwendung von Arzneimitteln außerhalb des zugelassenen Indikationsbereichs* BfArM, 2006, May 01, 2009; available from http://www.bfarm.de/nn_424278/DE/Arzneimittel/3__nachDerZulassung/offLabel/offlabel-node.html__nnn=true; Internet; accessed May 06, 2009.
[98] Stöcker, S. and Ruhaltinger, D. *Optimale Anwendung intravenöser Immunglobuline: Internationale Konferenz am Paul-Ehrlich-Institut in Langen* PEI, 2001; available from

http://www.pei.de/cln_048/nn_154580/sid_D993ED83BA58C4CCD8D3F53025627DDA/DE/infos/presse/pm/2001/16.html?__nnn=true; Internet; accessed August 02, 2007.
[99] See endnote 88
[100] Higher social court Berlin L 15 B 34/02 KR ER. September 11, 2002.*
[101] Appleby, J. et al. *'Off-label' drugs denied to patients in Medicare D* USA Today, 2007, August 02, 2007; available from http://www.usatoday.com/money/industries/health/2007-08-01-medicare-drugs_N.htm; Internet; accessed May 06, 2009.
[102] Sanmaier, C. et al. *Langzyklus: Verhütung ohne Pause* PZ, 2005; available from http://www.pharmazeutische-zeitung.de/fileadmin/pza/2005-13/pharm2.htm; Internet; accessed August 02, 2007.
[103] Hoffmeister, C. et al. *Off-Label-Use* Landessozialgericht München; available from http://www.sanofi-aventis.de/live/de/de/layout.jsp?cnt=C70E505C-53EA-4B55-8772-93C680D46276; Internet; accessed May 06, 2009.
[104] Seyberth, JH. "Mehr Arzneimittelsicherheit für Kinder." *Dtsch Arztebl* 96 (1999): 547–50.
[105] See endnote 7
[106] Fritze, J. and Schmauß, M. "Off-Label-Use in der Psychopharmakotherapie." *Psychoneuro* 28, no. 8 (2002): 431–39.
[107] Bavarian Higher social court L 12 KA 107/03. March 02, 2005.*
[108] Higher social court Berlin L 15 B 43/02 KR ER. September 11, 2002.*
[109] Higher social court Berlin L 9 KR 70/00. April 02, 2003.*
[110] Higher social court Hamburg L 1 KR 115/04. March 30, 2006.*
[111] Higher social court North Rhine-Westphalia L 5 KR 144/03. September 20, 2005.*
[112] Higher social court North Rhine-Westphalia L 5 KR 171/04. September 20, 2005.*
[113] Higher social court Saxony-Anhalt Az.: L 4 KR 114/04. April 25, 2006.*
[114] Federal social court B 1 KR 27/05 R. September 26, 2006.*
[115] Federal social court B 1 KR 15/06 R. September 26, 2006.*
[116] Federal social court B 1 KR 14/06 R. September 26, 2006.*
[117] Higher social court Saxony-Anhalt L 4 KR 36/99. December 10, 2002.*
[118] Higher social court Hamburg L 1 KR 46/03. July 14, 2004.*
[119] Higher social court Hamburg S 23 KR 871/02. April 14, 2003.*
[120] "Familienplanungs-Rundbrief." Pro familia, 11.2006; available from www.profamilia.de; Internet.
[121] BVHK. *Aus der Rechtsprechung 2005* BVHK; available from http://www.bvhk.de/dokument_8.33.583.html; Internet; accessed May 21, 2008.
[122] Bücheler, R. et al. "„Off-label “Verschreibung von Arzneimitteln in der ambulanten Versorgung von Kindern und Jugendlichen." *Deutsche medizinische Wochenschrift* 127, no. 48 (2002): 2551.
[123] Knöppel, C. et al. "Anwendung von Medikamenten außerhalb der Zulassung oder ohne Zulassung bei Kindern." *Monatsschrift Kinderheilkunde* 148, no. 10 (2000): 904–08.
[124] "Beschluss des Gemeinsamen Bundesausschusses zur Erteilung von Auftraegen zur Erstellung von Bewertungen an die Expertengruppen Off-Label nach § 1 Abs. 3 des Erlasses über die Einrichtung von Expertengruppen Off-Label nach § 35b Abs. 3 SGB V." In February 21, 2006; available from www.g-ba.de; Internet.
[125] Rabe, T., and Brucker, C. *Gemeinsame Stellungnahme der Deutschen Gesellschaft für Gynaekologische Endokrinologie undFortpflanzungsmedizin e.V. (DGGEFe.V.) in Zusammenarbeit mit demBerufsverband der Frauenaerzte e.V.:Empfaengnisverhütung -Familienplanung in Deutschland* 2004; available from http://www.kup.at/kup/pdf/4698.pdf; Internet; accessed December 13, 2009.
[126] Horen, B. et al. "Adverse drug reactions and off-label drug use in paediatric outpatients." *British journal of clinical pharmacology* 54, no. 6 (2002): 665.
[127] Zylka-Menhorn, V. "Bayer/Lipobay: Ringen um die Arzneimittelsicherheit." *Dtsch Arztebl* 98, no. 33 (2001): 51–52.
[128] See endnote 13
[129] Kompetenzzentrum Verordnungs-Management. *Generika: Kostenbewusstsein ohne Qualitaetsverlust* Kassenaerztlichen Vereinigung Bayerns, 2005; available from www.kvb.de/servlet/PB/show/1005741/Arzneimittel-im-Fokus-Generika-1.05.pdf; Internet; accessed February 14, 2009.
[130] Anonymus. *Zaepfchen* Hexal; available from http://www.hexal.de/subdomains/praeparate/arzneimittel-richtig-anwenden/zaepfchen/hinweise-tipps-zaepfchen.php; Internet; accessed December 13, 2009.

[131] Anonymus. "Fachinformation Proleukin®." Novartis Pharma, 03.2003; available from www.fachinfo.de; Internet, accessed December 13, 2008.
[132] Ibid.
[133] Bock, F. et al. "Antiangiogene Therapie am vorderen Augenabschnitt." *Ophthalmologe* 104, no. 4 (2007): 336–44.
[134] Shivas, T. et al. *Compassionate use of experimental drugs* 1999, January 21, 1999; available from http://bioethics.net/articles.php?viewCat=7&articleId=116; Internet; accessed May 06, 2009.
[135] Tolle, A., and Meyer-Sabellek, W. "Off-Label-Use." *Bundesgesundheitsblatt, Gesundheitsforschung, Gesundheitsschutz*, no. 6 (2003): 504–07, accessed May 06, 2009.
[136] Copeland, JG. et al. "Cardiac Replacement with a Total Artificial Heart as a Bridge to Transplantation." *The NEJM* 351, no. 9 (2004): 859–67, accessed May 06, 2009; available from http://journal.shouxi.net/qikan/article.php?id=209921; Internet.
[137] Neubert, A. et al. "Defining off-label and unlicensed use of medicines for children: Results of a Delphi survey." *Pharmacological research* 58, no. 5-6 (2008): 316–22, accessed May 06, 2009; available from http://www.sciencedirect.com/science?_ob=ArticleURL&_udi=B6WP9-4TG9HV6-1&_user=1848530&_rdoc=1&_fmt=&_orig=search&_sort=d&view=c&_acct=C000055082&_version=1&_urlVersion=0&_userid=1848530&md5=d10ca3cdbf9402f52ef6814d9a2eecaf; Internet.
[138] Jones, M. "Policy for Patient Group Directions (PGDs)." In . Harrogate and District NHS Foundation Trust, 04.2006: 1–23; available from http://www.hdft.nhs.uk/site-info/?asset=2082; Internet, accessed May 06, 2009.
[139] ABDA. *Umstrittene Rezepturen und Nischenarzneimittel* Eschborn, 2008, September 30, 2008; available from http://www.pharmazeutische-zeitung.de/fileadmin/nrf/PDF/1-Umstrittene-Rezepturen.pdf; Internet; accessed May 06, 2009.
[140] See endnote 332
[141] See endnote 88
[142] Turner, S. et al. "Adverse drug reactions to unlicensed and off-label drugs on paediatric wards: a prospective study." *Acta Paediatrica* 88, no. 9 (1999): 965–68.
[143] Conroy, S. et al. "Extemporaneous (magistral) preparation of oral medicines for children in European hospitals." *Acta Paediatrica* 92 (2003): 408–10.
[144] See endnote 332
[145] Nies, P. *Auswirkungen des Off-Label -, Unlicensed- & Compassionate-use auf das System der Arzneimittelzulassung sowie auf die Qualitaet der Arzneimitteltherapie und –versorgung* Bonn: Rheinische Friedrich-Wilhelms-Universitaet, 2006; available from http://home.arcor.de/schweim.privat/Nies.pdf; Internet; accessed February 13, 2009.
[146] Harvey, E. D. et al. "Early/Expanded Access Provisions for Unapproved/Investigational Medical Devices.": Food and Law Institute, April 08, 2005; available from http://www.fda.gov/cdrh/present/fdli-apr05-harvey/index_files/textonly/slide1.html; Internet; accessed May 05, 2009.
[147] Jassal, SS. et al. *Basic symptom control in paeditric palliative care- The rainbows children's hospice guidelines*; available from http://www.act.org.uk/dmdocuments/Microsoft_Word_-_2008_Symptom_Control_Manual.pdf; Internet; accessed February 13, 2009.
[148] Conroy, S. et al. "Unlicensed and off-label drug use: issues and recommendations." *Paediatric drugs* 4, no. 6 (2002): 353–59.
[149] Turner, S. et al. "Unlicensed and Off-label Drug Use in Australia." *Paediatric and perinatal drug therapy* 4, no. 1 (2000): 24.
[150] Kay, L. et al. "Pharmaproduce innovative products- patients can't access them." Autumn Symposium 2007 of the Guild of Healthcare pharmacists; available from www.ghp.org.uk/ContentFiles/ghppdig0711a.ppt; Internet; accessed February 13, 2009.
[151] Scottish Quality Assurance Specialist Interest Group. "Guidelines on unlicensed medicines ('specials')." (2001); available from www.astcp.scot.nhs.uk/QASIG/QASIG%20Specials/Specials.doc; Internet, accessed February 13, 2009.
[152] Cancer Network Pharmacists Forum & British Oncology Pharmacy Association. *Joint Position Statement on Access to Unlicensed Drugs Outside of Clinical Trials* Cancer Network Pharmacists Forum & British Oncology Pharmacy Association, 2006; available from www.bopawebsite.org/tiki-download_file.php?fileId=10; Internet; accessed December 13, 2009.
[153] Hill, R. and Box, J. *Unlicensed medicines policy* CNWL NHS Foundation Trust, 2008.
[154] Federal Constitutional Court BvR 1071/95. March 05, 1997.*
[155] Federal social court B 1 KR 19/96. July 23, 1998.*

[156] Blumer, JL. et al. "Off-Label Uses of Drugs in Children." *Pediatrics* 104, no. 3 (1999): 598–602.
[157] Hanna, K. et al. "Intravenous immune globulin use in Canada." *The Canadian journal of clinical pharmacology* 10, no. 1 (2003): 11–16.
[158] Parisse-Brassens, J. et al. *Survey: 4th Eurordis Survey on Orphan Drugs Availability in Europe (2007)* EurOrDis, 2007; available from http://www.eurordis.org/article.php3?id_article=1644; Internet; accessed February 14, 2009.
[159] Jensen, V. et al. *An Overview of the FDA's Drug Shortage Program* P&T, 03.2005; available from http://www.ptcommunity.com/ptjournal/fulltext/30/3/PTJ3003174.pdf; Internet; accessed February 14, 2009.
[160] O'day, M. et al. "Availability of Immune Globulin Intravenous for Treatment of Immune Deficient Patients -- United States, 1997-19." *MMWR* 48, no. 8 (1999): 159–62, accessed February 14, 2009; available from http://www.cdc.gov/mmwr/preview/mmwrhtml/00056604.htm; Internet.
[161] Hartnell, GG. and Gates, J. "The case of Abbokinase and the FDA: the events leading to the suspension of Abbokinase supplies in the United States." *J Vasc Interv Radiol* 11, no. 7 (2000): 841–47.
[162] Arrowsmith, JE. et al. "Shortage of isoproterenol (isoprenaline) hydrochloride." *British Journal of Anaesthesia* 89, no. 3 (2002): 528, accessed February 14, 2009; available from http://bja.oxfordjournals.org/cgi/content/full/89/3/528; Internet.
[163] Medicines and Healthcare products Regulatory Agency. *Global shortage of acetonitrile: Advice to the pharmaceutical industry on changes requiring variation submissions to update Marketing Authorisations* Internetdokument: Medicines and Healthcare products Regulatory Agency, 2009, January 26, 2009; available from http://www.mhra.gov.uk/Howweregulate/Medicines/Medicinesregulatorynews/CON036276; Internet; accessed February 25, 2009.
[164] t'Jong, GW. et al. "A Survey of the Use of Off-Label and Unlicensed Drugs in a Dutch Children's Hospital." *Pediatrics* 108, no. 5 (2001): 1089.
[165] Nahata, MC. et al. "Lack of Pediatric Drug Formulations." *Pediatrics* 104, no. 3 (1999): 607–09.
[166] Pientka, L. "Krebs + Alter = keine Hoffnung." Versorgungsforschung in der Onkologie. MEK-Forum (Gebaeude 42): Universitaetsklinik zu Köln, September 10, 2008.
[167] Wedding, U. and Höffken, K. ""Go go-slow go-no go"." *Der Onkologe* 8, no. 2 (2002): 111.
[168] See endnote 166
[169] Jacoby, A. "Deutschlands Gesundheitsbranche geht es blendend - noch: Pharma & Co." *Frankfurter Allgemeine Zeitung,* January 29, 2007; available from http://www.faz.net/s/RubB1763F30EEC64854802A79B116C9E00A/Doc~E35D75FD46FE5421BB014973EA1BF365C~ATpl~Ecommon~Scontent.html; Internet, accessed February 14, 2009.
[170] Plate, V. et al. "Reducing Off-Label use in paediatrics by improving drug information: Comparative study of approvals of children's medicines since 2001 and a database for approved children's medicines." In . DIA 19th Annual EuroMeeting. Wien, 2007. *Drug Information Journal:* P-273.
[171] Arbeitsgemeinschaft der Wissenschaftlichen Medizinischen Fachgesellschaften. *Leitlinie Sozialpaediatrie und Jugendmedizin:: Diagnostik und Therapie bei ADHS (Aufmerksamkeits-Defizit-Hyperaktivitaets- Störung)* 2001; available from http://www.helpster.de/groups/adhs/ADHS-Leitlinien.pdf; Internet; accessed February 16, 2009.
[172] Anonymus. *Das NRF im Kurzportraet* Pharmazeutische Zeitung online, 2009; available from http://www.pharmazeutische-zeitung.de/index.php?id=2266; Internet; accessed February 16, 2009.
[173] Nunn, AJ. et al. "Making medicines that children can take." *Archives of disease in childhood* 88, no. 5 (2003): 369.
[174] Brion, F. et al. "Extemporaneous (magistral) preparation of oral medicines for children in European hospitals." *Acta Paediatrica* 92, no. 4 (2003): 486–90.
[175] See endnote 292
[176] Feiden, K. and Pabel, HJ. Arzneimittelrecht (for Windows XP Professional). WVGmbH, Stuttgart.
[177] Zapf, T. "Standardzulassung." Swissmedic. Pharmacopoea Helvetica – Informationen und Visionen. Olten, Switzerland: Swissmedic, September 28, 2006; available from http://www.swissmedic.ch/bewilligungen/00487/00489/00491/index.html?lang=de&download=NHzLpZeg7t,lnp6I0NTU042l2Z6ln1acy4Zn4Z2qZpnO2Yuq2Z6gpJCDdH16fmym162epYbg2c_JjKbNoKSn6A--; Internet; accessed February 16, 2009.
[178] Medicines and Healthcare products Regulatory Agency. " Guidance Note 14 The supply of unlicensed relevant medicinal products for individual patients." available from http://www.mhra.gov.uk/home/idcplg?IdcService=GET_FILE&dDocName=CON007547&RevisionSelectionMethod=Latest accessed June 29, 2009

[179] The Department of Health. "Medicines management in NHS Trusts: hospital medicines management framework."; available from http://www.dh.gov.uk/en/Publicationsandstatistics/Publications/PublicationsPolicyAndGuidance/DH_4072184; Internet, accessed February 16, 2009.
[180]Greenwich NHS Teaching primary care trust. "Guidance for the use of unlicensed medicinal products and the use of medicines outside of their licensed indications." available from http://www.greenwichpct.nhs.uk/publications/file.aspx?int_version_id=2091, accessed June 29, 2009
[181] Morecambe Bay NHS Primary care trust. "Policy for Off-label use of medicines." available from www.mbht.nhs.uk, accessed June 29, 2009
[182] Pennine Care NHS trust. "The use of licensed medicines outside the conditions of their product license." available from http://www.penninecare.nhs.uk/documents/2293.pdf, accessed June 29, 2009
[183] Somerset Partneship NHS & Social Care Trust. "Policy for the use of unlicensed medicines." available from http://www.sompar.nhs.uk/pdf/Medicines%20Policy%20-%20Appendix%204%20Policy%20for%20the%20Use%20of%20Unlicensed%20Medicines.pdf, accessed June 29, 2009
[184] Pharmacy Services South West Yorkshire Mental Health Trust. "Request for the supply of a medicine for an unlicensed ("off label") indication." available from www.southwestyorkshire.nhs.uk/documents/326.pdf , accessed June 29, 2009
[185] The Dudley Group of hospital NHS trust. "Use of unlicensed medicines." (2003): 1–5; available from http://www.dudley.nhs.uk/sections/publications/documents/FOI24383864250.pdf; Internet, accessed February 16, 2009.
[186] See endnote 151
[187] Brighton and Hove City NHS Teaching Primary care trust. "Policy on prescribing and supply of unlicensed medicines or those used off-label." (2005): 1–11; available from http://www.brightonandhovepct.nhs.uk/healthprofessionals/clinical-areas/prescribing/documents/BHCPCTUnlicensedmedicinespolicy2006.pdf; Internet, accessed February 16, 2009.
[188] NHS Lothian. "Policy for the use of unlicensed (and off label use) medicines in NHS Lothian." (2004). available from http://www.ljf.scot.nhs.uk/resources/unlicensed_medicines_policy.pdf accessed June 29, 2009
[189] NHS Fife Board by Fife Area Drug and therapeutics committee. "Policy for the Use of Unlicensed (and Off-label use) Medicines." (2006). available from www.fifeadtc.scot.nhs.uk/Unlicensed%20medicines%20policy.doc, accessed June 29, 2009
[190] Medicines Management of the Liverpool women's NHS foundation trust. "Prescribing, Supply and use of unlicensed medicines." available from www.lwh.me.uk, accessed June 29, 2009
[191] Royal Pharmaceutical Society of Great Britain. "Records of Supplies of Unlicensed medicinal products." (11.2007): 1–2; available from http://www.rpsgb.org/pdfs/restoolsupplyunlic.pdf; Internet, accessed February 16, 2009.
[192] Royal Pharmaceutical Society of Great Britain. "The Use of Unlicensed Medicines in Pharmacy.": 1–9; available from http://www.rpsgb.org.uk/pdfs/factsheet5.pdf; Internet, accessed February 16, 2009.
[193] Central and North West London NHS Foundation trust. "Unlicensed Medicines Policy.": 1–11; available from http://www.cnwl.nhs.uk/uploads/Unlicensed_Medicines.pdf; Internet, accessed February 16, 2009.
[194] NHS Fife Board by Fife Area Drug and therapeutics committee. "Fife UMP database." In . NHS Fife Board by Fife Area Drug and therapeutics committee
[195] Townsend, P. et al. "Developing a database to manage use of unlicensed medicines." *Hospital Pharmacist* 13, no. 8 (2006): 299–300.
[196] Health Canada. "Guidance Document for Industry and Practitioners - Special Access Programme for Drugs." (2008); available from http://www.hc-sc.gc.ca/dhp-mps/acces/drugs-drogues/sapg3_pasg3-eng.php; Internet, accessed February 16, 2009.
[197] Health Canada. *Special Access Request Form A* 2008; available from http://www.hc-sc.gc.ca/dhp-mps/alt_formats/hpfb-dgpsa/pdf/acces/sapf1_pasf1-eng.pdf; Internet; accessed February 16, 2009.
[198] Health Canada. *Instructions for Completing the Application Form for Custom-Made Devices and Medical Devices for Special Access* 2007; available from http://www.hc-sc.gc.ca/dhp-mps/acces/md-im/sapmd_pasmd_inst_v2-eng.php; Internet; accessed February 16, 2009.

[199] Health Canada. *Special Access Programme - Drugs* 2002; available from http://www.hc-sc.gc.ca/dhp-mps/acces/drugs-drogues/sapfs_pasfd_2002-eng.php; Internet; accessed February 16, 2009.
[200] Ibid.
[201] Health Canada. *Single-Patient Access to Non-marketed Therapeutic Drugs* 2007; available from http://26448.vws.magma.ca/dhp-mps/homologation-licensing/docs/exception/exception02-eng.php; Internet; accessed February 16, 2009.
[202] BC Cancer Agency Systemic Therapy Update 10 (7); available from http://www.bccancer.bc.ca/HPI/stupdate.htm; Internet; accessed February 16, 2009.
[203] "Marketing Authorization Procedures (Canada): Temporary Use authorization (compassionate use/emergency use)." Thomson Reuters, 02.2007.
[204] Health Canada. *Health Canada's Special Access Programme (SAP) Instructions for Making a Special Access Future Use Request FORM B* 2008; available from http://www.coalition-nationale-714x.com/pas_formb_en.pdf; Internet; accessed February 16, 2009.
[205] Der Institutsrat des Schweizerischen Heilmittelinstituts. "Verordnung des Schweizerischen Heilmittelinstituts über die vereinfachte Zulassung von Arzneimitteln und die Zulassung von Arzneimitteln im Meldeverfahren." AS 2006 3623; available from http://www.admin.ch/ch/d/sr/8/812.212.23.de.pdf; Internet, accessed February 16, 2009.
[206] Swissmedic. *Erlaeuterungen zur Befristeten Zulassung von Arzneimitteln gegen lebensbedrohende Krankheiten* (Art. 18 – 22 VAZV)* 2007; available from http://www.swissmedic.ch/org/00064/00067/00331/00632/index.html?lang=en&download...JjKbNoK Sn6A; Internet; accessed February 16, 2009.
[207] Anonymus. *Erlaeuterungen zur Befristeten Zulassung von Arzneimitteln gegen lebensbedrohende Krankheiten* (Art. 18 – 22 VAZV)* Swissmedic, 2006; available from http://www.swissmedic.ch/org/00064/00065/00318/index.html?download=NHzLpZeg7t; Internet; accessed February 16, 2009.
(http://www.swissmedic.ch/files/pdf/09_2006.pdf October 2008
[208] Anonymus. "Humanarzneimittel."; available from http://www.swissmedic.ch/daten/00081/index.html?lang=de&download=NHzLpZeg7t,lnp6I0NTU042l2Z6ln1acy4Zn4Z2qZpnO2Yuq2Z6gpJCDdH55fGym162epYbg2c_JjKbNoKSn6A--; Internet, accessed February 16, 2009.
[209] Swissmedic. "Geschaeftsbericht." 2005; available from http://www.swissmedic.ch/org/00064/00066/00323/index.html?lang=de&download=NHzLpZeg7t,lnp6I0NTU042l2Z6ln1acy4Zn4Z2qZpnO2Yuq2Z6gpJCDdIF3f2ym162epYbg2c_JjKbNoKSn6A--; Internet, accessed February 19, 2009.
[210] "Regeln der Guten Herstellungspraxis in kleinen Mengen." In *Ph.Helv.*, vol. 10 available from http://www.swissmedic.ch/bewilligungen/00009/00082/index.html?lang=de&download=NHzLpZeg7t,lnp6I0NTU042l2Z6ln1acy4Zn4Z2qZpnO2Yuq2Z6gpJCDdH9_gGym162epYbg2c_JjKbNoKSn6A-- accessed June 29, 2009
[211] Swissmedic. "Sonderbewilligung für einen Einsatz im Einzelfall." In ; available from http://www.lamprene.com/uploads/media/swissmedic_form.pdf; Internet, accessed February 16, 2009
[212] Swissmedic. *Sonderbewilligung für Compassionate Use*; available from http://www.spitalpharmazie-basel.ch/dienstleistungen/pdf/Formular_Sonderbewilligungen_Compassionate%20Use.pdf; Internet.
[213] Czank, A. Swissmedic Swiss Agency for Therapeutic Products. Sonderbewilligung. E-Mail to Vanessa Plate. Bern. May 07, 2009.
[214] Gesellschaft Schweizer Amts- und Spitalapotheker (GSASA). Voraussetzungen für die Zusammenarbeit unter Spitalpharmazien: Rechtsgutachten vom 6. April 2004 Bern: Pharmalex GmbH, 2004; available from http://files.hplus.ch/pages/HPlusDocument4622.pdf; Internet; accessed June 25, 2009.
[215] Nationalrat. "Arzneiwareneinfuhrgesetz." *Bundesgesetzblatt für die Republik Österreich* (2002); available from http://www.argepgh.at/kwpc_Downloads/Pharmarecht%20%D6sterreich/Arzneiwareneinfuhrgesetz.pdf; Internet, accessed February 16, 2009.
[216] See endnote 159
[217] National Cancer Institute. *A Manual for Participants in Clinical Trials of Investigational Agents Sponsored by DCTD, NCI* 2002; available from

http://ctep.cancer.gov/investigatorResources/docs/hndbk.pdf; Internet; accessed February 16, 2009.
[218] Shoemaker, D. et al. "Access to Investigational Agents for Patients Unable to Participate in Clinical Trials." Workshop on Pediatric Oncology Drug Development. Advisors and Consultants Conference Room at 5630 Fishers Lane, Rockville, MD: FDA, July 18, 2002; available from www.fda.gov/cder/cancer/presentations/shoemaker.ppt; Internet; accessed February 16, 2009.
[219] See endnote 17
[220] Akbarian, GS. "Fragen zum Thema Compassionate-Use." Besuch der japanischen Delegation. Bonn: BfArM, January 29, 2008.
[221] Schwarz, G. "Fragen zum Thema GCP-Inspektion." Besuch der japanischen Delegation. Bonn: BfArM, January 29, 2008.
[222] See endnote 142
[223] Horen, B. et al. "Adverse drug reactions and off-label drug use in paediatric outpatients." *British journal of clinical pharmacology* 54, no. 6 (2002): 665.
[224] Autret-Leca, E. et al. "L'enfant et les médicaments: application à la prescription en pédiatrie." *Archives de pédiatrie* 13, no. 2 (2006): 181.
[225] See endnote 88
[226] Altenstetter, C. et al. "Regulatory Governance of Medical Devices in the European Union beyond Theories of European Integration." 5th European Conference on Health Economics London, 8-11.092004; available from http://158.143.192.210/collections/LSEHealth/ResearchNetworks/EHPGSEPTEMBER2004/EHPG3 Altenstetter.doc; Internet, accessed February 16, 2009.
[227] Beckmann, J. "Arzneimittelrisiken: Seminar 6 (12 h)." Weiterbildungsseminare im Gebiet Arzneimittelinformation. Munich: Bayerische LAK, May 11, 2007.
[228] See endnote 176 Teil A1.0 § 5 Anmerkungen zu Absatz 2 (20.)
[229] European Medicines Agency. "Regulation (EC) No 1901/2006 of the European Parliament and of the Council of 12 December 2006 on medicinal products for paediatric use." *Official Journal of the European Union*; available from http://ec.europa.eu/enterprise/pharmaceuticals/eudralex/vol-1/reg_2006_1901/reg_2006_1901_en.pdf; Internet, accessed February 16, 2009.
[230] European Medicines Agency, "Meeting highlights from the Committee for Medicinal Products for Human Use, 20-23 October 2008," press statement, October 24, 2008; available from http://www.emea.europa.eu/pdfs/human/press/pr/55020608en.pdf; Internet, accessed February 16, 2009.
[231] *Task-force in Europe for Drug Development for the Young (TEDDY): European Paediatric Medicines Database (EPMD)* 16.02.2009, February 16, 2009; available from http://www.teddyoung.org/index.php; Internet.
[232] Medicines and Healthcare products Regulatory Agency. *The Blue Guide* Norwich, 2005; available from http://www.mhra.gov.uk/home/groups/pl-a/documents/websiteresources/con007552.pdf; Internet; accessed February 16, 2009.
[233] Medicines and Healthcare products Regulatory Agency. *Paediatric Medicines Expert Advisory Group of the Commission on Human Medicines* 2009, February 16, 2009; available from http://www.mhra.gov.uk/Committees/Medicinesadvisorybodies/CommissiononHumanMedicines/ExpertAdvisoryGroups/PaediatricMedicines/index.htm; Internet.
[234] Yeates, N. et al. "Health Canada's Progressive Licensing Framework." *CMAJ* 176, no. 13 (2007): 1845.
[235] See endnote 196
[236] Japan Pharmaceutical Manufacturers Association. "Pharmaceutical Administration and Regulations in Japan." Tokyo, 11.2005: 23, 29; available from http://www.jpma.or.jp/english/parj/pdf/2006.pdf; Internet, accessed February 16, 2009.
[237] Schweizerische Gesellschaft der Vertrauens- und Versicherungsaerzte. *Empfehlungen im off-label-use* 16.02.2009, February 16, 2009; available from http://www.vertrauensaerzte.ch/expertcom/oncology/recommendations.html; Internet.
[238] Österreichische Gesellschaft für Dermatologie und Venerologie. *BidDbase: Biologicals in der Dermatologie off-label* 16.02.2009, February 16, 2009; available from http://www.biddbase.at/; Internet.
[239] Bélorgey, C. "Temporary Authorisations for Use (ATU)." 06.2001.
[240] FDA. *Early/Expanded Access* 2003; available from http://www.fda.gov/CDRH/devadvice/ide/early.shtml; Internet; accessed February 16, 2009.

[241] Dickenson, JG. "FDA's off-label guidance may be up for review." *Washington insider,* March 13, 2009; available from http://www.mmm-online.com/FDAs-off-label-guidance-may-be-up-for-review/article/129910/; Internet, accessed June 16, 2009.
[242] "Medicare expands coverage of off-label cancer treatments." DIA communications 27.01.2009.
[243] See endnote 15
[244] See endnote 16
[245] AOK. *Aktuelle Informationen zum Thema Onkologie: 9/06 Anlage 9 (off-label-use) des Abschnitts H der Arzneimittelrichtlinien im Bundesanzeiger veröffentlicht*; available from http://www.aok-beratungsapotheker.de/redirect.html?http://www.aok-beratungsapotheker.de/11_aktuelles/OnkologieAktArchiv.htm; Internet; accessed February 16, 2009.
[246] Deutsche Gesellschaft für Gynaekologie und Geburtshilfe. *Anwendung von Prostaglandinen in Geburtshilfe und Gynaekologie: AWMF 015/031 (SI)* 08.2008; available from http://neu.dggg.de/_download/unprotected/g_03_03_02_anwendung_prostaglandinen_geburtshilfe_gynaekologie.pdf; Internet; accessed February 16, 2009.
[247] Straeter, B. "Haftung und Verantwortung nach dem AMG." Spezielle Rechtsgebiete für Apotheker. Bonn: Rheinische Friedrich-Wilhelms-Universitaet Bonn; available from http://www.pharma.uni-bonn.de/fachgruppe/html/skripte.php; Internet; accessed February 16, 2009.
[248] See endnote 176
[249] See endnote 176
[250] See endnote 176
[251] Völler, R. "Off-label Use und Compassionate Use in der Dermatologie." *Dermotopics*, no. 03 (2001).
[252] Bundesministerium für Gesundheit. "Gesetz zur AEnderung des Arzneimittelgesetzes und anderer Vorschriften." (2008); available from http://www.bmg.bund.de/cln_110/nn_1168258/sid_30F8EF599792099FB36F61F824A24DDB/nsc_true/SharedDocs/Downloads/DE/GV/GT/Entwuerfe/publizierte-Entwuerfe/Referentenentwurf__15.AMG__Novelle.html?__nnn=true; Internet, accessed February 16, 2009.
[253] See endnote 176
[254] Namjoshi, S. et al. "A Primer om: Off-label marketing of pharmaceuticals." *American Medical Student Association (*2005).
[255] Fugh-Berman, A. and Melnick, D. "Off-Label Promotion, On-Target Sales." *PLoS medicine* 5, no. 10 (2008): e210.
[256] Graves, DA. and Baker, RP. "The core curriculum for medical communications professionals practicing in the pharmaceutical industry." *Drug Information Journal*, no. 34 (2000): 995–1000.
[257] Iserson, KV. et al. "Politely Refuse the Pen and Note Pad: Gifts From Industry to Physicians Harm Patients." *The Annals of thoracic surgery* 84, no. 4 (2007): 1077.
[258] Steinman, MA. et al. "Characteristics and Impact of Drug Detailing for Gabapentin." *PLoS medicine* 4, no. 4 (2007): e134.
[259] Anderson, GM. et al. "Newly Approved Does Not Always Mean New and Improved." *JAMA* 299, no. 13 (2008): 1598.
[260] Rising, K. et al. "Reporting bias in drug trials submitted to the Food and Drug Administration: A review of publication and presentation." *PLoS medicine* 5, no. 11 (2008): e217.
[261] Sheldon, T. et al. "Focus on the Funding and Production of Evidence Rather Than Its Publication." *PLoS medicine* 2, no. 7 (2005): e222.
[262] See endnote 43
[263] Drug Information Association, "MSLs help drug companies legally discuss off-label uses.," June 26, 2009; available from DIA.custombriefings.com; Internet, accessed June 26, 2009.
[264] Helm, KA. *Protecting Public Health from Outside the Physician's Office: A Century of FDA Regulation from Drug Safety Labeling to Off-Label Drug Promotion* Fordham University, 2007; available from http://law.fordham.edu/publications/article.ihtml?pubID=200&id=2578; Internet; accessed February 16, 2009.
[265] Rowley, BR. and Van Harrison, R. "Professionalism and Gifts to Physicians from Industry." *American Medical Association (*2003): 2, accessed February 16, 2009; available from http://www.ama-assn.org/ama1/pub/upload/mm/437/ama_m3_pg.pdf; Internet.
[266] Ratner, M. and Gura, T. "Off-label or off-limits?". *Nature biotechnology* 26, no. 8 (2008): 867.
[267] Bratulic, A. "Proposed U.S. bill would require drugmakers to disclose payments to doctors of $100 or more." *FirstWord,* 2009; available from

http://www.firstwordplus.com/Fws.do?articleid=FA2C4D75CEE04D7EAA3A9B566332BB06; Internet, accessed February 16, 2009.
[268] See endnote 266
[269] "Corporate integrity agreement between the office of inspector general of the department of health and human services and Bristol-Myers Sqibb company.": 10, 25ff, 29ff, 43, 68
[270] DIA Communications, "Lawmakers may take action to reverse FDA guidelines on off-label drug use," press statement, February 02, 2009.
[271] Schweim, HG. "Praeklinische Studien in der Entwicklung und Zulassung von Arzneimitteln." Rheinische Friedrich-Wilhelms-Universitaet Bonn. Drug Regulatory Affairs, Masterstudiengang Drug Research. Bonn: Pharmazeutisches Institut Bonn, June 10, 2009.
[272] See endnote 129
[273] Heijmans, T. Aut idem Substitution. E-Mail to V. Plate. Starnberg. November 06, 2006.
[274] "Tragende Gründe zum Beschluss des Gemeinsamen Bundesausschusses über eine AEnderung der Arzneimittel-Richtlinie: Aktualisierung von Festbetragsgruppen Makrolide, neuere, Gruppe 1, in Stufe 2." 16.08.2007; available from http://www.g-ba.de/downloads/40-268-438/2007-08-16-AMR2-Makrolide1_TrGr.pdf; Internet, accessed February 16, 2009.
[275] Medicines and Healthcare products Regulatory Agency. *Delivering High Standards in Medicines Advertising Regulation - Annual Report September 2007 – August 2008* 2008; available from http://www.mhra.gov.uk/Howweregulate/Medicines/Advertisingofmedicines/index.htm; Internet; accessed February 16, 2009.
[276] Gerver, K. "U.K. Medical experts to recommend gift ban for pharmaceutical companies." *FirstWord,* January 30, 2009.
[277] DeMonaco, HJ. Innovative Diagnostics and Therapeutics Committee. E-Mail to V. Plate. Boston. January 20, 2009.
[278] *IDIS: managing named-patient medicines*; available from www.idispharma.com; Internet; accessed February 16, 2009.
[279] *Orphanet: The portal for rare disease and orphan drugs.* Orphanet database of orphan drugs; available from http://www.orpha.net; Internet; accessed February 16, 2009.
[280] National Organization for Rare Disorders. *NORD: Orphan Drug database*; available from www.rarediseases.org; Internet; accessed February 16, 2009.
[281] See endnote 237
[282] See endnote 208
[283] See endnote 238
[284] U.S. Food and Drug Administration. *Treatment Investigational New Drugs (IND) Allowed to Proceed* 2001; available from http://www.fda.gov/oashi/patrep/treatind.html; Internet; accessed February 16, 2009.
[285] U.S. Food and Drug Administration. *List of Orphan Designations and Approvals* 2008; available from http://www.fda.gov/orphan/designat/list.htm; Internet; accessed February 16, 2009.
[286] See endnote 231
[287] European Commission. *Register of designated Orphan Medicinal Products (by number)*; available from http://ec.europa.eu/enterprise/pharmaceuticals/register/orphreg.htm; Internet; accessed February 16, 2009.
[288] Hexal- Initiative Kinderarzneimittel. *Zugelassene Arzneimittel für Kinder ZAK(R)*; available from http://www.zak-kinderarzneimittel.de/; Internet; accessed February 16, 2009.
[289] Fritze, J. and Schmauß, M. "Off-Label-Use in der Psychopharmakotherapie." *Psychoneuro* 28, no. 8 (2002): 431–39.
[290] "Richtlinien des Bundesausschusses der AErzte und Krankenkassen über die Verordnung von Arzneimitteln in der vertragsaerztlichen Versorgung („Arzneimittel-Richtlinien")." *Bundesanzeiger,* no. 181 (2008): 4261; available from http://www.g-ba.de/downloads/62-492-305/RL-AMR-2008-10-16.pdf; Internet, accessed April 30, 2009.
[291] Verband Forschender Arzneimittelhersteller e.V. *Orphan-Arzneimittel nach Indikationen*; available from http://www.vfa.de/download/SHOW/de/politik/positionen/orphan-drugs.html/orphan-drugs-list.pdf; Internet; accessed February 16, 2009.
[292] Enzmann, H. "Klinische Studien/Zulassung." Symposium des Pharma Zentrums Bonn: Bundesinstitut für Arzneimittel und Medizinprodukte, August 14, 2008; available from http://www.uni-bonn.tv/search?Subject_usage:ignore_empty=operator:and&Subject:list=Pharma-Zentrum; Internet; accessed February 19, 2009.
[293] Laeer, S. "Europa und die Chancen für eine Kindgerechte Arzneimitteltherapie." Pharmazeutisches Kolloquium. Bonn: Rheinische Friedrich-Wilhelms-Universitaet Bonn, June 30, 2008.

[294] "Losartan künftig auch für Kinder zugelassen." *@rzneimittelnews,* November 15, 2008.
[295] Elbers, R. "Orphan Drugs BfArM im Dialog: Wir in Europa.": Bundesinstitut für Arzneimittel und Medizinprodukte, October 09, 2001; available from http://www.bfarm.de/cln_029/nn_1232318/SharedDocs/Publikationen/DE/BfArM/publ/praesent/dialog__2001-2005/dialog-011009/elbers__dialog,templateId=raw,property=publicationFile.pdf/elbers_dialog.pdf; Internet; accessed February 16, 2009.
[296] Laeer, S. et al. "Termination of automatic atrial tachycardia in an infant by adequate sotalol dosing. Indication of clinically relevant age-dependent pharmacokinetics of sotalol." *European journal of clinical pharmacology* 57, no. 2 (2001): 181–82.
[297] Laer, S. et al. "Development of a Safe and Effective Pediatric Dosing Regimen for Sotalol Based on Population Pharmacokinetics and Pharmacodynamics in Children With Supraventricular Tachycardia." *Journal of the American College of Cardiology* 46, no. 7 (2005): 1322.
[298] *Aut-idem-Regelung: BMG haelt an extensiver Auslegung fest* 2009; available from http://www.deutscher-apotheker-verlag.de/daz_neu/public/tagesnews/Mai/tagesnews20090513a.html; Internet; accessed May 22, 2009.
[299] Süverkrüp, R. "Rezeptur und Defektur: Möglichkeiten und Grenzen." Abteilung "Aus- und Fortbildung" AKNR. Bonn: Rheinische Friedrich-Wilhelms-Universitaet Bonn, September 09, 2008.
[300] Sickmüller, B. "Das BfArM im Dialog: Wir in Europa." Das BfArM im Dialog: Wir in Europa. Bonn: Bundesinstitut für Arzneimittel und Medizinprodukte, October 09, 2001; available from http://www.bfarm.de/cln_029/nn_1232318/SharedDocs/Publikationen/DE/BfArM/publ/praesent/dialog__2001-2005/dialog-011009/sickmueller__dialog,templateId=raw,property=publicationFile.pdf/sickmueller_dialog.pdf; Internet; accessed February 16, 2009.
[301] Straeter, B. "Klinische Prüfung von Arzneimittel." Spezielle Rechtsgebiete für Apotheker. Bonn: Rheinische Friedrich-Wilhelms-Universitaet Bonn; available from http://www.pharma.uni-bonn.de/fachgruppe/html/skripte.php; Internet; accessed February 16, 2009.
[302] See endnote 177
[303] "Marketing Authorisation Procedures (U.K.) Procedure for variation/changes/supplements." IDRAC(R), 03.2007.
[304] Shaddy, R. E. et al. "Carvedilol for Children and Adolescents With Heart Failure: A Randomized Controlled Trial." *JAMA* 298, no. 10 (2007): 1171.
[305] Laer, S. et al. "Carvedilol therapy in pediatric patients with congestive heart failure: A study investigating clinical and pharmacokinetic parameters." *The American Heart Journal* 143, no. 5 (2002): 916.
[306] Albers, S. et al. "Population pharmacokinetics and dose simulation of carvedilol in paediatric patients with congestive heart failure." *British Journal of Cinical Pharmacology* 65, no. 4 (2008): 511.
[307] See endnote 293
[308] Adebare, A. "Data Exclusivity: The Implications for India." (2005); available from http://www.articlealley.com/article_16562_18.html; Internet.
[309] Bücheler, R. et al. "Off-Label-Verordnungen in der Paediatrie." *Bundesgesundheitsblatt, Gesundheitsforschung, Gesundheitsschutz* 46, no. 6 (2003): 467.
[310] Bundesverband Niedergelassener Diabetologen e.V. *Bericht des Hauptgeschaeftsführers über seine Taetigkeit im Zeitraum vom 09.Februar bis 09. Mai 2002* Bundesverband Niedergelassener Diabetologen e.V; available from http://www.bvnd.de/download/taetigkeitsbericht052002.pdf; Internet; accessed November 17, 2008.
[311] Deitermann, B. et al. "Mehr Qualitaet in der Arzneimitteltherapie." Gesellschaft für Arzneimittelanwendungsforschung und Arzneimittelepidemiologie e.V., October 17, 2003.
[312] The European Parliament and the Council of the European Union. "Regulation (EC) No 726/2004 of the European Parliament and of the Council of 31 March 2004." *Official Journal of the European Union (*2004); available from http://ec.europa.eu/enterprise/pharmaceuticals/eudralex/vol-1/reg_2004_726/reg_2004_726_en.pdf; Internet, accessed February 13, 2009.
[313] The European Parliament and the Council of the European Union. "Directive 2001/83/EC of the European Parliament and of the Council 6 November 2001." *Official Journal of the European Union (*2001); available from http://ec.europa.eu/enterprise/pharmaceuticals/eudralex/vol-1/dir_2001_83_cons/dir2001_83_cons_en.pdf; Internet, accessed February 13, 2009.

[314] Schwarz, JA. et al. "Therapieversuche mit nicht zugelassenen Prüfsubstanzen (Compassassionate use) and zugelassenen Arzneimitteln (Off-label Use)." *Pharm. Ind.* 61, no. 4 (1999): 309.
[315] Barnscheid, L. et al. "Kindgerechte Arzneizubereitungen mit diuretischen Wirkstoffen." Dissertation, Heinrich-Heine-Universitaet Düsseldorf, Düsseldorf, 11.2007; available from http://docserv.uni-duesseldorf.de/servlets/DerivateServlet/Derivate-6929/Barnscheid-Diss.pdf; Internet, accessed February 13, 2009.
[316] Thaler, M. and Plank, M-L. *Heilmittel und Komplementaermedizin in der Krankenversicherung.* Wien: Manz, 2005.
[317] "Compassionate Use." AGES. Anwendungsbeobachtung und Compassionate Use: AGES, November 29, 2007; available from http://www.basg.at/web/ages/content.nsf/73b5f92ac245b957c1256a9a004e1676/c79a7cc9ba97cb06c1257367003d0a5e/$FILE/Compassionate%20Use.pdf; Internet; accessed February 13, 2009.
[318] Anonymus. *Référentiels nationaux pour un bon usage des médicaments onéreux et innovants* Afssaps, 2007; available from http://www.e-cancer.fr/v1/fichiers/public/dp_medicaments_innovants_260307.pdf; Internet; accessed February 13, 2009.
[319] Chalumeau, M. et al. "Off label and unlicensed drug use among French office based paediatricians." *Archives of disease in childhood* 83, no. 6 (2000): 502.
[320] See endnote 7
[321] Anonymus. *Your medicines – useful sources of information* BMA, 2007; available from http://www.bma.org.uk/ap.nsf/Content/Youmedicinesusefulsourcesofinformation.jsp; Internet; accessed February 13, 2009.
[322] Royal Pharmaceutical Society of Great Britain. *Standards and Guidance Documents to support the revised Code of Ethics* Royal Pharmaceutical Society of Great Britain, 2007; available from http://www.rpsgb.org.uk/pdfs/coun0706-C-54.pdf; Internet; accessed February 13, 2009.
[323] Nunn, T. et al. *Medicines: Tried And Tested - In Children?* The Association of the British Pharmaceutical Industry; available from http://www.abpi.org.uk/publications/publication_details/mttur/mttur_children.asp; Internet; accessed February 13, 2009.
[324] Ibid.
[325] Moremcambe Bay NHS Primary care trust. "Policy for the Off-label use of medicines." Moremcambe Bay NHS Primary care trust, 06.2004.
[326] See endnote 7
[327] Medicines and Healthcare products Regulatory Agency. *Medicines that do not need a licence (Exemptions from licensing)* Medicines and Healthcare products Regulatory Agency; available from http://www.mhra.gov.uk/Howweregulate/Medicines/Doesmyproductneedalicence/Medicinesthatdonotneedalicence/index.htm; Internet; accessed February 13, 2009.
[328] National Institute for Health and Clinical Excellence. *Ranibizumab and pegaptanib for the treatment of age-related macular degeneration: a systematic review and economic evaluation* National Institute for Health and Clinical Excellence, 2006; available from http://www.nice.org.uk/nicemedia/pdf/PegaptanibRanbizumabAssessmentReport.pdf; Internet; accessed February 13, 2009.
[329] Lamb, L. and Biffignande, PM. "Review 2001:The future of European pharmaceutical legislation." *Drug Information Journal*, no. 36 (2002): 899–907.
[330] See endnote 88
[331] Collier, J. et al. "Paediatric prescribing: using unlicensed drugs and medicines outside their licensed indications." *British journal of clinical pharmacology* 48, no. 1 (1999): 5.
[332] European Medicines Agency. "Guideline on conduct of Pharmacovigilance for medicines used by the paediatric population." *Official Journal of the European Union (*2007); available from http://www.emea.europa.eu/pdfs/human/phvwp/23591005enfinal.pdf; Internet, accessed February 13, 2009.
[333] Behles C. "Off-label use und Arzneimittelzulassung." Colloquium Pharmaceuticum GmbH. Off-label/no-label-use und Studien in der GKV. Bonn, April 19, 2007.
[334] Steurer, M. et al. "Low-Dose Thalidomide for Multiple Myeloma: Interim Analysis of a Compassionate Use Program." *Onkologie* 27, no. 2 (2004): 150.
[335] See endnote 332
[336] See endnote 50

[337] Die Bundesbehörden der Schweizerischen Eidgenossenschaft. "Bundesgesetz vom 15. Dezember 2000 über Arzneimittel und Medizinprodukte." Art. 9 Abs. 2; available from http://www.admin.ch/ch/d/sr/8/812.21.de.pdf; Internet, accessed February 13, 2009.
[338] BGE 130 V 532 Erw. 6
[339] BGE 131 V 349 Erw. 3
[340] Swissmedic. *Faktenblatt: Kinder und Arzneimittel: Situation heute* Swissmedic, 2005; available from http://www.swissmedic.ch/files/pdf/Merkblatt_Arzneimittel_fuer_Kinder.pdf; Internet; accessed December 15, 2008.
[341] Ibid.
[342] Jagger, S. F., and U.S. *Prescription drugs: implications of drug labeling and off-label use: Statement of Sarah F. Jagger, Director of Health Services Quality and Public Health Issues, Health, Education, and Human Services Division before the Subcommittee on Human Resources and Intergovernmental Relations, Committee on Government Reform and Oversight, U.S. House of Representatives / United States General Accounting Office* GAO, 1996; available from <http://purl.access.gpo.gov/GPO/LPS12207>; Internet; accessed February 13, 2009.
[343] Former, M. J. et al. "The Ins & Outs of Compassionate Use Programs." *Oncology Times (*2005): 10, 12-14.
[344] Mintzes, B. et al. *Drug regulatory failure in Canada: The case of Diane-35* Canada: Women and Health Protection, 2004; available from http://www.whp-apsf.ca/pdf/diane35.pdf; Internet; accessed February 13, 2009.
[345] PMSB/ELD. "Notification Nr. 104." PMSB/ELD, February 01, 1999.

ibidem-Verlag / *ibidem* Press
Melchiorstr. 15
70439 Stuttgart
Germany

ibidem@ibidem.eu
www.ibidem-verlag.com
www.ibidem.eu